SINUOUS OBJECTS

Revaluing Women's Wealth
in the Contemporary Pacific

SINUOUS OBJECTS

Revaluing Women's Wealth in the Contemporary Pacific

EDITED BY
ANNA-KARINA HERMKENS
& KATHERINE LEPANI

Australian
National
University

PRESS

PACIFIC SERIES

ANU PRESS

Published by ANU Press
The Australian National University
Acton ACT 2601, Australia
Email: anupress@anu.edu.au
This title is also available online at press.anu.edu.au

National Library of Australia Cataloguing-in-Publication entry

Title:	Sinuous objects : revaluing women's wealth in the contemporary Pacific / editors: Anna-Karina Hermkens, Katherine Lepani.
ISBN:	9781760461331 (paperback) 9781760461348 (ebook)
Subjects:	Women--Pacific Area--Social conditions Pacific Area--Social life and customs. Oceania--Social life and customs.
Other Creators/Contributors:	Hermkens, Anna-Karina, 1969- editor. Lepani, Katherine, editor.

Cover design and layout by ANU Press

Cover image: *Untitled 1996*, Wendi Choulai. Hand-painted, acrylic, shredded plastic and raffia on canvas, inspired by Papuan coastal grass skirts.

*To Wendi Choulai (1954–2001), and to all
other creative women in the Pacific*

Contents

Illustrations

Figures

Maps

Table

Acknowledgements

The initial idea for this book was inspired by a panel convened by Margaret Jolly and Anna-Karina Hermkens titled 'Engendering Persons, Transforming Things: Christianities and Commodities in Oceania' at the 9th European Society for Oceanists Conference in December 2012, in Bergen, Norway. Both Katherine Lepani and Michelle MacCarthy participated in this panel, while several of the other authors contributed to other panels at the same conference. We extend our gratitude to Professor Margaret Jolly for her enduring encouragement and guidance, and to all the contributing authors for their enthusiasm, commitment and patience in seeing this project to its fruition. We thank the reviewers for their insightful comments and encouragement. Special thanks are extended to Dr Carolyn Brewer for her meticulous and thoughtful editing work.

The volume was made possible with support from the Australian Research Council through the Laureate Fellowship awarded to Professor Jolly, 'Engendering Persons, Transforming Things: Christianities, Commodities and Individualism in Oceania' (FL100100196), 2010–2015. We are grateful to ANU Press for awarding a publication subsidy grant to support the costs of publication. Finally, we wish to express our sincere gratitude to the family of the late Wendi Choulai for giving permission to use the cover image.

Abbreviations and Glossary

Abbreviations

AL	Austronesian Languages
B	Bislima
CI	Cook Islands
F	Fiji
KI	Kilivila
KO	Korafe
MAI	Maisin
MAO	Māori
Ő	Őmie
POH	Pohnpei
POL	Polynesia
PNG	Papua New Guinea
PP	Proto-Polynesian
S	Samoa
T	Tonga
TK	Tok Pisin
U	Ubir

Glossary

Vernacular	English
'api (T)	the household group
aabo (U)	'first-born' initiations

Vernacular	**English**
ara (U)	tapa loin cloth worn by men
aro'a (CI)	love
áti (KO)	string bag; string bags
áti ghayáfa (KO)	string bag filled with cloth or barkcloth presented as a gift; wealth exchange goods
áti jojegári (KO)	unfurling a new string bag before it is used for the first time
áti yabámara (KO)	large string bag, intended for carrying mats, pillows, blankets and clothes, or other voluminous but not too heavy items
avàri (KO)	rubbing fibres between the palm of the hand and one's leg to make string by rolling fibres together
baitab nokwat (U)	cooking pots
banìngu (KO)	tree that produces resin used for making black dye
barè-barè (MAI)	large, elevated shelter next to main domestic dwelling
beber (U)	tapa loin cloth worn by women
biga yakidasi (KI)	our language
bíkororo (KO)	ficus wassa tree used for its sandpaper-like leaves
bilum (TK)	string bag
bilum meri (TK)	*bilum* woman
binóno (KO)	plain stitches in string bags
boinboinghari (KO)	to swing or bounce a string bag (to calm the baby inside it)
bondìba (KO)	stitch for forming the mouth of a string bag
bukubaku (KI)	central clearing in hamlet or village
buro seraman (MAI)	work for which *seraman* is needed
bwagau (KI)	sorcery
dala (KI)	matrilineal sub-clan
dimdim (KI)	foreigner; white person

Vernacular	English
diti (KO)	lit. eyes; stitches used in making pandanus mats
doba (KI)	banana fibre skirts and bundles of dried banana leaves
dun (MAI)	red pigment
durári (KO)	laying out a mat
'ei (CI)	neck garland made from artificial flowers, lollies, shells, ribbons and cash money notes
'enua'ānau (CI)	place of birth
embobi (MAI)	tapa loin cloth worn by women
ésa (KO)	plain; not dyed; undecorated
evovi (MAI)	inalienable clan designs
fa'e tangata (T)	attendants at wedding ceremony; biological and classificatory brothers of the mothers of the bride and groom (also called *tu'asine*)
fai fatongia (T)	ceremonial gifting
faka'ofa'ofa (T)	beautiful
fakalāngilangi (T)	bringing splendour
fala (T)	mats
fāmili (T)	family; village-based action group
fautaukoka (T)	hibiscus fibre dye wringer
fenua (PP, AL)	lit. land, earth; the sacred connection between land and people; homeland
fiemālie (T)	feelings of being comfortable and contented
fofóra (KO)	type of mangrove tree: its bark is used to make red dye
fonua (PP, AL)	land and people; the sacred connection between land and people; homeland
gaghári (*korafe*)	folding a *gháito* mat according to a specific sequence similar to folding a map
gámo áti (KO)	string bag for carrying large amounts of tubers and other produce
gebila (KI)	to carry on one's head

Vernacular	English
gháito (KO)	pandanus mat
ghaséga (KO)	songs
gonia (KO)	lit. buttocks; stitches visible on the side of the mat on which people sit
guguá (KO)	lit. 'roll of pandanus mats'; possessions or wealth items assembled to take on a trading voyage
gulagula (KI)	manners and customs associated with the ancestors
ha'a (T)	a form of societal ranking by which titles and their holders are organised
hila (PP)	personification of the Mother Goddess Earth
hina (PP)	personification of the Mother Goddess Earth
hou'eiki [s. *'eiki*] (T)	chiefs
'ie toga (S)	permanent paraphernalia
ih likauih seli (POH)	she'll wear it around
íivura ári (KO)	separating inner from outer bark to achieve fibres for string making
ipukarea (CI)	homeland
jávo (KO)	man's personal string bag
javuregári (KO)	unfurling a mat
jégha (KO)	Pandanus tectorius; Pandanus sanderi: the leaves are used to weave mats
kafu niti (T)	crocheted bedspreads
kafu sipi (T)	fleece blankets
kai (T)	food
kàina (KO)	three-ply string
kāinga (T)	kinsmen; extended family
kāinga 'i fa'ē (T)	extended family on mother's side
kāinga 'i tamai (T)	extended family on father's side
kaitomom (U)	a singular thing
kaitomom orot (U)	20 *kaitomom* or one man

Vernacular	English
karekwa (KI)	calico or cotton cloth
kastom (TK, B)	custom; traditional practices
kato kakala (T)	flat woven coconut palm leaf baskets
kato lole (T)	plastic containers or Chinese rattan baskets filled with sweets
kātoanga (T)	ceremony
katubayasi (KI)	preparing oneself for public presentation
kautaha (T)	textile wealth-making group; organisation
kautaha nō paʻanga (T)	financial establishments
kawo (MAI)	clan emblems
keke (T)	cakes
kekes (U)	bride price
kie hingoa (T)	fine mats with genealogies
kina (PNG)	official currency of PNG
kisakis ieu (POH)	a gift
koefi (MAI)	tapa loin cloth worn by men
koka (T)	Bischofia javanica tree
kokaʻanga (T)	assembling and staining of barkcloth
kóke (KO)	stitch resembling the footprints of *kóke* bowerbirds
koloa (T)	gendered or prestigious objects such as textile valuables but also coconut oil and sometimes baskets
koloa faka (T)	gendered objects such as textile valuables but also coconut oil and sometimes baskets
koloa fakatonga (T)	*koloa* of the highest value
koloa siʻi (T)	lesser or minor *koloa*
kōpū tangata (CI)	extended kin
kula (KI)	large scale exchange system in Massim region of PNG
kumas (MAI)	to buy

Vernacular	**English**
kumila (KI)	four main clans each comprised of numerous sub-clans (*dala*)
kundu (TP)	handheld wooden drum
lakeda (KI)	the road or way
lakeda tapwaroru (KI)	the way of the church
lālanga (T)	woven textiles
langa fonua (T)	lit. 'build up the nation'; organised groups whose aim is to fulfil particular communal purposes
langanga (T)	a section of about 40 cm barkcloth
laplap (TK)	cloth wrap worn like a sarong
lisaladabu sagali (KI)	specific set of transactions in *sagali*
lolo niu (T)	scented coconut oil
mala'e kula (T)	royal tombs
mana (AL)	spiritual power
mapula (KI)	to purchase or pay
marawawe (MAI)	balancing relationships between groups of people
masi (F)	barkcloth
meri (TK)	woman
misinale (T)	yearly church donations
misini tutu (T)	barkcloth beating machine
mohenga mali (T)	wedding bed
mon (MAI)	knowledge; thinking
mon seraman (MAI)	knowledge and abilities of a person; social being; person
mónga (KO)	Pandanus pistillaris, the largest pandanus: its aerial roots are used in making rope and its leaves in mats
monomono (T)	patchwork quilts
mu'umu'u (CI)	Mother Hubbard-style dress

Vernacular	English
na'esaesa (KI)	woman of wealth; woman who performs strongly in the production and distribution of exchange valuables
nakodana (KI)	idle or lazy woman
nasa (MAI)	brush used to paint tapa
nayo'udila (KI)	hard-working woman
ngatu (T)	barkcloth
ngatu 'uli (T)	dark barkcloth
ngatu lau tefuhi (T)	a 100 *langanga* (section of about 40 cm) long barkcloth
ngāue (T)	products derived from agricultural work and animal husbandry; closely connected to the 'work' men do for a ceremonial presentation
ngāue fakame'a'a (T)	material treasures
ngoue (T)	agricultural produce
nioge (Ő)	barkcloth
noa (POL)	free; nothing; unmarked; unconstrained
nokwat (U)	pot
nunug (U)	shell necklaces
nununiga (KI)	individual bundles of dried banana leaves (*doba*)
'o'ora (CI)	gift-giving event
'ofa (T)	love
'oloa (S)	objects that belong to the husband; all kinds of valued objects
ogi darag (U)	type of banana
orot (U)	the numbers one to 20 may be conceived of as a unity or the completion of a whole: 'one man' *orot* is 'a man'
paisewa (KI)	work; staging and partaking in *sagali*
pākoti'anga 'o'ora (CI)	haircutting ceremony
pāreu (CI)	type of fabric

Vernacular	**English**
peula (KI)	strong
Pulotu (T)	afterworld
pupagatu (KI)	dirty
pweia (KI)	large baskets
ramo (U)	eating or serving vessel
rùvi (KO)	stitch for strengthening the mouth of a string bag
sabed (U)	ceremonial feasting vessel
sagali (KI)	mortuary distributions
saságha (KO)	Pandanus englerianus or Pandanus kruaelianus: their leaves are used for weaving *savásava* mats
savásava (KO)	mat made out of leaves from the *jégha* tree
sekunona (KI)	large trays made from coconut fronds
sepwana (KI)	mourning skirts
seraman (MAI)	social, technical and creative abilities
sewaf (U)	eating or serving vessel
simon (U)	water storage vessels
Sina (PP)	personification of the Mother Goddess Earth
siria (KO)	tree species Gnetum gnemon – Gnetaceae: its bark is used for making strings
siva veyowi (MAI)	lit. 'washing shoulders'; ceremony to repay someone who has helped out in time of need
sokifa (KO)	close-knit loops
songa (KO)	small tree: its inner bark is used to sew pandanus mats
ta'ovala (T)	waist mats
tambuta, taubutu (MAI)	red blood; ripe
taonga (MAO)	treasure
tapu (P)	contained potency of some thing, place or person; forbidden or dangerous

Vernacular	English
tapu lole (T)	rectangular screens with two legs, covered with shiny wrapping paper
tapwaroru (KI)	Christian faith, prayer, church
tatáu (KO)	string bag for carrying one's last-born baby
tino (KO)	stitch to make the strap of a string bag; strap of a string bag
tivaivai (CI)	quilts
tivaivai manu (CI)	quilt with a pattern cut from one piece of fabric that is then appliquéd to a base fabric
tivaivai taorei (CI)	quilt made using the patchwork technique
tivaivai tātaura (CI)	quilt with several colours of appliquéd fabric with embroidery embellishment
tofiʻa (T)	estate
tok ples (PNG)	local language in PNG
tok pisin (PNG)	pidgin language used commonly throughout much of PNG
tonua (PP, AL)	land and people; the sacred connection between land and people
toulālanga (T)	mat-weaving group
toulanganga (T)	barkcloth-making group
tuʻa (T)	commoners
tuʻasine (T)	biological and classificatory brothers of the mothers of the bride and groom (also called *faʻe tangata*)
tuʻuvala (KO)	wedding ceremony
tufunga (T)	skilled male professionals
tukunibogwa (KI)	former time; days of old
túmo áti (KO)	woman's personal string bag
urohs (POH)	machine embroidered and appliquéd skirts made by Pohnpeian women from Pohnpei Island, Federated States of Micronesia
valova (KI)	transactions of material objects or money for *doba*

Vernacular	**English**
vanua (PP, AL)	used in, amongst others, Fiji and Vanuatu, meaning: land, people and custom; the sacred connection between land and people
vina (MAI)	formal and informal repayments; exchanges
vujári (KO)	lit. to decorate; term used for ceremonial decoration of first born at initiation or of a widow/widower at the end of mourning
wakaya (KI)	particular species of banana tree used for *doba* manufacture
wakèki (MAI)	red spondylus shell necklaces from Milne Bay known as *bagi*
wasa motob (U)	village land
wuwusi (MAI)	paper mulberry tree
ya'udila kaupatala (KI)	one bundle of fresh banana leaves used for *doba* manufacture
yabogwa (KI)	object that is too old to be useful
yamigileu (KI)	clean, fresh face
yapupagatu (KI)	wet or dirty
yavau (KI)	fresh and new

Contributors

Ping-Ann Addo is Associate Professor of Anthropology at the University of Massachusetts Boston, where she teaches courses on the anthropology of art and material culture, critical multiculturalism, race, ethnicity, nationalism and anthropological approaches to art. Her book, *Creating a Nation with Cloth: Women, Wealth, and Tradition in the Tongan Diaspora*, was published with Berghahn Books in 2013. She currently researches the politics of Caribbean-Boston's Carnival-related art production as it relates to bodily adornment, performativity and gendered entrepreneurship.

Elizabeth Bonshek is Senior Curator, Pacific Cultures at Museums Victoria, Melbourne. She completed her doctorate at The Australian National University, carrying out fieldwork in Collingwood Bay, Papua New Guinea. She held a joint postdoctoral research position at the British Museum, London, and the University of Cambridge, working on collections from Melanesia prior to teaching museum studies at the University of Canberra. Her research focuses on Pacific material culture, the creation of cultural heritage and contemporary interpretations of museum collections, and the use of objects as vehicles for memory making. Her most recent book, *Tikopia Collected: Raymond Firth and the Creation of from Solomon Islands Cultural Heritage* (2017), examines Firth's collection and collecting in Tikopia. She has written on museums and the creation of memory, 'Making Museum Objects: A Silent Performance of Connection and Loss in Solmon Islands', in *Beyond Memory: Silence and the Aesthetics of Remembrance*, ed. Alexandre Dessingué and Jay Winter (2015), and is co-editor of *Melanesia: Art and Encounter* (2013), a major research project focused on the British Museum's collections from Melanesia.

Elisabetta Gnecchi-Ruscone has a PhD in anthropology from The Australian National University. She has conducted fieldwork among Korafe speakers in Tufi, Oro Province, Papua New Guinea. Currently, she teaches a Master's course on 'Cultures and Societies of the Pacific' at the University of Milano-Bicocca. She has acted as consultant for the Castello D'Albertis Museo delle Culture del Mondo in Genova, for the Museo delle Culture in Lugano, and for Museo delle Culture (MUDEC) in Milano. In 2008, she was co-convener of the 7th European Society for Oceanists Conference in Verona. Her main publications include *Antropologia dell'Oceania* (ed. with Anna Paini, 2009); *Oceania* (2010), French edition: *Les Arts d'Océanie* (2011); *Putting People First. Dialogo interculturale, immaginando il futuro in Oceania* (ed. with Anna Paini, 2011); and a special edition of *La Ricerca Folklorica* (2011). Her latest publication is *Tides of Innovation in Oceania: Value, Materiality and Place* (ed. with Anna Paini, 2017).

Anna-Karina Hermkens is a lecturer and researcher interested in cultural anthropology, museum collections, gender studies and art. She has been doing research in Indonesia, Papua New Guinea and Solomon Islands on the interplay between gender and art, and between gender, religion and violence. She was a senior postdoctoral research fellow with Professor Margaret Jolly's Australian Research Council Laureate Fellowship project, 'Engendering Persons: Transforming Things: Christianities, Commodities and Individualism in Oceania' (FL100100196), 2010–2015. She currently works at the Department of Anthropology at Macquarie University, and is a visiting research fellow in Professor Nicholas Thomas' Pacific Presences Project at the Museum of Archaeology and Anthropology, University of Cambridge, UK (2016–2018). Her aim is to explore and establish an 'anthropology-in-art' practice that fuses academic theory and research on gender and art with her ceramics and painting.

Jane Horan received her PhD in social anthropology from the University of Auckland in 2012. In her thesis, she explored the interactions of value, values and valuables in the Cook Islands' ceremonial economy in New Zealand. She currently holds a research associate's position in the Property Department of the University of Auckland Business School to look at the escalation of value and price in the Auckland housing market from an economic marketing perspective.

Margaret Jolly (Fellow of the Academy of the Social Sciences in Australia) is an Australian Research Council Laureate Fellow and Professor in the School of Culture, History and Language in the College of Asia and the Pacific at The Australian National University. She has taught at The Australian National University, Macquarie University, the University of Hawai'i and the University of California, and been a visiting scholar in anthropology at the University of Cambridge and at the Centre de

Recherche et Documentation sur l'Océanie in Marseille, and a visiting professor with the Centre National de la Recherche Scientifique in France. She is a historical anthropologist who has written extensively on gender in the Pacific, on exploratory voyages and travel writing, missions and contemporary Christianity, maternity and sexuality, cinema and art. Her books include *Women of the Place: Kastom, Colonialism and Gender in Vanuatu* (1994); *Sites of Desire, Economies of Pleasure: Sexualities in Asia and the Pacific* (ed. with Lenore Manderson, 1997); *Maternities and Modernities: Colonial and Postcolonial Experiences in Asia and the Pacific* (ed. with Kalpana Ram, 1998); *Borders of Being: Citizenship, Fertility and Sexuality in Asia and the Pacific* (ed. with Kalpana Ram, 2001); *Oceanic Encounters: Exchange, Desire, Violence* (ed. with Serge Tcherkézoff and Darrell Tryon, 2009); *Engendering Violence in Papua New Guinea* (ed. with Christine Stewart and Carolyn Brewer, 2012); *Divine Domesticities: Christian Paradoxes in Asia and the Pacific* (ed. with Hyaeweol Choi, 2014) and *Gender Violence and Human Rights: Seeking Justice in Fiji, Papua New Guinea and Vanuatu* (ed. with Aletta Biersack and Martha Macintyre, 2016).

Emelihter Kihleng completed her PhD in Va'aomanū Pasifika, Pacific Studies from Victoria University of Wellington in Aotearoa New Zealand. Her dissertation, '*Menginpehn Lien Pohnpei*: A Poetic Ethnography of *Urohs* (Pohnpeian Skirts)', is a bilingual and creative exploration of a genealogy of Pohnpeian women's *menginpeh* or handiwork from tattooing to cloth production to poetry, another kind of dynamic textual and textured 'writing' that responds to *urohs*, a highly valued textile and distinct form of female dress. Emeli has worked as an interim Curator, Pacific Cultures at the Museum of New Zealand Te Papa Tongarewa, and taught at the University of Hawai'i at Mānoa, the University of Guam and the College of Micronesia-FSM (Federated States of Micronesia). Her first collection of poetry, *My Urohs*, was published by Kahuaomānoa Press in 2008. Her work has also appeared in other national and international literary journals and anthologies. Most recently, Emelihter was the Fall 2015 Distinguished Writer in Residence in the English Department at the University of Hawai'i at Mānoa. Since July 2016, she has been working as the Cultural Anthropologist for the Pohnpei Historic Preservation Program in Pohnpei Island, Micronesia.

Katherine Lepani is an anthropologist with a research focus on gender and health. She lives in Papua New Guinea (PNG) and is currently working as gender equity specialist for the PNG Governance Facility, a joint initiative between the governments of PNG and Australia. She was recently a senior research associate with Professor Margaret Jolly's Australian Research Council Laureate Fellowship project, 'Engendering Persons, Transforming Things: Christianities, Commodities and Individualism in Oceania' (FL100100196), 2010–2015. Lepani's book *Islands of Love, Islands of Risk: Culture and HIV in the Trobriands* (2012), based on her PhD thesis, is the first full-length ethnography that examines the interface between global and local understandings of gender, sexuality and HIV in a Melanesian cultural context.

Michelle MacCarthy is an Assistant Professor in the Department of Anthropology at Saint Mary's University in Halifax, Canada. She was previously a Postdoctoral Fellow in the Department of Social Anthropology at the University of Bergen (where she undertook the research and writing of the chapter in this book), and where she was a contributor to Annelin Eriksen's Norwegian Research Council–funded project on gender and Pentecostalism in Africa and Melanesia. She completed her PhD at the University of Auckland in 2012. She has conducted a total of 22 months of fieldwork in the Trobriand Islands between 2009 and 2016, and based on this research, has written about tourism, performance, food security, witchcraft, gender and Pentecostalism. Her monograph is entitled *Making the Modern Primitive: Cultural Tourism in the Trobriand Islands* (2016). She recently co-edited (with Annelin Eriksen) a special issue of *The Australian Journal of Anthropology* on Gender and Pentecostalism in Melanesia (August 2016). A co-edited volume entitled *Pentecostalism and Witchcraft: Spiritual Warfare in Africa and Melanesia* (with Knut Rio and Ruy Blanes) is forthcoming from Palgrave Macmillan.

Tessa Miller is a creative facilitator with Namana Fiji Arts, engaging women to develop their crafts and maintain agriculture for handicrafts and medicine gardens as a mainstay for improved livelihoods. She is the country editor (Fiji) for World Crafts Council online encyclopedia. Her paper 'Masi Making and Marking' (2014) is published in *TAPA: From Tree Bark to Cloth, An Ancient Art of Oceania* (2017). She lives in Fiji and uses the arts and creative facilitation as a means to re-establish peaceful coexistence within communities and nature.

Fanny Wonu Veys is Curator for Oceania (51,000 objects) at the National Museum of World Cultures in the Netherlands. For her PhD thesis at the University of East Anglia, UK, she researched Western Polynesian barkcloth, focusing on historical material and contemporary royal ceremonies in the Kingdom of Tonga. She has worked at the Museum of Archaeology and Anthropology in Cambridge, UK (2004–2006, 2008–2009), and has held postdoctoral fellowships at the Metropolitan Museum of Art, New York (2006–2007), and at the Musée du quai Branly, Paris (2007–2008). She co-curated a barkcloth exhibition, 'Tapa, Étoffes cosmiques d'Océanie', in Cahors, France, and curated the 'Mana Māori' exhibition (2010–2011) at the National Museum of Ethnology in Leiden. Her fieldwork sites include New Zealand (since 2000), Tonga (since 2003) and more recently Arnhem Land, Australia (since 2014), in the context of the Australian Research Council–funded project entitled 'Globalization, Photography, and Race: The Circulation and Return of Aboriginal Photographs in Europe' (2011–ongoing). She is currently a research partner of the European Research Council–funded 'Pacific Presences' project at the Museum of Archaeology and Anthropology, University of Cambridge, researching the complex cross-cultural histories of the western New Guinea collections, their colonial lives and the salience to twenty-first-century communities and audiences (2015–2018). She regularly gives guest lectures to students attending Dutch universities. Her topics of interest and expertise include Pacific art and material culture, museums and cultures of collecting, Pacific musical instruments, Pacific textiles and the significance of historical objects in a contemporary setting.

Introduction: Revaluing women's wealth in the contemporary Pacific

Anna-Karina Hermkens and Katherine Lepani

A thick verdant swathe of freshly cut coconut leaves composes a wall of green at the top of the fashion runway. Ten small newly woven coconut mats are placed at equidistance on the runway like a resilient green spine, a measure of movement across space and time but grounded in accustomed purpose. At first sight, this evocation of Pacific plant life and the objects of daily labour seem oddly juxtaposed on a platform of modern fashion. But the aesthetic meshing of culture and style, of traditional knowledge and contemporary design, stirs anticipation in the overflowing venue as the audience waits for RUNWAY2015 to begin.

A unique fashion event highlighting eight Papua New Guinea (PNG) designers, six women and two men, RUNWAY2015 was staged at Gateway Hotel in Port Moresby, the nation's capital, on 9 August 2015. The event evolved out of the success of *Stella*, the 'thinking woman's magazine', celebrating its third year of publication covering fashion, design, art, health, travel and life in the contemporary Pacific (Spark 2014, 2015). One of the featured designers of RUNWAY2015, Florence Jaukae Kamel, widely known in PNG as the *Bilum Meri*, had recently returned from New York where one of her exquisite dresses created with the *bilum* (string bag) technique of weaving had been featured in the spring runway show. Her designs, at once elegant, playful and practical, exude a storied aesthetic enlivened by the creative energy of the women whose skilful labour turns the looping of fibre into contemporary fashion.

The lights dim and soft electronic riffs of PNG music announce the commencement of the show. From behind the coconut screen, an older woman emerges onto the runway. She wears a black *meri* blouse and *laplap*, and carries a bunch of coconut fronds. She walks steadily on bare feet to the far end of the runway, where in one graceful motion she sits down on the mat and begins to rhythmically weave the fronds into a basket. Her labouring presence on the runway establishes the source of creative inspiration, the embodied connection between design and purpose—quick and proficient plaiting for immediate utility, a basket to carry produce from the garden—and between design and enduring value—the transformation of measured labour into an object of beauty with gifting in mind.

Then from behind the screen the models begin to emerge, one by one and in twos and threes; a steady progression down the runway. They glide around the woman on the mat; their gentle gait distinctly PNG, hinting of traditional dance moves from the coast, the islands and the highlands. Each designer's collection is heralded in turn by another woman dressed in simple black and carrying coconut fronds, who again walks gracefully down the runway to the next mat in line, sits down cross-legged and begins plaiting a basket. The steady rhythm of nimble hands sets the pace for the runway models; the embodied knowledge and practice of weaving underscores the textures and colours, the motifs and patterns, and the shape and flow of the garments.

The designer showcase is crowned by a spectacular finale. The models reemerge in steady procession from behind the coconut screen, now dressed in loosely draped black fabric, hair adorned with leaves and flowers, each carrying or wearing an object of PNG cultural wealth—baskets, *bilums*, shell necklaces, breastplates, headdresses, barkcloth, drums, flutes, carved shields. Joined by the women weavers carrying the baskets they have made, the choreographed movement on the runway transitions seamlessly into a traditional dance—lilting steps and voices singing in unison. The overall effect is immediate and resounding: contemporary fashion is multilayered, sustained by the value of deep cultural knowledge and grounded connections to purpose and place.

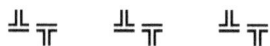

⏚ ⏚ ⏚

Everywhere in the Pacific, objects made by women—string bags, fibre skirts, barkcloth, pottery and mats—are used to decorate, wrap, cover, protect, contain and carry the human body. They are used as exchange valuables and commodities; they are critical for land claims and as indices of social relations; they are the embodiments of gender and clan identity and ancestral power. For the Ŏmie people living in Oro Province,

Papua New Guinea, barkcloth (*nioge*) is intimately associated with the beginning of time and the first ancestors. Ömie myth tells of the first mud-dyed barkcloth, which symbolises the female ancestor's menstrual blood and her capacity to produce children. From these origins, every new generation of Ömie women continues to make and paint barkcloth (Thomas 2012: 484; Modjeska 2012; National Gallery of Victoria 2009; ReDot Gallery n.d.; Thomas 2013: 20). These cloths now travel the world as highly valued objects of 'tribal art', displayed in modern art galleries and museums in Australia, Europe and the United States, and they have become an important source of monetary wealth for the painters and their communities.

As illustrated in the RUNAWAY2015 epigraph above, barkcloth and other fibre arts, such as string bags and fibre skirts, are a vital inspiration to contemporary Pacific artists and designers. Wendi Choulai, one of the Pacific region's most acclaimed textile designers, drew inspiration from the ritual, dance and skirts of her Papuan heritage and extended family. A publication dedicated to her corpus of work reveals that the late artist 'returned again and again to the grass skirt as a textile garment, an icon of ritual and a means of conveying her ideas' (Kinnear 2008: 11). Choulai saw the skirt as a multilayered metaphor that 'incorporated traditions and, through interaction with her clan, provided opportunities for legitimate innovation, the past and the future, inseparable and cohesive' (Kinnear 2008: 11).

The deep, intense and affective nature of fibre arts made by women is revealed through the perspectives and experiences of the Ömie and Choulai, and through the work of other contemporary Pacific artists and designers. There is an enduring dialectic between the sensuous nature of these objects—often intimately intertwined with the body, reproduction, motherhood and social identity—and the artistic and the economic values they are ascribed (see, for example, Addo 2013; Hermkens 2013; Lepani 2012; Veys 2017; Young Leslie and Addo 2007). Animated by women's agency, these precious objects travel across Pacific ethnoscapes, are carried into diasporas, and are creatively remixed with new ideas and new materials. Yet apart from the success and international appreciation of contemporary Pacific fashion, such as that showcased in RUNWAY2015, and the work of contemporary artists such as Choulai and the Ömie women, the genealogy of Pacific women's creative productivity has received far less attention and validation, especially in the western world. What becomes apparent when considering the historical and current validations of objects such as *bilums*, barkcloth and clay pots are the pervasive colonial legacies that have privileged the 'western sensorium' (Edwards, Gosden and Philips 2006: 1), or a Eurocentric aesthetic perspective and preference. These legacies continue to accord greater value to objects made by men, while devaluing and overlooking objects made by women.

This volume engages critically with debates about wealth and value, materiality, relationality and the social life and agency of things (Gell 1998; Kopytoff 1986), but specifically through a gender lens by bringing woman's creative productivity to the fore. The chapters draw on ethnographic material from the Trobriand Islands and Oro Province in Papua New Guinea, and Tonga, and from diasporic Tongans and Cook Islanders living in Aotearoa New Zealand. Through a comparative perspective and by situating women's work and their lives in the *longue durée* of Christian conversion, colonialism, commoditisation and globalisation in the Pacific, from the nineteenth century to the present, the chapters in this volume question, explore and engage in debate with each other about how 'women's wealth' is defined, valued and contested in current exchanges, church programs, sustainable development projects, art and tourist markets, and the challenges of living in diaspora. We celebrate the multilayered sources of inspiration and identity and the connections between deeply held cultural knowledge and contemporary art and design.

Interlocking domains of value and devaluation

> Telefol women know the value of their skills, but do not idealise their bilum making tasks. The contexts in which they spin and loop, and the manner in which they pass on their knowledge to one another, reflect the very qualities of the looping itself, in that they are open, flexible and unpretentious (MacKenzie 1991: 108).

Value—or the differential regard, importance and worth attributed to something—is a central concept in our contemporary world of ever-expanding capitalism. Value is also a culturally mediated category that finds various expressions in different social contexts. Moreover, it is foundational to academic scholarship and how we, as social researchers, focus on specific aspects of value that we think are worth exploring. The projection of value onto 'things' and into 'actions' is essential in all these processes.

David Graeber, in his influential *Toward an Anthropological Theory of Value*, identifies three major streams of thought that converge in the term value. These are:

1. 'values' in the sociological sense: conceptions of what is ultimately good, proper, or desirable in human life
2. 'value' in the economic sense: the degree to which an object is desired, particularly, as measured by how much others are willing to give up to get them
3. 'value' in the linguistic sense, which goes back to the structural linguistics of Ferdinand de Saussure (1966), and might be most simply glossed as 'meaningful difference' (2001: 1–2).

Graeber's work revisits previous attempts to come up with a theory of value and, while trying to retain a fundamental link between relativist conceptions of value, such as described by Nancy Munn for the Gawa people of Milne Bay in PNG (1986), and a more universal source of value (Miller 2008), Graeber ultimately recasts value as a model of human meaning making.

Starting with Marxist definitions of consumption and production as universal processes, Graeber introduces Marcel Mauss's idea of 'objects that are not consumed' and posits that most human practice consists of activities that cannot be separately categorised as either consumption or production. Graeber writes:

> One cannot hope to understand circulation of valuables in a 'gift economy' … without first taking into account more fundamental processes by which the human person is created and dissolved. And that when such general principles as action and reflection, or the movement between abstract potential and concrete form do appear—which they generally do— these too are always aspects of persons before they are aspects of things (2001: 167).

In short, Graeber argues that the core process of value making involves the creation of people (142). Value emerges from the actions of individuals aimed at reproducing social persons, relations and structures, and it provides the basis for comparison and regulation. In a similar way, Terence Turner argues that values 'constitute the most general purposes of social action and the most important qualities of personal identity' (2012: 501).[1]

While acknowledging the quest for a universal source and definition of value, our approach in this volume resonates more directly with Marilyn Strathern's (1988) work and her emphasis on the local. We each start with an ethnographic concern for what value means and does in particular societies and for particular people, instead of conceiving of value as *a priori* based on labour, or looking for a foundational basis for value (see also Miller 2008). We see our work as consonant with Maureen MacKenzie's exploration of Telefol string bags (*bilum*), which, as she argues, highlights that objects are not just valued because they derive from secret knowledge, as has sometimes been argued in the context of men's ritual objects and practices. Value also, and perhaps especially, lies in the physical creation of meaningful objects. MacKenzie observes, 'Women create cultural value by extending their repertoire of looping technology to make more functional, more aesthetic and more culturally powerful objects' (1991: 105). The intimate encounters with women and their objects of 'wealth' that we describe in this volume all show that value is ultimately about creating meaning; thus, we move beyond viewing value in mere economic terms to emphasise how value is generated in embodied practice.

Recently, value has become the subject of renewed scholarly interest (Angosto-Ferrandez and Presterudstuen 2016; Narotzky and Besnier 2014; Otto and Willerslev 2013a, 2013b; Turner 2008, 2012), with several studies taking up Graeber's quest and debating whether it is useful or even possible to develop an anthropological theory of value (Miller 2008; Otto and Willerslev 2013a: 19). While there exists ambiguity about the possibility of developing such a theory, the debate has elucidated the most prominent questions related to value creation. These questions ask how value is created in processes of exchange, how different value systems and hierarchies operate, and how value and action are interlinked (Otto and Willerslev 2013a: 19; 2013b). Such themes also pervade the chapters of this volume, although our quest is more directly concerned with issues of gender, power and change. While engaging with anthropological debates on value and with value as a theoretical and analytical tool, we foremost consider value as being part of the way people make sense of

---

1   Michael Lambek (2013: 149) considers any form of human action from the perspective of value creation.

their own social practice. The chapters in this volume aim to shed light on the processes through which 'economic' and 'cultural' dimensions of value are intertwined and mutually constitutive within contemporary Pacific worlds. But we also look at how objects made by women are part of the 'strategies communities use to materialize their social relations, desires and values' (Bell and Geismar 2009: 3).[2] The processual focus reveals how values (cultural, social, religious and economic) are materialised in objects as well as created in the very acts of their production and circulation; hence the focus on 'materialisation' (Bell and Geismar 2009: 3) rather than just objects per se. This perspective allows us to move beyond classificatory distinctions between art and artefacts—objects of symbolic, creative value, and objects of daily utility—that have been valued differently in time, not only by local and international agents but also by the gendered perspectives of observers, whose differential valuations have been amplified by the passage of time and historical change (Jolly 1992). When we place women and their work in the *longue durée* of western imperialism, we can see several interlocking domains of devaluation.

Devaluation by colonial agents, missionaries and art collectors

Importantly, objects have been attributed and denied different forms of value (Henry, Otto and Wood 2013: 34). Women's artefacts have historically been given less attention in western valuations; colonists, missionaries and traders, at times each participating in the collection of 'primitive' art, attributed more value to the material objects made by men. Nicholas Thomas observes, 'artifacts produced by women were often neglected by the early collectors, and subsequently by the tribal art market, partly because they were classified as craft rather than art' (1995: 132). These hierarchical categories reflect outsiders' valuations of the relative importance of representation, aesthetics and authenticity when

---

2   Tim Ingold (2012) suggests we differentiate between things and objects. A thing is a process of becoming, while an object is standing over and against its perceiver, with value being created in the 'very tension or contradiction between flow and fixity, thing and object' (Henry, Otto and Wood 2012: 34–35). In this volume, we move beyond categorical differentiations according to process and/ or perspective. What our material suggests is that objects are always social things, whether static or in motion, concealed or revealed, hidden away in the rafters, carried proudly, or animated through being worn in the public sphere.

validating what constitutes 'art' in the viewed objects, which are informed by the 'western sensorium' with its emphasis on five autonomous senses and preference for the visual.

Especially in the past, collectors of nonwestern material objects have tended to place emphasis on iconographic meaning when evaluating artefacts as art. This means there has been a strong preference for mimetic and representational objects and images (Errington 1998: 87). This preference is based on what Dutton calls, 'ethnocentric aesthetic absolutism' (1995: para. 8), the view that naturalistic (western) art is more developed or sophisticated than nonnaturalistic art with origins outside the European oeuvre. Significantly, the preference for naturalism determines the market value for ethnographic art. 'The most desirable tribal carvings in the Western market for such art continue to be renderings of the human form' (Dutton 1998: para. 5), which in Oceania are objects predominantly made by men.

Several scholars have raised the problem of cross-cultural aesthetic understanding in evaluating ethnographic objects (Danto 1988; Dutton 1993; Errington 1998; Price 1989). Alfred Gell argues that 'the desire to see art of other cultures aesthetically tells us more about our own ideology and its quasi-religious veneration of objects as aesthetic talismans, than it does about these other cultures' (1998: 3). Instead, he describes art as a system of action that is meant to 'do' something. Thus, the visual complexity of Trobriand canoe prows is made to captivate *kula* trading partners and stimulate them to give more valuable exchange goods than they initially intended (Gell 1998: 68). In a similar way, the colourful and shiny appearance of Maisin dancers (Hermkens this volume) is meant to evoke a particular response from the audience. However, it is not just the dancers' visual appearance that is a significant modality. The strong fragrance of the flowers, other plant decorations and the dancers' abundantly coconut-oiled glistening skins, the rhythm of the drums and feet shuffling, and the balanced composition of the dances all come together in a sensory experience that is meant to overwhelm the audience. With the ancestors embodied in each dancer through clan ornaments and designs, the sensory efficacy of the dancers and their performance displays the degree of strength and support of the ancestors. If the performance is strong, it induces their hosts to give them an abundance of food. If their visual and physical performance is weak, the dancers may receive little in return; their hosts may even ridicule the dancers, as well as their ancestors.

The valuing of objects (carvings, canoes, barkcloth and body ornaments), in terms of western aesthetics, risks overlooking indigenous sensoriums, intentions and validations. Contemporary collectors of tribal art tend to value 'authentic' objects (see Shiner 1994); that is, those objects made before major social change took place. The enigma of 'tourist art' signalled the demise of the authentic (Errington 1998: 99, 118, 128). As such, aesthetic and commercial valuations of Pacific material culture seldom take recent developments and creative productions into account; in effect, contemporary material culture is devalued. Consequently, 'Western connoisseurs' determine what ethnic art should be, how much it is worth (Price 1989: 69), and whether it should be collected and displayed in museums and art galleries.

Within this hierarchy of foreign validations, textiles hold a unique position as works of art and of utility, as material sources of sacred ancestral power and as instruments of Christian conversion. Thomas observes that barkcloth (tapa) 'has long aroused the interest of Europeans' (1995: 132) and, consequently, has been collected abundantly by missionaries, art collectors and anthropologists. In fact, Margaret Jolly (2014: 429, 431) argues that tapa and other textiles have been intimate partners of Christianity in Oceania, especially as icons of conversion. Jolly makes the case that it was the affinity between Oceanic and western textiles as women's creations that was recognised by early missionaries. However, while they noticed the sanctity of male-created images of ancestors, which were then burned, buried and collected by missionaries as 'idols', they failed to register the sanctity of Oceanic cloths, such as tapa and pandanus and banana leaves, in protecting *mana*, wrapping the dead and honouring rank (Jolly 1996).

While barkcloth stirred the interest of colonial agents (see also Hermkens 2014), like many other indigenous fabrics it was often quickly replaced by western-style garments, and missionary sewing classes replaced indigenous techniques of making cloth (see Lepani this volume). This is viewed by some as proof of conversion, whereby Oceanic people have succumbed to western models of gender and sexuality through the experience of colonisation (Jolly 2014: 429). Yet, as Jolly demonstrates, such a view ignores how both indigenous and introduced objects of gendered labour, including creolisations, are 'saturated with values of indigenous sanctity and rank, anticolonial resistance, cultural pride, women's collectivities, national identities and transnational connections in an increasingly globalised world' (433). In this volume, we acknowledge that these deep layers of value, meaning and agency are inherent in cloth and other objects made by Oceanic women.

Significantly, the historical interest in and commodification of tapa by missionaries and other colonial agents continues to influence local valuations of this object. This is revealed in Elizabeth Bonshek's chapter on the barter exchange of clay pots for tapa in Collingwood Bay. Here, recent attempts to commercialise tapa have unintentionally redistributed or recalibrated values that were previously coequal. This shows how the value and materiality of objects are not only situated in contemporary local and global power relations but are part of the historical processes in the *longue durée* of imperial interaction and exchange (Ingold 2012: 434). Moreover, Bonshek's chapter points us to the fact that in many places, mass-produced items, such as plastic containers and cloth, have replaced objects locally made by women. As Bonshek observes, today most women do *not* make pots, as pottery making has declined significantly in the context of social and economic changes.

Similar transformations are noted in Jane Horan's chapter about the Cook Island diaspora in Aotearoa New Zealand, where women are making fewer *tivaivai* quilts for ceremonial gift giving and purchased duvets are becoming acceptable substitutes. Horan argues that the value of these commodities resides in their social meaning rather than in the female creativity embodied in the mats and *tivaivai* that women have made in the past. Earlier substitutes, such as calico and quilts, were still linked to women, but through more Christian notions of women as mothers. Horan's example is an indication of the way that recently introduced commodities *replace* the objects of women's wealth. But does this also mean that the value of gift exchange is rendered gender neutral? Commensurate measures of value continue to frame gift giving in gender-specific ways. Transactions retain the gendered nature of the gift along relational lines and through the work of women in organising and staging ceremonial events. Whether gifts are purchased commodities and envelopes of money, or objects that have come into being through women's creative labour, the coherent value in meaning making is still legitimated by gender.

The processes, dialogues and tensions by which commodities gain commensurability with or replace women's wealth are also detailed in the chapters that deal with *doba*, the banana fibre skirts and bundles of dried banana leaves made by Trobriand women. Michelle MacCarthy

considers how people simultaneously engage in different 'spheres' or 'regimes' of value in their daily life (Appadurai 1986; Bloch and Parry 1989). She invokes Dumont's (1980) hierarchy of values to understand how Trobrianders reconcile values ascribed by the church in relation to values embodied in *gulagula*, or the manners and customs associated with the ancestors. If the more individualistic discourses advocated by the church, particularly the emerging evangelical denominations, assume ascendancy over *gulagula* with respect to women's domestic labour and economic productivity, the result is not only a change in the orientation of values but also a change in how both objects, such as *doba*, and actions are assigned value, increasingly in more economic and monetary terms. Katherine Lepani deals with similar issues in her chapter on the enduring material value of *doba*. While the incorporation of cloth, cash and introduced commodities has produced an efflorescence of new forms of exchange (Gregory 1982, 2015), this has not supplanted the importance of *doba*, which continues to comprise the central transaction in mortuary distributions. However, both chapters reveal that some people complain about 'women wasting their time' with *doba*, and that it diverts women away from more appropriate forms of work. The effects of these shifting regimes and valuations of women's work are especially significant in relation to the current emphasis of development policy on women's empowerment and economic participation, a theme that we consider later in this introduction.

Academic regimes of value

The categorical division between art and craft promulgated by western valuations has not only informed colonial collecting practices but has had a continuing influence on the visibility and valuation of objects made by Pacific women in the contemporary global economy. The preoccupation with classifying objects as either art or artefact has also influenced anthropological analyses of indigenous objects and subsistence economies. The earlier work of anthropologists generated theoretical claims that not only the modern western world but also 'primitive man' makes a distinction between craft and art, wherein craft, such as weaving and pottery, is relegated by indigenous men to 'inferiors' (i.e. women), while arts such as sculpture are reserved for men (Fraser 1962: 13). Douglas Fraser also argued that indigenous values were attributed differentially to craft made by women and art made by men. While objects of craft are deemed 'practical and secular' and thus easily replaced, the highly valued works of art made by men are not mundane and can only be parted with 'if properly despiritualized' (Fraser 1962: 13). It is obvious that Fraser's perception and definition of 'primitive art' is grounded in a decidedly masculinist value system. Moreover, it is grounded in the western sensorium (Edwards, Gosden and Philips 2006: 1), which recognises (only) five autonomous senses, with vision ('reading') elevated to the highest position (Hamilakis 2011: 210).

The result of this gendered differentiation and emphasis on the visual, instead of on touch, taste, hearing, smell, or a juncture of these or other modalities such as balance (Hamilakis 2011: 210), is that objects have predominantly been approached from aesthetic and functional viewpoints. The 'anthropology of art' field has often used semiotics and structuralism to explain objects of 'art' as profoundly cultural phenomena (for example, Boas 1927; Forge 1979; Gerbrands 1990; Layton 1991, 2003; Morphy 1994; Price 1989), whereas studies of objects classified as artefacts have focused mainly on form, style, technology and function. Examples of such latter analyses are found in museum and archaeological studies. However, since Nicholas Thomas's *Entangled Objects* (1991) and his more recent works (for example, Thomas et al. 2013), much has changed in the way ethnographic and also archaeological collections are examined. Contemporary academics working in museum contexts, such as volume contributors Elizabeth Bonshek, Elisabetta Gnecchi-Ruscone and Fanny Wonu Veys, have pointed out that they are 'unpacking the collection' and engaging in 'assemblage analysis', which means exploring the origins and provenance of the collections, as well as collectors' and indigenous motivations. As Bonshek stresses, we are looking for signs of indigenous agency in museum collections. Many museum projects, such as Thomas's most recent *Pacific Presences Project*, are about creating connections between museum objects and the descendants of those who created these objects. In addition to the 'anthropology of art' field and museum studies, anthropology has traditionally placed emphasis on the cultural significance and economic value of objects, concentrating in particular on exchange values (for example, Jeudy-Ballini and Juillerat 2002; Mauss 1990).

Importantly, the categorical and hierarchical valuations of material objects as art or artefact are replicated in anthropology's traditional focus on reciprocal exchange (see Myers 2001). This comes to the fore in Annette Weiner's (1976, 1980 and 1989) critique of Bronisław Malinowski's (1922) work and his focus on what men do in the context of Trobriand *kula* exchanges. While Malinowski defined Trobriand women's fibre skirts and banana leaf bundles as crafts and obscured them from his analyses, Weiner's work was critical for establishing an anthropological focus on the significance of women's objects in local cosmologies and subsistence economies. Weiner's ethnography of Trobriand mortuary exchange, *Women of Value, Men of Renown* (1976), firmly established the concept of 'women's wealth' and provided an ethnographic benchmark for interpreting the meaning and value of objects produced by women, and the investments of women's productivity in processes of social reproduction and reciprocal exchange.

Anthropological thinking about objects and exchange also involves the distinction between gift and commodity. These ideas are grounded in the important theoretical contributions of Karl Marx and Marcel Mauss, which have influenced concepts of value and understandings of the relations of production and consumption, reciprocity and nonreciprocity, and equality and inequality. In his influential book, *Gifts and Commodities*, Chris Gregory (1982: 19) brings together Marx's critique of the capitalist system of commodity production and consumption, and Mauss's perspective on reciprocity in gift exchange, with the premise that commodity exchange establishes a relationship between the objects exchanged, whereas gift exchange establishes a relationship between the subjects. Gregory further defines gift exchange as an exchange of inalienable things between persons who are in a state of reciprocal dependence (1982: 19; 2015). The main purpose of the gift is to establish and maintain social relationships. Commodities, on the other hand, represent relations between 'aliens', or strangers, by means of alienable things, with the main purpose of exchanging things of commensurate value. In short, Gregory (1982: 41) advocates a firm relationship between personhood and modes of exchange, stating that 'things and people assume the social form of objects in a commodity economy while they assume the social form of persons in a gift economy'. Gregory (1982: 23) acknowledges that empirical reality is much more complex and diverse; for example, a single object can assume different social forms depending upon the context (see Godelier 1977: 128). Moreover, people themselves may not draw such clear distinctions between these forms of exchange, and their attributed social contexts may differ from those ascribed by western scholars (Firth 1959: 138). In fact, the possibility of distinguishing between gift and commodity exchange, and the extent to which their social implications can be determined, has been strongly contested (for example, Appadurai 1986). Further, 'their widespread copresence demands careful revelation of how these forms of exchange mutually articulate and how they crystallise and engender different dynamics of sociality and agency' (Morgain and Taylor 2015: 3).[3]

The ambiguity in distinguishing between objects and persons, and the copresence of gifts and commodities, as for example in bride-price exchanges (Jolly 2015), is visible in Anna-Karina Hermkens' chapter. Hermkens details the significance of women's objects and their shifting roles in gift, barter and commodity exchanges, and the tension between local and international valuations of these objects and women's work and activities. Her chapter reveals the importance of local definitions of value and exchange, and how value is intimately intertwined with exchanges—the 'invisible chains that link relations between things to relations between people' (Gregory 1997: 12). Accordingly, value is not an abstract, independent entity; value has valuers who judge and determine what is good about specific ways of living together (Gregory 2009; Sykes 2013). All the chapters in this volume make visible the power relations and gendered agency imbued in the objects that women produce, which register differential degrees of value through networks of exchange.

Yet anthropological theories of exchange continue to skew and delimit the scope of what is made visible along gender lines. Weiner observed that 'exchange theories reveal strongly enhanced gender biases because the relevant subject matter remains what males exchange between one another' (Weiner 1992: 12). In general, theories ignore female-produced objects and exchanges performed by women; this exclusion suggests that women's objects do not have the qualities of gifts (or 'art') and that their forms of exchange do not play a significant role in social life (see also MacKenzie 1991: 21–22). Weiner (1992: x) argues that exchange theories that segregate women and men into domestic and political spheres respectively are at the heart of this distorted view (see also Strathern 1988). The emphasis on public, male-dominated activities is clearly visible in the anthropological focus on gift exchange (Humphrey and Hugh-Jones 1992). Yet types of exchanges embedded in daily social practice, including practices of sharing are often overlooked. Consequently, women's objects, such as mats and string bags, which are typically described as utilitarian

---

3   See Gregory (2015) for a reflective essay on various theoretical debates subsequent to the initial publication of *Gifts and Commodities*.

by collectors and anthropologists alike, and women's roles and actions in these different spheres of production and exchange, appear to have lesser value.

Weiner's work demonstrates that Trobriand women's banana leaf bundles and skirts, neglected by earlier anthropologists including Malinowski, are in fact important aspects of men's exchange, including the complex transactions of the *kula* trade (Weiner 1980, 1983). Her ethnographic accounts predominantly focus on the economic properties of bundles and skirts in mortuary exchanges; she argues that these female objects represent women's wealth and power in the cosmological domain of Trobriand matrilineal society (1983: 20). However, Weiner's emphasis on universal cosmological power positions women's reproductive agency, and the objects they make, outside of historical processes (Jolly 1992; Strathern 1981). Her analysis fails to address how women's power results from 'the relation between the interior world of the Trobriands and the exterior world in which it is situated' (Jolly 1992: 57). That women control the production and distribution of textiles and other material objects of exchange does not confer positions of high social status and economic power unequivocally. Weiner later acknowledged:

> [Women's] power may be skewed in particular ways ... but the extent of the symbolic density in cloth and women's involvement in its production and control are a measure of how this gender-based power is organized (1994: 397–98).

Weiner's focus on women's wealth inspired other scholars to focus on the gendered dimensions of materiality, productivity and exchange. This work (for example, Addo 2013; Bolton 1996, 2003; Ewins 2009; Hermkens 2013; Kaeppler 1980, 1995; MacKenzie 1991) has contributed significantly to our understanding of the importance of, for example, fibre arts in Pacific societies. Lissant Bolton's work illustrates the interconnections between women, pandanus textiles and landscapes, elucidating their central position on Ambae Island (1996, 2003). Here, the production of plaited pandanus textiles is intertwined with women's knowledge, notions about *kastom*, and agency (2003). Christian Kaufmann (1997: 146) credits Bolton, as well as Annie Walter (1996), for having 'rediscovered plaited mats made by women', thereby acknowledging the importance of these objects for ni-Vanuatu people. Earlier, in her study of highland Papua New Guinean string bags, Maureen MacKenzie (1991) emphasised the ontology of string bags as a complex social construction and product. She acknowledged that both men and women contribute to their production and social significance. By tracing the social life of a string bag, MacKenzie showed how this object is a material model of the social dynamics of gender relations and helped men and women explore and comprehend their coexistence, and understand their respective roles in society.

In this volume, Elisabetta Gnecchi-Ruscone equally explores the social and cultural significance of the string bag, but among the Korafe people living on the northeastern coast of Papua New Guinea. She shows how the mundane string bag expresses different values in various contexts, exploring its entanglement with diverse fields of action, as well as with gender and gender relations. The gender of women's 'wealth' is also addressed in Fanny Wonu Veys' chapter on Tongan textile wealth (*koloa*). She argues that Tongan women and their work are complemented by men and the work of men. *Koloa* are, like the women themselves, valuable, while *ngāue* (objects made by men) are, like men, powerful. The differentiated qualities of these gendered objects do not simply represent the division of labour, or ideas about what it means to be a woman or a man in Tongan society. *Koloa* indexes the *mana* of Tongan women by virtue of the work and love they have put in it; it is not solely a category of objects made by women. In fact, both *koloa* and *ngāue* are values that take different meanings depending on the context in which they are circulating.

The chapters in this volume show that although it is important to bring women's work to the fore of scholarly attention, we also need to include a theoretical emphasis on gender, and gender relations, to elucidate the intricacies of objects, and their fluctuating uses, meanings and values. This was the focus of Strathern's epic work *The Gender of the Gift*, which revisits and synthesises her own and other ethnographic studies on political economy and gender relations in Melanesia. Strathern (1988: 7–8) rests her analysis upon what she calls binary 'fictions'; for example, the us/them binary of 'the West' and 'Melanesia'; 'commodity' and 'gift' distinctions; and 'individual' and 'dividual' notions of the person. Strathern's innovation was to view gender as 'much more than the existence of male and female as sociological categories' (Jolly 1992: 137), rendering persons, objects, events and sequences as gendered relationally between male and female and other markers of difference. Indeed, gender can be viewed as being a relational value (Eriksen 2014). Strathern's work, as well as that of other scholars, reveals that objects come into being with specific identities, names and histories, that they have their own social biographies (for example, Hoskins 1998), and that they are animated through the relational value of gender. With this volume, we build upon this work and aim for a critical intervention into anthropological theories of value, exchange and local economies by exploring and comparing local gendered processes of production and consumption, and the value attributed to women's work and the objects they make and transact.

The value of women's work in development discourse

Cultural, social, economic and hierarchical forms and materialisations of value are all interlinked with people's livelihoods and the social relations that make possible the production and circulation of objects. In the contemporary context, the expansion of the capitalist market system as the dominant mode of resource allocation and distribution is a powerful metonym of the global economy (Narotzky and Besnier 2014).[4] Especially in the Pacific, a large body of anthropological work has been devoted to how value is created and contested through different types of local, regional and international exchanges, including participation in commodity markets and monetary transactions.[5]

Increasingly, women's labour and productive capacity are gaining attention in relation to the issues of rights and equity of opportunity in the global economy. The current emphasis of development policy on women's empowerment is focused not only on educational attainment and political leadership, but on economic participation, particularly in the formal employment sector and in entrepreneurial and business enterprises (Klugman et al. 2014; Jolly et al. 2015). Yet development discourse is infused with market valuations that regard the labour invested in the materialisation of objects such as tapa, string bags, mats, pottery, fibre skirts and banana leaf bundles, and in the acts of exchange that animate their value, as incommensurate with wage labour or the production of market commodities. Consequently, the material objects made by women

---

4   Susana Narotzky and Niko Besnier (2014) investigate the economy in terms of focusing on social reproduction, that is, continuity and change of human collective life-sustaining systems. This focus is also present in our volume, with all of the papers focusing on social reproduction in different but significant ways.

5   Among the many scholars focusing on exchange and market transactions in Oceania are: Cecile Barraud, Daniel de Coppet, André Iteanu and Raymond Jamous (1994); James Carrier (1991, 1992); Frederick Damon (1978, 1980, 1983, 1989, 1993, 1995); Jane Fajans (1993a, 1993b); Robert Foster (1985, 1990, 1992, 1993, 1995, 2008); Alfred Gell (1999); Maurice Godelier (1977, 1986, 1996); Christopher Gregory (1980, 1982, 1983, 1996, 1997, 2009, 2015); John Liep (1990); Nancy Munn (1986); Marilyn Strathern (1984a, 1984b, 1988, 1992); and Paige West (2012).

are themselves ascribed less economic value; wages and manufactured goods take precedence over 'traditional' objects in the hierarchy of values propagated by modern individualist capitalism. Women's work is relegated to the domestic sphere and the informal sector, where it becomes invisible and where the services and products of women's labour are deemed to have minimal economic value in the global market.

Our volume tackles these issues and the hierarchical and gendered projection of value over women's objects, and we articulate our perspectives in relation to the current development discourse and policy focus on women's economic empowerment. For example, in her chapter on the values of Tongan fine mats and barkcloth (*koloa*), Ping-Ann Addo asserts that even in the capitalist economy of the Aotearoa New Zealand diaspora, notions of wealth do not necessarily index the success of individuals in securing the financial means to purchase and display material commodities. Rather, the tangibility of wealth is made apparent through the material adornment of valued social relations. In her chapter on the Cook Islands hair-cutting ceremony, Horan illuminates how cash is imbued with value beyond its monetary worth through the public honouring of social indebtedness and obligations. These examples show the limitations of the dominant capitalist development perspective, and its inherent devaluation of women's labour and work. Indeed, one of our aims is to provide ways of rethinking economic empowerment that better resonate the forms and values of women's contribution to the sustainability of informal economies and the prospects they hold for improving opportunities for participation in larger spheres of exchange and for shared prosperity in the global economy (Jolly et al. 2015). We resist valuations that divide domestic and public spheres and informal and formal economies, and look instead at the embodied practice of women's productive and creative labour which links these spheres in complex ways. Following Karen Sykes, we endorse critical analysis of the contexts and conditions within which different regimes of value converge, where 'women's esteem comes to the foreground and dignity becomes a key issue in posing the value question' (2013: 98).

The complimentary show bags given to audience members at RUNWAY2015 included an information flyer from the Australian High Commission in PNG, one of the event's major sponsors, about the Australian Government's aid policy priority for supporting private-sector development in PNG and women's economic empowerment, with the objective to create income opportunities and greater participation in formal markets. One of the key initiatives of the policy is the PNG Bilum Pilot Project, with funding of AU$1.8 million over the three-year period from 2013 to 2016, which 'supports rural women to utilise traditional knowledge and create new markets for *bilum* products' (Australian High Commission in Papua New Guinea 2015). To echo MacKenzie's insights on the contexts of Telefol women's *bilum* making (1991: 108), we see the potential in such initiatives as expanding the values of inclusivity and flexibility, and creating resilient pathways to new avenues of wealth that are grounded in respected purpose and embodied practice.

The conceptual design for the staging of RUNWAY2015 suggests that the devaluing of women's objects in the global economy of goods and ideas has little purchase in how contemporary Pacific designers and artists source their inspiration and empower their creativity. The sinuous, or the intricate, supple material objects that women produce through their labour—coiling, weaving, stitching, looping, pounding, painting—are the very things that create, sustain and hold together social relations; securing the future by staying connected to deep genealogies of creative practice. We argue that the move towards commercialisation of value in the global marketplace as the avenue for women's greater economic participation must not displace the enduring social value of the objects that Pacific women create.

Gender and the value of things in the contemporary Pacific

While seeking to contribute to wider and more generalised debates on gender, objects and value, the individual authors in this volume are all careful to foreground the specific social, cultural and economic contexts within which their research and analyses are based. Each of the eight chapters offers a closely observed ethnographic account of the embodied practices of value making, and conveys the individual and collective perspectives of people involved in the production and exchange of 'women's wealth', and the social events in which meaning takes tangible expression. The chapters are paired and clustered to invite direct comparison of distinct geographical and cultural areas, and to invigorate dialogue on key themes and questions. The first pairing represents a return to the beginning of the women's wealth debate, with both chapters situated in the Trobriand Islands in Milne Bay Province, PNG. This is followed by a cluster of chapters on the cultural objects made by women from the coastal villages of Maisin, Wanigela and Korafe in Collingwood Bay in Oro Province, PNG. The final trio focuses on the endurance of cultural knowledge in Tonga and among the Tongan and Cook Islands diaspora communities in Auckland, Aotearoa New Zealand. The volume is wrapped up with an epilogue by Margaret Jolly. Woven between the sections and the epilogue are three creative reflections on women's wealth—a poem about Trobriand fibre skirts and dried banana leaf bundles, a poem about Fijian barkcloth, and a poem about *urohs* (Pohnpeian women's skirts).[6]

The chapters by Katherine Lepani and Michelle MacCarthy explore the social life of *doba*, the bundles of dried banana leaves and fibre skirts made by Trobriand women for *sagali*, or mortuary distributions, with questions about the endurance and transmutability of *doba*, and how Christianity provides a frame of reference for changing materiality and economic valuation. The chapters convey how the symbolic and tangible value of *doba* is activated in response to death, when women's investments of their labour into *doba* production signify matrilineal reconstitution and regeneration. Both chapters signal how the value of *doba* is analogous to the value of yams in Trobriand society, and the attendant relations of exchange and regeneration that men's cultivation and distribution of yams involves.

The starting point for Lepani's chapter about the durability of *doba* is not Weiner's (1976) classification of women's wealth to theoretically assert women's social and economic status and make claims about the universality of female reproductive power. Rather, Lepani situates *doba* in relation to the deep sedimentation of Christianity in Trobriand women's value making by tracing recollections from the early years of the twentieth century when pieces of cotton fabric were first introduced into mortuary distributions at the Methodist mission station. Lepani further traces the material transformations of mortuary exchange and the translocal dimensions of value creation in the ways Trobriand women continue to work for *doba* in urban settings. The commensurability of banana leaf bundles and cloth raises the question of the inevitable replacement of one form for the other through the increasing commoditisation of exchange, and what this signals about the position of women in the Trobriand regenerative economy.

---

6   Creative writing offers an important means for understanding and celebrating the value of material objects created by Pacific women. For example, the publication *Twisting Knowledge and Emotion: Modern Bilums of Papua New Guinea* (Garnier 2009) includes numerous poems and creative prose about the value of *bilums*, written by students at the University of Papua New Guinea.

MacCarthy's starting point is a vivid description of the embodied work of *doba* in the frenzy of *sagali* distributions, deeply symbolic of matrilineal strength and vitality. She explores the meaning of 'proper Trobriand womanhood' as redefined by evangelical Christianity, and the contestations among Trobrianders about changing cultural values and the changing value of material culture as people accommodate the influences of capitalism in their daily lives. Some Trobriand women are asserting the power of their productivity in ways that articulate directly with the market economy—providing food for their families by having more immediate access to cash through the production and sale of baskets and mats. The debate compels difficult questions about the perceived wastefulness of *doba* as an investment of women's time and labour in light of the demands and desires of modernity and the moral edicts of Christianity. To what extent do identity and kinship hinge on the materiality of *doba*, and the labour and exchange relations that *doba* signifies in *sagali* transactions? What might the devaluation of *doba* mean for women's status?

The trio of chapters on Collingwood Bay, by Anna-Karina Hermkens, Elizabeth Bonshek and Elisabetta Gnecchi-Ruscone, also explore the tensions between enduring cultural forms and changing valuations as the pathways of women's wealth take new directions, particularly as objects produced for commercial sale in the context of sustainable development projects. Hermkens opens her chapter on the moral economies of Maisin tapa, or barkcloth, with a stirring vignette of an Anglican Church festival that shows how the value of tapa is animated in ceremonial dance. The chapter explores the embodied value of tapa through gendered space and time—the intimate exchange of women's bodily substances in the making of tapa, and how once imbued with women's regenerative powers tapa carries clan identity into broader networks of exchange. Hermkens elucidates the mental and physical investment of individual women's labour in creating material and aesthetic value, and in reproducing gendered knowledge and personhood. She considers how tapa contributes to the moral economy of *vina*, or the principle of reciprocity, where people are compelled by the desire and necessity to give as the means to define and sustain social relations. Further, Hermkens observes how exchanges between men are amplifications of women's labour, but with important repercussions for gender relations and women's workloads when tapa transactions are controlled by men in the market economy. In such contexts, tapa no longer registers as the material embodiment of individual women's labour and their family and clan identity; rather, the value of tapa is assessed as a generic, genderless commodity in the global tribal art market.

Bonshek's chapter examines the changing context of pottery production and use in Wanigela since the arrival of the first Christian missionaries at the turn of the twentieth century. The chapter reveals how these highly desirable objects have assumed multiple values in complex sets of transactions, including in regional exchange networks where pots now command a monetary price. As commodities with price tags, no longer are pots valued foremost as material expressions of cultural life and social relations. Bonshek chronicles resistance to the commoditisation of women's objects as she joins five senior women potters on an expedition to exchange pots for barkcloth with the neighbouring Maisin. She describes the unexpected effects of a Greenpeace sustainable development project established to prevent logging of timber in the region, and how the desire for monetary gain through the production of barkcloth, as an alternative to the wealth promised by destructive logging, has upset longstanding exchange relations between Wanigela and Maisin people and established regimes of value.

Gnecchi-Ruscone's chapter challenges the usefulness of the concept of 'women's wealth' in understanding gendered productivity and value, whether the focus is on highly symbolic, ceremonial objects or mundane, everyday utilitarian products such as mats and bags. She argues that ordinary objects also assume extraordinary value in communicating social identity and connections as they become activated through production, performance and exchange in the course of their life histories. Gnecchi-Ruscone provides an in-depth account of the biographies of objects, including the intimate rapport between makers, materials and the objects as they come into being. These biographies illustrate how value registers differently depending on context, whether expressed in the making, in everyday use, in ritual contexts, and informal and ceremonial exchange, and how these transformations maintain internal integrity within diverse fields of action.

The final three chapters in the collection explore the endurance and efficacy of cultural values in Tonga and among the Pacific diaspora in Aotearoa New Zealand. Wonu Veys' chapter brings us to Tonga where we are introduced to the sensuous world of *koloa* (Tongan textile wealth). Wonu Veys shows that Tongan women and their products bring human life into the world; they nurture life, protect it and accompany it on its journey out of the world. This cycle of nurturing is more than physical; it spiritually embeds a person within culture, and by doing so incorporates them into society, thus generating and reproducing social and cultural life. Moreover, by participating in rituals and contributing with their products of labour, women ensure that the transitions in a person's life are appropriately facilitated.

Ping-Ann Addo's chapter guides us from Tonga to the Tongan diaspora in Aotearoa New Zealand. We are brought into the world of Kalo, a revered elder and focal woman in the Tongan community who provisions members of her extended family with *koloa*, the fine mats and barkcloth produced for ceremonial exchange. The close portrait of Kalo provides unique insights on the domestic spaces and relations of intergenerational transference of cultural values and knowledge throughout the life course and in anticipation of death. The chapter evokes the integral ties between cultural wealth, women's productive energy and the church, and explores why it matters that particular forms of wealth are valued differently as they change hands, contexts, generations and locations. Of significance is that the tangibility of wealth is made apparent through the material adornment of valued social relations. Addo's chapter as well as the final chapter by Jane Horan, describes in intimate detail how the exquisite material objects made by women—barkcloth, mats and quilts—inextricably link people to their place of cultural origin, and adorn social relations with value and meaning.

Adornment as a measure of respect, and as a performance of identity, is powerfully conveyed in Horan's chapter on the Cook Islands hair-cutting ceremony—a young boy's rite of passage into manhood, which involves the display and draping of *tivaivai* quilts on the initiate. The materialisation of cultural identity is palpable—layers of *tivaivai* embellish the young boy while cohering the values of community belonging and cultural connectedness. Horan poignantly illuminates how the hair-cutting ceremony articulates with the capitalist economy in the diaspora; the layered quilts not only signify the relational ties of nurture and support but they dignify the gifting of money. Cash is imbued with value beyond its monetary worth through the public honouring of social indebtedness and obligations.

Horan's and the other chapters elucidate the complex and sometimes contested nature of processes of commodification, commensurability and alienability. All contributors emphasise that creations made by women not only embody their labour, but have value in exchanges precisely because female creativity has engendered in them a constant relationship to the maker. But what does the alienability of some objects mean for their valuation? How mass-produced items and money gain commensurability with the value embodied in women's objects such as tapa, pots, quilts or banana fibre skirts is the question here. And how might environmental pressures be recalibrating scales of value where the organic materials for creative production are becoming harder to source, cultivate and sustain? The chapters herein offer a range of different perspectives on these questions, but consistent throughout this volume is the observation that the relationality at the core of women's gift giving confers commensurate value and meaning in exchanges, whether the objects are created through women's embodied labour or purchased and transacted as commodities. Women preserve and activate the value and meaning themselves.

As such, this volume is a tribute to Pacific women whose creative innovations of cultural objects at once reinforce attachments to place, even, and perhaps especially, in diasporic contexts, while projecting to the world the material and social value of local resources and deeply connected knowledge of the land. The incorporation of new commodity forms and manufactured materials in the production and exchange of cultural objects registers relational value as well, illuminating how the aesthetic, social and moral value of relationships is at once transformed, reinforced and sustained. The objects made by women are not classified as aesthetic objects, or as pure disposable commodities, but as practices that engage the local and the global in potent and valuable ways.

References

Addo, Ping-Ann. 2013. *Creating a Nation with Cloth: Women, Wealth, and Tradition in the Tongan Diaspora*. Volume 4. ASAO Studies in Pacific Anthropology. New York and Oxford: Berghahn.

Akins, David and Joel Robbins (eds). 1999. *Money and Modernity: State and Local Currencies in Melanesia*. Pittsburgh: University of Pittsburgh Press.

Angosto-Ferrandez, Luis Fernando, and Geir Henning Presterudstuen (eds). 2016. *Anthropologies of Value, Cultures of Accumulation Across the Global North and South*. London: Pluto Press.

Appadurai, Arjun (ed). 1986. *The Social Life of Things: Commodities in Cultural Perspective*. Cambridge: Cambridge University Press.

Australian High Commission in Papua New Guinea. 2015. *Supporting Private Sector Development in PNG: Innovation and Partnerships*. Online: png.embassy.gov.au/files/pmsb/PMD15%20 43993%20%20G2253_FACT%20SHEET_PILLAR%203_WEB. pdf (accessed 11 October 2015).

Barraud, Cecile, Daniel de Coppet, André Iteanu and Raymond Jamous. 1994. *Of Relations and the Dead: Four Societies Viewed from the Angle of their Exchanges*, trans. Stephen J. Suffern. Oxford: Berg Press.

Bell, Joshua A. and Heidi Geismar. 2009. 'Materialising Oceania: New Ethnographies of Things in Melanesia and Polynesia'. *The Australian Journal of Anthropology* 20(1): 3–27. DOI: 10.1111/j.1757-6547.2009.00001.x.

Bloch, Maurice and Jonathan Parry. 1989. 'Introduction: Money and the Morality of Exchange'. In *Money and the Morality of Exchange*, ed. Jonathan Parry and Maurice Bloch, pp. 1–32. Cambridge: Cambridge University Press.

Boas, Franz. 1927. *Primitive Art*. Cambridge, MA: Harvard University Press.

Bolton, Lissant M. 1993. 'Dancing in Mats: Extending *Kastom* to Women in Vanuatu'. PhD thesis. Manchester: Manchester University.

——. 1996. 'Tahigogona's sisters: women, mats and landscape on Ambae'. In *Arts of Vanuatu*, ed. J. Bonnemaison, K. Huffman, C. Kaufmann and D. Tryon, pp. 112–119. Bathurst: Crawford House.

——. 2003. *Unfolding the Moon: Enacting Women's* Kastom *in Vanuatu*. Honolulu: University of Hawai'i Press.

Bonnemaison, Joël, Kirk Huffman, Christian Kaufmann and Darrell Tryon (eds). 1996. *Arts of Vanuatu*. Bathurst: Crawford House.

Carrier, James G. 1991. 'Gifts, Commodities, and Social Relations: A Maussian View of Exchange'. *Sociological Forum* 6: 119–136. DOI: 10.1007/BF01112730.

——. 1992. 'The Gift in Theory and Practice in Melanesia: A Note on the Centrality of Gift Exchange'. *Ethnology* 31: 185–193. DOI: 10.2307/3773620.

Damon, Fredrick H. 1978. 'Modes of Production and the Circulation of Value on the Other Side of the Kula Ring'. PhD thesis. Princeton: Princeton University.

——. 1980. 'The Kula and Generalized Exchange: Considering Some Unconsidered Aspects of the Elementary Structures of Kinship'. *Man* (n.s.) 15: 267–292. DOI: 10.2307/2801671.

——. 1983. 'Muyuw Kinship and the Metamorphosis of Gendered Labor'. *Man* (n.s.) 18(2): 305–326. DOI: 10.2307/2801437.

——. 1989. 'The Muyuw Lo'un and the End of Marriage'. In *Death Rituals and Life in the Societies of the Kula Ring*, ed. Fredrick Damon and Roy Wagner, pp. 73–94. DeKalb: Northern Illinois University Press.

——. 1993. 'Representation and Experience in Kula and Western Exchange Spheres (or, Billy)'. *Research in Economic Anthropology* 14: S235–S254.

——. 1995. 'The Problem of the Kula on Woodlark Island: Expansion, Accumulation, and Overproduction'. *Ethnos* 3–4: 176–201. DOI: 10.1080/00141844.1980.9981198.

Damon, Fredrick and Roy Wagner (eds). 1989. *Death Rituals and Life in the Societies of the Kula Ring*. DeKalb: Northern Illinois University Press.

Danto, Arthur. 1988. 'Artifact and Art'. In *ART/Artifact*, ed. Susan Vogel, pp. 18–32. New York: Center for African Art.

Dumont, Louis. 1980. *Homo Hierarchicus: The Caste System and its Implications*. Chicago: University of Chicago Press.

——. 1982. 'On Value'. *Proceedings of the British Academy* 66: 207–241. London: Oxford University Press.

Dutton, Denis. 1993. 'Tribal Art and Artifact'. *Journal of Aesthetics and Art Criticism* 51: 13–21. DOI: 10.2307/431966.

———. 1995. 'Mythologies of Tribal Art'. *African Arts* 28(3): 32–43, 90–91. DOI: 10.2307/3337269.

———. 1998. 'Tribal Art'. In *The Encyclopedia of Aesthetics*, vol. 4, ed. Michael Kelly, pp. 404–406. New York: Oxford University Press. Online: www.denisdutton.com/tribal_art.htm (accessed 21 September 2010).

Edwards, Elizabeth, Chris Gosden and Ruth B. Philips (eds). 2006. *Sensible Objects. Colonialism, Museums and Material Culture*. Oxford and New York: Berg.

Eriksen, Annelin. 2014. 'Sarah's sinfulness: Egalitarianism, Denied Difference, and Gender in Pentecostal Christianity'. *Current Anthropology* 55(sup. 10): S226–S237. DOI: 10.1086/678288.

Errington, Sally. 1998. *The Death of Authentic Primitive Art and Other Tales of Progress*. Berkeley: University of California Press.

Etienne, Mona and Eleanor Leacock (eds). 1980. *Women and Colonisation, Anthropological Perspectives*. New York: Praeger Publications.

Ewins, Roderick. 2009. *Staying Fijian: Vatulele Island Barkcloth and Society Identity*. Honolulu: University of Hawai'i Press.

Fajans, Jane. 1993a. *Exchanging Products: Producing Exchange*. Sydney: Oceania Monographs, University of Sydney.

———. 1993b. 'The Alimentary Structures of Kinship: Food and Exchange Among the Baining of Papua New Guinea'. In *Exchanging Products: Producing Exchange*, ed. Jane Fajans, pp. 59–75. Sydney: Oceania Monographs, University of Sydney.

———. 1997. *They Make Themselves: Work and Play among the Baining of Papua New Guinea*. Chicago: University of Chicago Press.

Firth, Raymond. 1959. *Social Change in Tikopia*. London: George Allen and Unwin.

Forge, Anthony. 1979. 'The Problem of Meaning in Art'. In *Exploring the Visual Art of Oceania. Australia, Melanesia, Micronesia and Polynesia*, ed. Sidney M. Mead, pp. 279–286. Honolulu: The University Press of Hawaii.

Foster, Robert J. 1985. 'Production and Value in the Enga Tee'. *Oceania* 55: 182–196.

——. 1990. 'Value Without Equivalence: Exchange and Replacement in a Melanesian Society'. *Man* (n.s.) 25: 54–69. DOI: 10.2307/2804109.

——. 1992. 'Commoditization and the Emergence of "Kastom" as a Cultural Category: A New Ireland Case in Comparative Perspective'. *Oceania* 62: 284–294. DOI: 10.1002/j.1834-4461.1992.tb00358.x.

——. 1993. 'Dangerous Circulation and Revelatory Display: Exchange Practices in a New Ireland Society'. In *Exchanging Products: Producing Exchange*, ed. Jane Fajans, pp. 15–31. Sydney: Oceania Monographs, University of Sydney.

——. 1995. *Social Reproduction and History in Melanesia: Mortuary Ritual, Gift Exchange, and Custom in the Tanga Islands*. Cambridge: Cambridge University Press.

——. 2008. 'Commodities, Brands, Love and Kula. Comparative Notes on Value Creation. In Honor of Nancy Munn'. *Anthropological Theory* 8(1): 9–15. DOI: 10.1177/1463499607087492.

Fraser, Douglas. 1962. *Primitive Art*. London: Thames and Hudson.

Garnier, Nicolas (ed.). 2009. *Twisting Knowledge and Emotion: Modern Bilums of Papua New Guinea*. Port Moresby: Alliance Francaise de Port Moresby and University of Papua New Guinea.

Gell, Alfred. 1998. *Art and Agency: Towards a New Anthropological Theory*. Oxford: Clarendon Press.

——. 1999. *The Art of Anthropology: Essays and Diagrams*. London: Athlone.

Gerbrands, Adriaan A. 1990. 'Made by Man. Cultural Anthropological Reflections on the Theme of Ethnocommunication'. In *The Language of Things*, vol. 25, ed. Pieter ter Keurs and Dirk Smidt, pp. 45–74. Leiden: Mededelingen van het Rijksmuseum voor Volkenkunde, Leiden.

Godelier, Maurice (ed.). 1977 [1973]. *Perspectives in Marxist Anthropology*. Cambridge: Cambridge University Press.

———. 1986. *The Making of Great Men: Male Domination and Power among the New Guinea Baruya*. Cambridge: Cambridge University Press.

———. 1996. *L'Enigme du don*. Paris: Libraire Arthéme Fayard. Trans. Nora Scott. 1999. *The Enigma of the Gift*. Chicago: University of Chicago Press.

Graeber, David. 2001. *Toward an Anthropological Theory of Value: The False Coin of Our Own Dreams*. New York: Palgrave.

Gregory, Christopher A. 1980. 'Gifts to Men and Gifts to God: Gift Exchange and Capital Accumulation in Contemporary Papua'. *Man* (n.s.): 15(4): 626–652. DOI: 10.2307/2801537.

———. 1982. *Gifts and Commodities*. New York: Academic Press.

———. 1983. 'Kula Gift Exchange and Capitalist Commodity Exchange: A Comparison'. In *The Kula: New Perspectives on Massim Exchange*, ed. James Leach and Edmund Leach, pp. 103–117. Cambridge: Cambridge University Press.

———. 1996. 'Cowries and Conquest: Towards a Subalternate Quality Theory of Money'. *Comparative Studies in Society and History* 38(2): 195–217.

———. 1997. *Savage Money: The Anthropology and Politics of Commodity Exchange*. Amsterdam: Harwood Academic Publishers.

———. 2009. 'Whatever Happened to Economic Anthropology?' *The Australian Journal of Anthropology* 20(3): 285–300. DOI: 10.1111/j.1757-6547.2009.00037.x.

———. 2015. 'Preface to the Second Edition'. In *Gifts and Commodities* (2nd edition), Chris Gregory, pp. xi–xli. Chicago: HAU Books.

Hamilakis, Yannis. 2011. 'Archaeologies of the Senses'. In *The Oxford Handbook of the Archaeology of Ritual and Religion*, ed. Timothy Insoll, pp. 208–225. New York: Oxford University Press.

Henry, Rosita, Ton Otto and Michael Wood. 2013. 'Ethnographic Artifacts and Value Transformations'. *HAU: Journal of Ethnographic Theory* 3(2): 33–51. DOI: 10.14318/hau3.2.004.

Hermkens, Anna-Karina. 2013. *Engendering Objects: Dynamics of Barkcloth and Gender among the Maisin in Papua New Guinea.* Leiden: Sidestone Press.

——. 2014. 'The Materiality of Missionisation in Collingwood Bay, Papua New Guinea'. In *Divine Domesticities: Christian Paradoxes in Asia and the Pacific*, ed. Hyaeweol Choi and Margaret Jolly, pp. 349–380. Canberra: ANU Press. Online: press-files.anu.edu.au/downloads/press/p298891/pdf/ch152.pdf (accessed 19 January 2017).

Hermkens, Anna-Karina, John Taylor and Rachel Morgain (eds). 2015. *Gender and Person in Oceania.* Special issue of *Oceania* 85(1).

Hirschon, Renée (ed.). 1984. *Women and Property – Women as Property.* New York: St Martin's Press.

Hoskins, Janet. 1998. *Biographical Objects. How Things Tell the Stories of People's Lives.* New York: Routledge.

Humphrey, Caroline and Stephen Hugh-Jones (eds). 1992. *Barter, Exchange and Value: An Anthropological Approach.* Cambridge: Cambridge University Press.

Ingold, Tim. 2012. 'Toward an Ecology of Materials'. *Annual Review of Anthropology* 41: 427–442. DOI: 10.1146/annurev-anthro-081309-145920.

Ingold, Tim (ed.). 1994. *Companion Encyclopaedia of Anthropology, Humanity, Culture and Social Life.* London: Routledge.

Jeudy-Ballini, Monique and Bernard Juillerat. 2002. 'The Social Life of Objects'. In *People and Things, Social Mediations in Oceania*, ed. Monique Jeudy-Ballini and Bernard Juillerat, pp. 3–25. Durham: Carolina Academic Press.

Jolly, Margaret. 1992. 'Banana Leaf Bundles and Skirts: A Pacific Penelope's Web?' In *History and Tradition in Melanesian Anthropology*, ed. James G. Carrier, pp. 38–63. Berkeley: University of Los Angeles Press.

———.1996. 'European Perceptions of the Arts of Vanuatu: Engendering Colonial Interests'. In *Arts of Vanuatu*, ed. Joël Bonnemaison, Kirk Huffman, Christian Kaufman and Darrel Tryon, pp. 264, 267–277. Honolulu: University of Hawai'i Press.

———. 2014. 'A Saturated History of Christianity and Cloth in Oceania'. In *Divine Domesticities: Christian Paradoxes in Asia and the Pacific*, ed. Hyaeweol Choi and Margaret Jolly, pp. 429–454. Canberra: ANU Press. Online: press-files.anu.edu.au/downloads/press/p298891/pdf/ch162.pdf (accessed 11 November 2015).

———. 2015. '*Braed Praes* in Vanuatu: Beyond the Binaries of Gifts and Commodities'. In *Gender and Person in Oceania*, ed. Anna-Karina Hermkens, John Taylor and Rachel Morgain. Special issue of *Oceania* 85(1): 63–78. DOI: 10.1002/ocea.5074.

Jolly, Margaret, Helen Lee, Katherine Lepani, Anna Naupa and Michelle Rooney. 2015. *Falling through the Net? Gender and Social Protection in the Pacific*. Discussion Paper for UN Women New York, Progress of the World's Women, 2015–16. Online: www.unwomen.org/en/digital-library/publications/2015/9/dps-gender-and-social-protection-in-the-pacific (accessed 11 November 2015).

Kaeppler, Adrianne. 1980. *Kapa: Hawaiian Bark Cloth*. Honolulu: Bernice Pauahi Bishop Museum.

———. 1995. 'Poetics and Politics of Tongan Barkcloth'. In *Pacific Material Culture*, ed. Dirk A.M. Smidt, Pieter ter Keurs and Albert Trouwborst, pp. 101–121. Leiden: Mededelingen van het Rijksmuseum voor Volkenkunde, Leiden 28.

Kaufmann, Christian. 1997. *Vanuatu-Kunst aus der Südsee. Museum der Kulturen*. Basel: Christoph Merian Verlag.

Kelly, Michael (ed.). 1998. *The Encyclopedia of Aesthetics*. New York: Oxford University Press.

ter Keurs, Pieter and Dirk Smidt (eds). 1990. *The Language of Things*, vol. 25. Leiden: Mededelingen van het Rijksmuseum voor Volkenkunde, Leiden.

Kinnear, Jill. 2008. 'Introduction'. In *Wendi Choulai*, by David Tenenbaum, pp. 6–12. Melbourne: Melbourne Books.

Klugman, Jeni, Lucis Hanmer, Sarah Twigg, Tazeen Hasan, Jennifer McCleary-Sills and Julieth Santamaria. 2014. *Voice and Agency: Empowering Women and Girls for Shared Prosperity*. Washington, DC: World Bank Group.

Kopytoff, Igor. 1986. 'The Cultural Biography of Things: Commoditization as Process'. In *The Social Life of Things: Commodities in Cultural Perspective*, ed. Arjun Appadurai, pp. 64–94. Cambridge: Cambridge University Press.

Lambek, Michael. 2008. 'Value and Virtue'. *Anthropological Theory* 8(2): 133–57.

——. 2013. 'The Value of (Performative) Acts'. *HAU: Journal of Ethnographic Theory* 3(2): 141–160. DOI: 10.14318/hau3.2.009.

Layton, Robert. 1991 [1981]. *The Anthropology of Art*. Cambridge: Cambridge University Press.

——. 2003. 'Art and Agency: A Reassessment'. *Journal of the Royal Anthropological Institute* (n.s.) 9: 447–464. DOI: 10.1111/1467-9655.00158.

Leach, James and Edmund Leach (eds). 1983. *The Kula: New Perspectives on Massim Exchange*. Cambridge: Cambridge University Press.

Lepani, Katherine. 2012. *Islands of Love, Islands of Risk: Culture and HIV in the Trobriands*. Nashville: Vanderbilt University Press.

Liep, John. 1990. 'Gift Exchange and the Construction of Identity'. In *Culture and History in the Pacific*, ed. Jukka Siikala, pp. 164–183. Helsinki: The Finnish Anthropological Society.

MacKenzie, Maureen A. 1991. *Androgynous Objects: String Bags and Gender in Central New Guinea*. Amsterdam: Harwood Academic Publishers.

Malinowski, Bronisław. 1922. *Argonauts of the Western Pacific: An Account of Native Enterprise and Adventure in the Archipelagoes of Melanesian New Guinea*. Studies in Economics and Political Science, no. 65. London: Routledge.

Mauss, Marcel. 1990 [1950]. *The Gift: The Form and Reason for Exchange in Archaic Societies*, trans. W.D. Halls. New York: W.W. Norton. Original edition, *Essai sur le don*, first published 1950 by Presses Universitaires de France en *Sociologie et Anthropologie*.

Mead, Sidney M. (ed.). 1979. *Exploring the Visual Art of Oceania. Australia, Melanesia, Micronesia and Polynesia*. Honolulu: The University Press of Hawaii.

Miller, Daniel. 2008. 'The Uses of Value'. *Geoform* vol. 39 (3): 1122–1132.

Modjeska, Drusilla. 2012. *The Mountain*. North Sydney, NSW: Random House Australia.

Morgain, Rachel and John Taylor. 2015. 'Transforming Relations of Gender, Person, and Agency in Oceania'. *Gender and Person in Oceania*, ed. Anna-Karina Hermkens, John Taylor and Rachel Morgain. Special issue of *Oceania* 85(1): 1–9. DOI: 10.1002/ocea.5069.

Morphy, Howard. 1994. 'The Anthropology of Art'. In *Companion Encyclopaedia of Anthropology, Humanity, Culture and Social Life*, ed. Tim Ingold, pp. 648–685. London: Routledge.

———. 2008. *Becoming Art. Exploring Cross-Cultural Categories*. London: Bloomsbury Publishers.

Munn, Nancy. 1986. *The Fame of Gawa: A Symbolic Study of Value Transformation in a Massim (Papua New Guinea) Society*. Cambridge: Cambridge University Press.

Myers, Fred (ed). 2001. *The Empire of Things: Regimes of Value and Material Culture*. Santa Fe: School of American Research Press.

———. 2002. *Painting Culture: The Making of an Aboriginal High Art*. Durham: Duke University Press.

Narotzky, Susana and Niko Besnier. 2014. 'Crisis, Value, and Hope: Rethinking the Economy. An Introduction to Supplement 9'. *Current Anthropology* 55(S9): S4–S15. DOI: 10.1086/676327.

National Gallery of Victoria. 2009. Wisdom of the Mountain: Art of the Ömie. Exhibition 27 November 2009 – 21 March 2010, Melbourne, Australia. Online: www.ngv.vic.gov.au/exhibition/wisdom-of-the-mountain/ (accessed 22 January 2017).

Otto, Ton and Rane Willerslev. 2013a. 'Introduction: Value as Theory: Comparison, Cultural Critique, and Guerilla Ethnographic Theory'. *HAU: Journal of Ethnographic Theory* 3(1): 1–20. DOI: 10.14318/hau3.1.

———. 2013b. 'Prologue: Value as Theory'. *HAU: Journal of Ethnographic Theory* 3(2): 1–10. DOI: 10.14318/hau3.2.

Price, Sally. 1989. *Primitive Art in Civilized Places*. Chicago: University of Chicago Press.

ReDot Fine Art Gallery n.d. Online: www.redotgallery.com/artist_detail2.php?artist=495&artwork=1618 (accessed 4 August 2015).

Saussure, Ferdinand de. 1966. *Course in General Linguistics*, trans. W. Bakins. New York: McGraw Hill.

Schneider, Jane and Annette Weiner (eds). 1989. *Cloth and Human Experience*. Washington, DC: Smithsonian Institution Press.

Shiner, Larry. 1994. 'Primitive Fakes, "Tourist Art", and the Ideology of Authenticity'. *Journal of Aesthetics and Art Criticism* 52(2): 225–234. DOI: DOI: 10.2307/431169.

Siikala, Jukka (ed.). 1990. *Culture and History in the Pacific*. Helsinki: The Finnish Anthropological Society.

Spark, Ceridwen. 2014. 'An Oceanic Revolution? *Stella* and the Construction of New Femininities in Papua New Guinea and the Pacific'. *The Australian Journal of Anthropology* 25: 54–72. DOI: 10.1111/taja.12066.

———. 2015. 'Working out What to Wear in Papua New Guinea: The Politics of Fashion in *Stella*'. *The Contemporary Pacific* 27: 39–70. DOI: 10.1353/cp.2015.0019.

Strathern, Marilyn. 1981. 'Culture in a Netbag: The Manufacture of a Subdiscipline in Anthropology'. *Man* (n.s.) 16: 665–688. DOI: 10.2307/2801494.

———. 1984a. 'Subject or Object? Women and the Circulation of Valuables in Highlands New Guinea'. In *Women and Property – Women as Property*, ed. Renée Hirschon, pp. 158–175. New York: St Martin's Press.

———. 1984b. 'Marriage Exchanges: A Melanesian Comment'. *Annual Review of Anthropology* 13: 41–73. DOI: 10.1146/annurev. an.13.100184.000353.

———. 1988. *The Gender of the Gift: Problems with Women and Problems with Society in Melanesia*. Berkeley: University of California Press.

———. 1992. 'Qualified Value: The Perspective of Gift Exchange'. In *Barter, Exchange and Value: An Anthropological Approach*, ed. Caroline Humphrey and Stephen Hugh-Jones, pp. 169–191. Cambridge: Cambridge University Press.

Sykes, Karen. 2013. 'Mortgaging the Bridewealth. Problems with Brothers and Problems with Value'. *HAU Journal of Ethnographic Theory* 3(2): 97–117. DOI: doi.org/10.14318/hau3.2.007.

Tenenbaum, David. 1986. *Wendi Choulai*. Melbourne: Melbourne Books.

Thomas, Nicholas. 1991. *Entangled Objects: Exchange, Material Culture and Colonialism in the Pacific*. Cambridge, London: Harvard University Press.

———. 1995. *Oceanic Art*. London: Thames and Hudson.

———. 2012. 'Spiderweb and Vine: The Art of Ömie'. In *Art in Oceania. A New History*, ed. Peter Brunt and Nicholas Thomas, pp. 484–485. London: Thames & Hudson.

———. 2013. 'Introduction'. In *Melanesia: Art and Encounter*, ed. Nicholas Thomas, Lissant Bolton, Elizabeth Bonshek, Julie Adams and Ben Burt, pp. xi–xix. London: British Museum Press.

Thomas, Nicholas, Lissant Bolton, Elizabeth Bonshek, Julie Adams and Ben Burt (eds). 2013. *Melanesia: Art and Encounter*. London: British Museum Press.

Turner, Terence. 2008. 'Marxian Value Theory: An Anthropological Perspective'. *Anthropological Theory* 8(1): 43–56. DOI: 10.1177/1463499607087494.

——. 2012. 'The Social Skin'. *Hau: Journal of Ethnographic Theory* 3(2): 219–243. DOI: 10.14318/hau2.2.026.

Veys, Fanny Wonu. 2017. *Unwrapping Tongan Barkcloth: Encounters, Creativity and Female Agency*. London: Bloomsbury.

Vogel, Susan (ed.). 1988. *ART/Artifact*. New York: Center for African Art.

Walter, Annie. 1996. 'The Feminine Art of Mat-weaving on Pentecost'. In *Arts of Vanuatu*, ed. Joël Bonnemaison, Kirk Huffman, Christian Kaufmann and Darrell Tryon, pp. 100–109. Bathurst: Crawford House.

Weiner, Annette B. 1976. *Women of Value, Men of Renown: New Perspectives in Trobriand Exchange*. Austin: University of Texas Press.

——. 1980. 'Stability in Banana Leaves: Colonisation and women in Kiriwina, Trobriand Islands'. In *Women and Colonisation, Anthropological Perspectives*, ed. Mona Etienne and Eleanor Leacock, pp. 270–293. New York: Praeger Publications.

——. 1989. 'Why Cloth? Wealth, Gender and Power in Oceania'. In *Cloth and Human Experience*, ed. Jane Schneider and Annette Weiner, pp. 33–72. Washington, DC: Smithsonian Institution Press.

——. 1992. *Inalienable Possessions. The Paradox of Keeping-While-Giving*. Berkeley: University of California Press.

——. 1994. 'Cultural Difference and the Density of Objects'. *American Ethnologist* 21(2): 391–403.

West, Paige. 2012. *From Modern Production to Imagined Primitive: The Social World of Coffee from Papua New Guinea*. Durham, North Carolina: Duke University Press.

Young Leslie, Heather E. and Ping-Ann Addo. 2007. 'Introduction. Pacific Textiles, Pacific Cultures: Hybridity and Pragmatic Creativity'. In *Hybrid Textiles: Pragmatic Creativity and Authentic Innovations in Pacific Cloth*, ed. Heather Young Leslie, Ping-Ann Addo and Phyllis Herda. Special issue of *Journal of Pacific Arts* 3(5): 12–21.

1

Doba and Ephemeral Durability: The Enduring Material Value of Women's Work in the Trobriand Regenerative Economy

Katherine Lepani

In the matrilineal Trobriand Islands, the intrinsic social value of sustaining interclan exchange relations and regenerating clan and *dala* (lineage) identity is invested largely in the productive work of *sagali*, or mortuary feasts. Organised and conducted primarily by women, the continued vitality of *sagali* is a significant measure of Trobriand cultural resilience in interaction with the material effects of modernity and the increasing commodification of exchange practices. The changing materiality of the Trobriand gift economy over the last several generations, marked by the incorporation of cash and commercial commodities, in particular manufactured cloth, has produced an efflorescence of new forms of exchange (Gregory 1982, 2015). Yet this dynamic process has not supplanted the value of *doba*—the banana fibre skirts and the bundles of dried banana leaves made by Trobriand women, which continue to comprise the central transactions in *sagali*. Distributed by the thousands during *sagali* events, the ephemeral banana leaf bundles retain centre stage in signifying the aesthetic and material worth of women's work in the regeneration of matrilineal identity. The durability of *doba* as both the subject and object of women's labour in mortuary distributions—

activating relationality between persons and between persons and things—heralds the enduring value of this particular form of gendered agency in the collective project of social reproduction.

Banana leaf bundles and fibre skirts have a modern equivalent; cloth, or *karekwa* after the English 'calico', has been fully integrated into *sagali* over the last several generations. Purchased from shops or acquired through elaborate networks of obligatory exchange, *karekwa* augments *doba* transactions in a number of forms—by the bolt, cut into 2-metre lengths, or sewn into skirts, blouses, shirts and pillow slips. The commensurability of pieces of cloth with banana leaf bundles and fibre skirts raises the question of the inevitable replacement of one form for the other through the increasing commodification of *sagali*. In this chapter, I explore the durability of *doba* in terms of form and value in relation to the escalated incorporation of cloth, cash and commodities into exchange relations, and what these reconfigurations signal about the work of women in the Trobriand regenerative economy.

Material transformations

The reconfiguration of *doba* over time reflects the deep sedimentation of Christianity in Trobriand cultural aesthetics and embodied practices, and speaks of the broader history of cloth as the icon of Christian conversion in the Pacific and the missionary vision of domesticity, gendered bodies and women's work (Jolly 2014: 3). In the early years of the twentieth century, Trobriand women first began cultivating their relational craft with *karekwa* at Oiabia, the Methodist Mission Station on the south coast of Kiriwina, by learning how to sew garments on Singer hand machines under the watchful eyes of expatriate missionaries (Akerman 2001: 5, 10). Paradoxically, Trobriand women were at once subject to the 1906 law of the Australian Territory of Papua, which prohibited Papuans from wearing cloth garments on the upper body (Connelly 2007: 70–71), while at the same time the skirts and blouses they crafted in mission station sewing classes were presented to visiting government officials as evidence of the 'tremendous force' the missionaries were having on transforming the moral bearing of the islanders (Akerman 2001: 41). The enterprise not only introduced new forms of gendered labour in the fashioning of Christian identity but it also marked emerging economic distinctions in the colonial landscape between Trobrianders residing within the moral boundaries of the mission station and villagers beyond (see Connelly 2007: 143).

According to an elderly woman from Orabesi village (aged 84 at time of interview in 2000), the initial incorporation of cloth skirts and pieces of fabric into *doba* distributions dates back to the 1920s, in the context of a general prohibition of the practice of *sagali* on the Oiabia mission station. It seems that the innovation was approved by the missionaries as a truncated form of traditional funeral rites in response to the death of a Trobriand man on the mission station.

> The time they started using clothes and materials [for *sagali*] we were still young … At the time they didn't use *doba* on the mission station. There was a death on the station and the clans had to go together to look for new clothes and some foods … they went together and they searched for materials and foods and money and they cooked food with chicken. At that time they were wearing black because of mourning so then they got rid of the black clothes and they got a bit of colour with the materials and new clothes. The *sagali* was just for those on the mission station. The European missionaries gave permission. My father's younger brother was the one who died. He died at the mission station so we had to make *sagali*. It wasn't like these days or before. We just had to do what we could on the station (Recorded interview, 20 December 2000).

Not allowed to invest their time and labour into the manufacture of banana leaf bundles, the first generation of Trobriand women living on the station also redirected the products of their sewing labour toward *sagali* distributions beyond the coral stone fence, which marked the mission boundaries. This deliberate transformation of the industriousness of Christian domesticity into a valued Trobriand form of embodied practice was dialectical. Similar to the early missionary encounters among the Suau people, also of the Milne Bay region in Papua New Guinea, Trobriand women discerned 'an image of themselves in the actions of the missionaries' (Demian 2007: 103), recognising their own valued capacities for *doba* production in the work of sewing. The materiality of form was also commensurate: measured lengths of *karekwa* and sewn skirts retained the value of women's work in sustaining interclan relations and reproducing matrilineal identity through mortuary exchange. Putting *karekwa* into circulation beyond the mission station no doubt carried new value as well—the image of Christian modernity and the material practicality of cotton—and forged new connections and transactional relationships in the elaborate networks of exchange linked to *sagali* distributions.

The relationality performed by these women through the sewing of garments and the exchange of pieces of *karekwa* undoubtedly expressed their Christian faith, or *tapwaroru*, as well. A letter to the *Australasian Methodist Missionary Review* in 1893, written by William Bromilow, the founder of the Methodist mission in British New Guinea, contains an account by Bromilow's wife that indicates the value with which cloth was assessed by Christian converts. In the letter, Lily Bromilow describes the catechism she imparted during sewing classes at the Methodist mission headquarters on Dobu Island, part of the D'Entrecasteaux Islands in Milne Bay with close cultural and historical ties to the Trobriands. In response to the missionary's instructive question, 'What is *taparoro*'? (Dobu language for Christian faith), a young Dobu girl said, '*Taparoro* is the calico we put on'. The missionary corrected her, saying, '*Taparoro* is not calico or anything that we use; but Jesus in your heart' (Bromilow 1893: 6).[1] I would suggest that the young girl's metonymic answer was likely misapprehended by the missionary, and that instead it was a direct expression of the perceived consonance between Christian faith and the value of relationality that productive labour, like sewing, makes visible. Similarly, in the Trobriands, calico as emblematic of Christian materiality resonates strongly with the enduring relational value of *doba* in gift exchange.

The initial material transformation of banana leaf bundles into cloth on the Oiabia mission station weaves through a deeper history of *doba* production. This is evidenced from the journal of Ethel Prisk, an Australian Methodist missionary whose six years in the Trobriands, from 1911 to 1916, overlapped with that of Bronisław Malinowski's period of ethnographic fieldwork. Prisk recorded the vernacular names and provided descriptions of 16 distinct types of banana, pandanus and coconut fibre skirts made for *sagali* (Prisk 1937). Considered in relation to Annette Weiner's pivotal ethnography on the status of women in Trobriand society (1976), which triggered debate about historical change and Malinowski's seemingly androcentric disregard of the central role of Trobriand women in mortuary distributions (see Jolly 1992; Strathern 1981), the evidence in Prisk's diary suggests that the woman missionary was more attentive than the male anthropologist when it came to contemporaneous observations of women's material culture (but see Bashkow 2011). The missionary women

---

1   I wish to acknowledge Ryan Schram for bringing this archival account to my attention, and for sharing with me his insights about missionaries' semiotic ideologies and the use of constructed dialogue in missionary records.

admired the methods and skills involved in weaving fibre skirts, and on at least one occasion they organised a demonstration of *doba* manufacture for Malinowski when he visited the mission station (Young 2004: 399). The remarkable array of different skirt types that Prisk encountered in the early twentieth century no longer exists today. However, creativity in design continues to flourish, and no two fibre skirts are ever identical but rather they carry unique stylistic signatures of the individual makers. The diminished quantity of form may provide a firm measure of historical change regarding the displacement of banana fibre for cloth in the skirts that women make, yet it does not account for the enduring value of *doba* in the Trobriand exchange economy.

Moral revaluations

Questions surrounding the durability of *doba* across time came to the fore in a circumstantial event recounted to me by Diana, one of three Trobriand women who collaborated with me on my ethnographic research on culture and HIV in 2003 (Lepani 2012). Late one Saturday evening in August that year, after an all-day *sagali* at Kavataria—one of the largest villages in the Trobriands with a population of over 1,000 people, and located next to Oiabia mission station—a sudden downpour caught a group of women as they were about to set off to their home village on the northern side of Kiriwina Island. The women rushed to take shelter under the thatched roof of a communal seating platform on the church grounds, setting down the large baskets they were carrying on their heads, each replete with the *doba* they had received in *sagali* distributions. Dark clouds were rolling in the night sky and the rain did not look like it would let up anytime soon. Assessing the situation, the women called out to Diana's husband, David, who managed the church canteen, and asked him if they could store their *doba* baskets in the cement brick building until morning. The women did not mind getting wet walking the two hours to their village in the rain, but they did not want their *doba* to get wet. Rain-drenched bundles are rendered useless. Diana said that David quietly scoffed at their request:

> Why should we look after their *doba* for the night? That's their problem, if they want to walk around with *doba* on their heads. Why are they wasting their time? They should be at home cooking for their families.

But the women's request was not contestable; the resplendent baskets were sheltered overnight on the dry concrete floor of the church canteen.

David's assessment about the value of *doba* in terms of women's labour and investment of time echoes the views of Joshua, the young Trobriand man who would sometimes drive Weiner around Kiriwina in the vehicle belonging to the district health centre during her period of fieldwork in the early 1970s (Weiner 1980). Joshua had recently returned home to the Trobriands to take up a nursing position at the health centre after living and working elsewhere in Papua New Guinea. Weiner recounts how during one road trip when they happened to drive by a *sagali* in progress off the main road, Joshua remarked to her that *doba* bundles were useless and a drain on other resources, particularly hard-earned money.

> We have to get those women to stop throwing their wealth, because they take our money. If the women would stop needing so many baskets of wealth ... then men would have plenty of money to pay for other things (Weiner 1980: 274).

Weiner inferred that Joshua's years living away from home and earning a wage income had caused him to revaluate *doba* in strictly 'Western capitalist terms', and she extended Joshua's comments with the proposition that *doba* as 'women's wealth' diminishes men's economic power (Weiner 1980: 273–74; but see Jolly 1992).

I have heard similar statements from women as well as men about the uselessness of *doba* as an exchange object and the extravagance of *sagali* as a social enterprise that diverts women away from more appropriate forms of work, like 'cooking for their families' (see also MacCarthy this volume). Banana leaf bundles are mere flimsy bits of fibre that get wet in the rain, take up storage space in large baskets in the recesses of small dwellings, turn musty and attract rats and cockroaches. The demands of *doba* manufacture, accumulation and storage in preparation for *sagali* are revaluated as disproportionate and wasteful in relation to the utility of commodity transactions. But I have also witnessed men helping women do the work of *doba* manufacture—scraping the strips of freshly cut banana leaves on incised *kaidawagu* boards and refreshing old bundles by pressing them with their hands. Men also channel substantial monetary resources into the work of *sagali*, supporting their wives and sisters to acquire bolts of material and purchasing trade-store food in bulk to augment men's *sagali* distributions of yams, taro, betel nut and pigs with rice, flour, sugar, tea and tin fish. *Doba* transactions correspond with the value of men's productive labour in yam cultivation and their complex networks of exchange (Weiner 1976), and the strength of men's exchange relations in the monetary economy—the ability to mobilise cash resources through obligatory ties (see Lepani 2012: 51–54).

Pieces of fabric are integral exchange items for *sagali*, which both replicate *doba* in form and value and supplement prime *doba* distributions (Figure 1). At present, there is no clear indication that fabric will eclipse banana leaf bundles as the preferred object of exchange.[2] The extent to which the incorporation of cloth and cash has put new and potentially unsustainable financial pressures on the stability of *sagali* is the topic of much contemplation and debate by Trobrianders: amongst themselves in the planning stages of an upcoming *sagali*; in rhetoric emanating from the church pulpit and expressed at community meetings—with resonances of the Protestant work ethic of Methodism; and in reflective dialogue with the circulating discourses in Papua New Guinea on economic development and the commoditisation of customary practices. The analogy between yams and fortnightly wages has long shaped evaluations of men's obligatory contributions in the gift economy. Likewise, the correlation between *doba* and cloth in *sagali* distributions, aesthetically and pragmatically, has set new monetary measures of exchange. Bundles themselves are sometimes ascribed a currency value in comparison with cash, and in *sagali* transactions they represent the most immediate equivalence of form with the metric system of accounting, where individual distributions are made in units of five bundles. A man in his 40s told me, 'Money is part of custom now. Everything is money now. It would be hard to *sagali* without money. We need money for *doba*' (Journal notes, 9 October 2003). Women and men express ambivalence about the 'burden' of *sagali*, both financially and productively, but they also say they cannot 'give it up' because '*sagali* keeps calling us'.

---

2   It is important to note the geographical variation of local practices in the Trobriand group of islands. *Sagali* practices on the outer islands, including Vakuta, Kitava and Kuyawa, do not involve the manufacture and distribution of banana leaf bundles like on the main island of Kiriwina. The diffusion and diversity of practice in such a critical element of Trobriand material culture necessarily reflects local political and historical interactions and processes, including that of broader trade networks and Christian missionisation.

Figure 1. Complementary values: *doba*, cloth, cash, Orabesi village, Kiriwina

Source. Photographed by Katherine Lepani, 12 June 2003

Most Trobrianders, men and women alike, cannot imagine dealing with death without working for *sagali*, and many people say it would be impossible to do *sagali* properly without banana leaf bundles. While *sagali* practices on the outer islands of the Trobriand group do not involve distributions of banana leaf bundles, people from these islands nonetheless acknowledge the value of *doba*, and women who participate in *sagali* on Kiriwina also receive *doba* bundles and then recycle them through their interisland exchange networks. To an important extent, the continued use of bundles is a measure of limited access to monetary resources in the local economy. One needs money to purchase bolts of fabric. By contrast, bundles are not used in *sagali* distributions in urban contexts for equally pragmatic reasons. Urban residents engaged in wage labour do not have the time or requisite supply of banana trees in amounts sufficient for *doba* production, and whereas yams, clay pots, fibre skirts and woven mats and baskets are routinely transported as cargo by sea or air from the islands to urban centres for use in *sagali*, it would be an impractical folly to transport the ephemeral pieces of *doba* over such distances.

About 20 years ago, a village on Kiriwina made the collective decision to give up *sagali* because it was viewed as too expensive and a wasteful preoccupation that kept people from other more important activities (see MacCarthy this volume). Despite this internal restriction, women and men from the village continue to attend and partake in *sagali* at other villages through their clan affiliations. Some women even redefined their relational position as entrepreneurs, producing and supplying woven mats and baskets as cash commodities for purchase by others to use in the hallmark *sepwana* and *deli* distributions (described below). The decision to cease *sagali* practice within the village has affected how young girls from the village view their marriage options. As one woman explained to me, 'Our girls don't want to marry here because no *sagali*. They want to marry other places so they can go there and *sagali*' (Group interview, 23 July 2003). The prospect of such diminished capacity in the moral economy of *sagali* suggests that, for women at least, the value of *doba* has not been displaced by frugal revaluations or commodity markets but continues to inhere in women's embodied contributions to the social reproduction of Trobriand values.

Joshua's statement to Weiner signalled the economic tensions affecting *sagali*, which have become more pronounced 40 years on, but I am curious whether he actually used the word 'wealth' to refer to *doba*. Trobrianders do not talk of *doba* as 'women's wealth', a decidedly anthropological term. The women I've asked about this descriptor find it a laughable fiction in translation: 'Oh, yes, we are very wealthy!' they exclaim with ironic humour. Clearly, their estimations are based on a notion of monetary affluence as conveyed by the English definition, in contrast to Weiner's conceptual use of the term 'women's wealth' to theorise the 'value of womanness' (1976: 230). The Trobriand word *na'esaesa* (*na*: female prefix; *esaesa* wealth) evokes wealth not in terms of acquired bounty but in the relational capacity to generate and redistribute objects of exchange. 'Valuable' is accepted by my interlocutors as an apt English word to qualify the importance of *doba*, yet it does not translate directly either. The Trobriand word for valuable, *veguwau*, classifies those exchange items that generally remain concealed until displayed and put into circulation (clay pots, stone axe blades, shell arm bands and necklaces); *doba* is not referred to as a valuable in this way. Nor do banana leaf bundles have commercial value in the monetary economy beyond the enterprise of *sagali*. Unlike woven mats and baskets, and banana fibre skirts to a lesser extent, *doba* bundles do not circulate beyond the Trobriands as valued exchange objects, nor do they convert to commodities for sale in the larger market place.

Trobriand women quite simply refer to *doba* as *paisewa*, or work. *Paisewa* also refers to staging and partaking in *sagali*, and to the act of mourning—observing food taboos, wearing black clothing, restricting activities. In this distinctive sense, value—both cultural and economic—is located not in the objects of exchange but in embodied practice. Work is valued for its performative effects on a continuum of purpose in the production and exchange of goods. Objects are imbued with the value of productivity and performativity, always oriented towards working with others in mind. Work produces and makes visible social relations; hence, the value of objects cannot be assessed separately from the relations activated through exchange. Valuation involves a dialectical process in which personhood embodies the reproductive value of lineage, clan identity and attachments to place, and is projected onto objects of exchange. Likewise, objects of exchange and their transactions are imbued with personhood and the value of clan identity within embodied contexts of action.

The imperative to work for *doba*, and in so doing to demonstrate the capacity and fitness of one's matriline, accounts for the endurance of *sagali* in Trobriand social life. The materiality of *doba* is patent and ever present in the Trobriand landscape, and is striking to the most casual observer. Women cut and scrape banana leaves on the incised *kaidawagu* boards to remove the outer layer of skin and create textured patterns on the thin green strips. Along pathways and beside dwellings, the imprinted strips lie in straight rows on the ground, bleaching in the sun, turning light beige. Women work alone on a beach, or sit in groups in patches of shade, busily tying strips by the hundreds into fresh *doba* bundles. Women with enormous baskets of *doba* balanced on their heads, walk purposively to *sagali* (Figure 2).

The death of a clansperson sets in motion the work of *sagali*; women commence making and accumulating bundles, acquiring bolts of material and sewing skirts. For women to produce and acquire *doba* when not working towards a specific *sagali* would be unthinkable and diminish the value of their labour. Likewise, to hoard *doba* would be shameful. As the preparatory work of *sagali* unfolds, women receive contributions of *doba* from their in-laws and friends, and they take careful note of who supports them since these people will be recipients of *doba* and food distributions in the upcoming *sagali*.

Figure 2. Women carrying baskets of *doba*, Losuia, Kiriwina
Source. Photographed by Katherine Lepani, 15 January 2000

Small transactions involving the exchange of various commodities for *doba* bundles—food items, firewood, kerosene and betel nut—become a daily occurrence as women work to build up their *doba* reserves. Called *valova*, these exchanges demonstrate the convertibility of *doba* as a unit of value (see MacCarthy this volume). Women will also purchase small items from the store—lollies, balloons, biscuits, tobacco—to exchange for *doba*. *Valova* transactions are one way that men become directly involved in supporting their mothers, sisters and wives with commodities and cash to acquire *doba*—an obligation subjected to moral evaluations, as conveyed by Joshua in his assessment of how *sagali* depletes men's monetary resources. However, the convertibility of cash for *doba* is strictly determined. Women would never make bundles as a commodity for monetary gain. Women *valova* to build their supply of *doba*, not to get rid of it; transactions are driven by a demand for *doba*, not a demand for cash. The only direct transaction involving cash for *doba* takes a very specific form—activating support through the village church by giving a cash donation to the women's fellowship group. In this way, a woman appeals to members of her church congregation to reciprocate collectively with a commensurate amount of *doba* as an obligatory contribution to support her work towards *sagali*.

Trobrianders tend to speak of the process of accumulating *doba* by using the verb *nene*, meaning 'to search'. The idiom 'searching for *doba*' suggests that productivity is inherently social and not something achieved in isolation of other people's efforts. The valuation of *doba* is more than the product of its labour; it reflects the effort that goes into mobilising resources through social networks of exchange. The search for *doba* often involves mobility beyond the islands. Men sometimes will give their reason for travelling to Alotau, the provincial capital, or to Port Moresby as 'looking for *doba*' to help their mothers or wives with the work of *sagali*. The *doba* they find are not banana leaf bundles, but bolts of fabric purchased at shops with money earned through wage labour or acquired by activating exchange relationships with people who have sources of cash income.

At times, the work of *sagali* seems perpetual and all consuming. I recall many times when my late mother-in-law would sigh with resignation while busily preparing for a feast, and utter under her breath, '*Sagali, sagali, sagali*'. Her sighs were tinged with ambivalent affection as she smoothed the neatly arranged *doba* bundles and patted the growing pile of folded pieces of cloth, momentarily pausing from her work to lean back against the wall and chew betel nut. In 2000, in preparation for the *sagali* for her deceased maternal uncle, the last clan member of his generation to pass away, my mother-in-law was intensely involved in sewing skirts and dresses. Her personal *doba* inventory included a huge basket measuring 2 metres in circumference and 1 metre in height, which contained hundreds of banana leaf bundles. In addition, she had eight fibre skirts, 40 cotton skirts, 22 cotton dresses, 20 pillow cases, six bolts of material that were cut into 2-metre lengths for distribution, and four cotton skirts made specifically for *sepwana* (see below). The heightened daily comings and goings of women at the house, bringing small contributions of *doba* and bits of material to support my mother-in-law's efforts, put in motion a domestic rhythm that intensified as the day of *sagali* drew closer. My mother-in-law kept close account of those who supported her, and recorded names of contributors and the items they gave on a sheet of paper she kept between the pages of her Bible. At the end of the *sagali*, she was exuberant with exhaustion. With careful planning and auditing, her ample distributions were comprehensive and received with satisfaction. With her *doba* supplies now fully depleted, nothing left ungiven, she was indeed *na'esaesa*, a woman of wealth.

Weiner underplays the incorporation of cloth into *sagali* even though it was well established during the time of her fieldwork in the mid-1970s. Cloth is not simply a substitute for bundles imposed by urban wage earners returning home to the islands, as Weiner infers from Joshua's comments, nor is cloth used by 'women who have been too lazy' to make bundles (1976: 113). Such moral revaluations fail to recognise the complementarity of form between banana leaf bundles and *karekwa*, both equally imbued with the enduring aesthetic and material value of women's agency in working for *sagali*, and simultaneously absorptive of commodity value set by the market economy. The fidelity to cultural values is remarkably stable in interaction with the accelerated flows of cash and manufactured goods incorporated in *sagali* transactions (Figure 3).

Figure 3. Lucianne Gilbert and the late Sarah Watson prepare pieces of *karekwa* for *sagali*, Orabesi village, Kiriwina

Source. Photographed by Katherine Lepani, 9 June 2003

Material innovations and consumer pleasures

Like their early missionary ancestors, Trobriand women continue to use their sewing skills to work for *sagali*. Cloth is highly valued because of its immediate utility in daily life: a simple *laplap*, or wrap, tied around the waist, or sewn into garments; and household items—sheets, pillowslips, tablecloths, curtains. Young men get pieces of cloth from their mothers and aunties to use for *buwala*, the obligatory gifts given by men to women after lovemaking, which connect intimate transactions to larger networks of exchange (Lepani 2012: 112–18). The bright colours and bold tropical designs of the bolts of fabric purchased for *sagali* animate the intertwining flows of exchange relations and enliven the template of the social landscape, weaving their way into the materiality of everyday life. The selection and precirculation of bolts of fabric have become part of the patterning and coding of *sagali* performance; ensembles of women collectively assign specific colours and designs to different generations of clanswomen taking part, and to signify clan and village affiliations as well as ways in which participants are related to the deceased.

The integral value of cloth in *doba* distributions is most prominently conveyed by *sepwana*, the hallmark of *sagali*. *Sepwana* signifies the mourning skirts made and worn by the clanswomen of the deceased's father and spouse (if the deceased was married), who in turn are the primary recipients of *sagali* transactions. *Sepwana* also takes the stately form of piles of freshly made bundles of *doba*, numbering in the hundreds, which are carefully arranged and balanced on flat woven baskets (Figure 4). Made by the deceased's clanswomen to acknowledge and compensate the principal mourners, the piles of fresh bundles measure at least 1 metre in height and are topped with new fibre skirts, pieces of cloth and cash. The number of *sepwana* piles at *sagali* is optional but minimally there must be two to represent the primary exchange relations between the deceased's clan and the clans of the deceased's father and spouse. Additional *sepwana* are made in the name of close friends of the deceased, favourite nephews or nieces, or brothers who work hard for their sisters to acquire *doba* for *sagali*.

Figure 4. Carrying *sepwana* to *sagali* on the road to Kwemtula village, Kiriwina

Source. Photographed by Katherine Lepani, 18 July 2003

The women who assemble the *sepwana* piles and carry them to *sagali* on their heads wear new skirts, which are also referred to as *sepwana*. These skirts are no longer woven with banana fibres as in the past, but now are sewn with cotton material, and their production involves vibrant skill and creativity—full swinging skirts with contrasting coloured panels and layers, adorned with rickrack, ribbon and lace. Innovations are the source of mirth and playful engagement with modern fashion, but they can also be serious reflections on changing gender practices. In 2003, I attended a *sagali* where the women who assembled the *sepwana* piles collectively decided to wear trousers instead of skirts; they fashioned them out of *sagali* fabric plus purchased some at the newly opened second-hand clothing store on the island. In special tribute to the deceased, a young woman who had a successful career as a primary school principal, this innovation was a powerful statement about women's agency in the modern world.

Sagali distributions of bundles, cloth and cash, carried out methodically over long stretches of time, become aesthetically heightened during *sepwana* presentations and then culminate in the delights of *deli*, the most extravagant and plentiful site of exchange. *Deli* is the last series of distributions in *sagali* and is a complementary follow-up to *sepwana* to inspire ongoing reciprocal support in future *sagali*. The Trobriand word *deli* is the preposition 'with', and it also means to 'follow behind' or 'line up one after another'. *Deli* items are paraded in long lines to the recipients, who are the chief mourners from the clans of the deceased's father and spouse. This is the high point in *sagali* when the mourners are 'cleaned' by ceremoniously removing their black mourning attire and tying freshly made fibre skirts and cloth material around their hips, fitting them with newly sewn skirts and shirts, and then showering them with a plenitude of manufactured goods. In addition to skirts, clay pots, woven mats and baskets, *deli* items include an array of practical domestic merchandise such as cooking pots, plates and cups, cutlery, umbrellas, towels, sheets, clothing, bras and underpants. The hallmark of display in *deli* parades are the poles and cut tree branches festooned with fabric, money and consumer goods. *Deli* signifies excessive consumption in the true sense of feasting, and pragmatic investments in the materiality of the modern world, providing recipients periodic access to goods otherwise difficult to attain. The practice of *deli* achieves a dazzling effect of valuation that merges women's productive agency and matrilineal regeneration with the monetary economy. This concentrated site of material consumerism is where *sagali* has undergone its most dramatic transformations to date, and it might prove to be the site that eclipses *doba* bundles as markers of indebtedness, categorically transforming the materiality of exchange into commercial products of consumption. *Deli* is likely to be the site most fraught with moral debate as Trobrianders face future decisions about embodied capacity, productivity and value, and the consequences of emerging economic inequalities and financial burdens on livelihoods.

In August 2010, I participated in the *sagali* for my mother-in-law, who had passed away peacefully in January 2010 at the age of 81 years. The *sagali* was a massive event in her residential village of Orabesi. With proceedings held over three days, the event involved nearly 1,000 participants, including people who travelled home to the Trobriands from elsewhere in Papua New Guinea and overseas. The considerable financial resources put into the feast by my husband Charles and members of his clan included the purchase of over 40 bolts of fabric from a wholesale store in Alotau, which were shipped to the Trobriands on a chartered cargo boat. Several of Charles's *dala* sisters and I, and our daughters and nieces, spent a day measuring and cutting the bolts of fabric into 2-metre and 5-metre lengths, and pile sorting them by colour, pattern and size in preparation for distribution. Such material largess might be evaluated by some observers as an inflationary distortion of women's wealth, where monetary inputs turn gifts into commodities and overshadow women's productive agency in working for *sagali*. Yet the scale and symbolic 'density' of the material objects of exchange (Weiner 1994) reflected the flows of support for the event and met the collective expectation of what Charles should be able to mobilise as sponsor of the *sagali*, or *toliu'ula*, acting on behalf of his matriline. My personal contribution as the daughter-in-law of the deceased was a further variation of the forms *doba* takes; in tribute to my mother-in-law's renown as a seamstress, I topped each of the 16 *sepwana* piles with sewing kits.

Material conversions, adjustments of scale and translocality

Trobrianders living in other locations in PNG and overseas express a strong sense of obligation and desire to participate in *sagali*. Such motivation attests to the importance of *sagali* as an integrative practice in social and economic life, and its essential role in regenerating matrilineal identity. The enterprising agency of a young single mother of three living in Port Moresby exemplifies the translocality of working for *sagali*, the shifting forms of *doba*, and the transactional pathways that turn commodities into gifts (Gregory 1997: 55). Born and raised in the nation's capital, the young woman's mother is from Central Province and her father was from the Trobriands. Several months after her father died in 2012, she text messaged me in Australia to say she was looking for help to start up a small food stall in the neighbourhood where she lives, to sell breakfast to public servants on their way to work. She appealed to me for support in the form of a cash contribution to help with initial expenses. She texted that she was ready to 'start work for my father's *sagali*' and intended to turn the anticipated income into bolts of fabric to take with her when she travelled to the Trobriands for the feast later that year, which then she would put into circulation to support the women of her father's *dala*, the organisers of the *sagali*. As the daughter of the deceased she was a principal mourner and a primary recipient of copious amounts of *doba* during the *sagali* distributions, yet she orientated her active participation towards working for her father's clan. Her contribution assumed a material form commensurate to the resources she was able to mobilise through her own labour—not bundles of dried banana leaves but cloth. The conversion was multiple: a gift of cash turned into commodity, turned back into cash and then commodity again, and ultimately turned into gift in *sagali* distributions. Her entrepreneurial initiative could be viewed as a form of fundraising, an enterprise that involved generating cash resources through the mobilisation of social relations. But central to her endeavour were the performative effects of her labour; a public reckoning of her personal capacity, on display and directed toward relational value by acting with others in mind.

The lived experience of increased engagement with the monetary economy is a transformative process, whether practised through distinctly cultural forms or through changing livelihood strategies and consumption patterns; whether one is involved in the fluctuating cycles and scales of exchange in a rural village or dependent on regular flows of cash income in an urban context. Material conversions are increasingly modifying the forms and valuations of relations of exchange. The young woman's enterprising agency in the urban informal sector, strategising her options as an unemployed single mother with a translocal objective in mind, poses important questions for policies that seek to promote gender equality and women's empowerment through increased economic participation. Interventions and programmatic efforts aimed at expanding opportunities for women as economic agents and consumers, primarily in formal-sector employment, must be attentive to the informal arena where women's creative and innovative practices are directed at upholding social relations, and where indebtedness to others is valued as a productive site of relational agency (see Jolly et al. 2015). Indeed, as the young woman's actions suggest, indebtedness can be understood as a form of empowerment. It is important to recognise the ways in which women negotiate their economic options at the collective level, strategically activating obligations and channelling their monetary resources towards others, even as they strive to carve out more autonomy in their individual lives (see Macintyre 2011). What many women seek is not economic independence per se but economic opportunities to fulfil social obligations and make stronger contributions to collective wellbeing and social cohesion.

The material production of objects for *sagali*—banana fibre and cotton skirts, woven mats and hand baskets—is comparative to the extraordinarily vibrant and creative *bilum* and *meri* blouse craft practised by women elsewhere in Papua New Guinea. Such products of labour carry multiple values and are highly convertible depending on how they get put into circulation and transacted. But they represent a vibrant dimension of gendered practice in the creative industry sector and beyond (see Teaiwa 2007), and are important indicators for evaluating and valuing women's economic productivity and wealth.

Material durability

As an in-law and ethnographic researcher, I have been witness to and participant in numerous *sagali* over a period of nearly 40 years, but my questions about value and transformation in relation to *doba* and gendered agency have been framed most directly in recent years by how Trobrianders are making sense of HIV (Lepani 2012). Clearly, *sagali* as the cultural strategy for resolving the disruption of death through regeneration has important implications for how Trobrianders respond to the impact of HIV on their ways of knowing and being. What is patently at stake is people's continued capacity to cope with the demands of social obligation in response to unprecedented disease and death. If such a scenario unfolds, the suspension of *sagali* obligations is the likely possibility. As a precedent, Trobrianders refer to a malaria epidemic in the mid-1990s, when scores of people died over a short period. In response to the overwhelming loss, the affected communities made a collective agreement to ease *sagali* obligations. Nonetheless, the ethos of *sagali*, where people work with others in mind, is a valuable cultural resource for cultivating a positive response to living in the midst of an epidemic and for alleviating the stigma and fear that continues to surround HIV in Papua New Guinea.

And yet other questions about the ethos of *sagali* come to the fore as well. The collective zeal of increasingly excessive display and consumption in *sepwana* and *deli* distributions prompts me to ponder what further transformations might unfold in the Trobriand moral economy, both within and beyond the practice of *sagali* exchange, especially when the out-of-the-way small coral atolls are subjected to increased environmental and population constraints. Will the effects of climate change impinge on the sustained cultivation of yams and banana trees to the extent that exchange practices and corresponding scales of valuation are irrevocably transformed? As the local economy becomes more entwined in wider monetary flows, as consumer desires and the acquisition of material goods become more individualised in interaction with global economic forces and wage labour, and as notions of personhood are reshaped by changing relations with the church and new articulations of Christian faith (see MacCarthy this volume), what might be new transformations of collective exchange practices, and how might gendered assessments of value be revised? When the exchange of one thing for another takes place on a more intimate scale, what might be the transformative material and moral effects on collective social relations? The longing gaze at an item in the shop and the eventual purchase with secretly saved cash; the exchange of a gift between two young lovers, not acquired through larger networks of exchange but purchased directly as a commodity transaction; the 'promising smell' of second-hand clothes, as one of my interlocutors described her sensory pleasure when we walked by the newly opened shop on the island, which then motivated her to bake scones and sell them in her village so she could have extra cash to make a purchase.

And how do people adjust for the burden of scale, especially when cash resources are scarce or have to be pooled through strategic conversions? Translocality has generated simplified forms of practice in urban centres as people cope with the demands of death, where airfares for transporting the deceased's body back home to the village for burial are the major expense. The male organisers of a *sagali* held in 2013 among Trobrianders living in the national capital determined it would be a modest 'Moresby-style' feast, recognising the financial constraints that face urban wage earners. Intended to be limited to a generic distribution of purchased food staples and cooked market food, plus several pigs and bunches of betel nut, the *sagali* manifested over the course of the afternoon with generous *doba* distributions—the women had arrived bearing brand-new plastic clothes baskets abundantly filled with 2-metre lengths of neatly folded fabric.

As a nondurable exchange item, banana leaf bundles continue to represent a deep genealogy of belonging that holds potency for future possibilities, even when transformed by pieces of cloth. A key factor to consider in making a prognosis about the stability of *sagali* is the enduring imperative, and motivation, to demonstrate *dala* capacity and vitality through investments of gendered labour. Questions of value and of measuring change should not insist on the durability of a form impenetrable to transformative processes. Investments of personhood in working for *sagali* ensure the sustainability of value regardless of form. The ephemeral bundles of dried banana leaves made by Trobriand women are durable in the Trobriand economy, at least now and for the foreseeable future, because they activate social relations—affiliations, obligations, indebtedness, transactions—through the productive value of labour. *Doba* offers a form of economic productivity that continues to be recognised and valued in *sagali* transactions, and in the wider Trobriand economy, for aesthetic purpose and pragmatic action, for reasons of equivalence and reasons of belonging (Figure 5).

Figure 5. *Sagali* gathering, Losuia, Kiriwina
Source. Photographed by Katherine Lepani, 19 July 2003

References

Akerman, Kim. 2001. *New Guinea Diaries of the Rev. S.B. Fellows*, Vol. 1. 21 July 1891 – 14 October 1893. Hobart, Tasmania: Tasmanian Museum and Art Gallery.

Bashkow, Ira. 2011. 'Old Light on a New Controversy: Alex Rentoul's Account of the Trobriand Women's *Sagali'*. *History of Anthropology Newsletter* 38(2): 9–18.

Bromilow, William E. 1893. 'Letter from Mr. Bromilow'. *Australasian Methodist Missionary Review*, 6 January: 6–7.

Carrier, James G. (ed.). 1992. *History and Tradition in Melanesian Anthropology*. Berkeley: University of California Press.

Choi, Hyaeweol and Margaret Jolly (eds). 2014. *Divine Domesticities: Christian Paradoxes in Asia and the Pacific*. Canberra: ANU Press. Online: press.anu.edu.au/publications/divine-domesticities (accessed 31 March 2017).

Connelly, Andrew James. 2007. 'Counting Coconuts: Patrol Reports from the Trobriand Islands, Part I: 1907–1934'. MA thesis. California State University.

Demian, Melissa. 2007. 'Canoe, Mission Boat, Freighter: The Life History of a Melanesia Relationship'. *Paideuma* 53: 89–109.

Etienne, Mona and Eleanor Burke Leacock (eds). 1980. *Women and Colonization: Anthropological Perspectives*. New York: J.F. Bergin.

Gregory, Chris A. 1982. *Gifts and Commodities*. New York: Academic Press.

——. 1997. *Savage Money: The Anthropology and Politics of Commodity Exchange*. Amsterdam: Harwood Academic Publishers.

——. 2015. 'Preface to the Second Edition'. In *Gifts and Commodities* (2nd edition), Chris Gregory, pp. xi–xii. Chicago: HAU Books.

Jolly, Margaret. 1992. 'Banana Leaf Bundles and Skirts: A Pacific Penelope's Web?' In *History and Tradition in Melanesian Anthropology*, ed. James G. Carrier, pp. 38–63. Berkeley: University of California Press.

——. 2014. 'A Saturated History of Christianity and Cloth in Oceania'. In *Divine Domesticities: Christian Paradoxes in Asia and the Pacific*, ed. Hyaeweol Choi and Margaret Jolly, pp. 429–454. Canberra: ANU Press. Online: press-files.anu.edu.au/downloads/press/p298891/pdf/ch162.pdf (accessed 23 January 2017).

Jolly, Margaret, Helen Lee, Katherine Lepani, Anna Naupa and Michelle Rooney. 2015. *Falling through the Net? Gender and Social Protection in the Pacific*. Discussion Paper for UN Women New York, Progress of the World's Women, 2015–16. Online: www.unwomen.org/en/digital-library/publications/2015/9/dps-gender-and-social-protection-in-the-pacific (accessed 11 November 2015).

Lepani, Katherine. 2012. *Islands of Risk, Islands of Love: Culture and HIV in the Trobriands*. Nashville, TN: Vanderbilt University Press.

Macintyre, Martha. 2011. 'Money Changes Everything: Papua New Guinean Women in the Modern Economy'. In *Managing Modernity in the Western Pacific*, ed. Mary Patterson and Martha Macintyre, pp. 90–120. St Lucia: University of Queensland Press.

Patterson, Mary and Martha Macintyre (eds). 2011. *Managing Modernity in the Western Pacific*. St Lucia: University of Queensland Press.

Prisk, Ethel M. 1937. *Photographs, Documents*. Adelaide: South Australia Museum.

Strathern, Marilyn. 1981. 'Culture in a Netbag: The Manufacture of a Subdiscipline in Anthropology'. *Man* (n.s.), 16(4): 665–688. DOI: 10.2307/2801494.

Teaiwa, Katerina Martina. 2007. 'On Sinking, Swimming, Floating, Flying and Dancing: The Potential of Cultural Industries in the Pacific Islands'. *Pacific Economic Bulletin* 22(2): 140–151.

Weiner, Annette B. 1976. *Women of Value, Men of Renown: New Perspectives in Trobriand Exchange*. Austin: University of Texas Press.

——. 1980. 'Stability in Banana Leaves: Colonialism, Economics and Trobriand Women'. In *Women and Colonization: Anthropological Perspectives*, ed. Mona Etienne and Eleanor Burke Leacock, pp. 270–293. New York: J.F. Bergin.

——. 1994. 'Cultural Difference and the Density of Objects'. *American Ethnologist* 21(2): 391–403. DOI: 10.1525/ae.1994.21.2.02a00090.

Young, Michael W. 2004. *Malinowski: Odyssey of an Anthropologist 1884–1920*. New Haven, CT: Yale University Press.

2

Doing away with *Doba*? Women's Wealth and Shifting Values in Trobriand Mortuary Distributions

Michelle MacCarthy

Introduction

The activity on the *bukubaku*, or centre of the hamlet, is frenzied. Throngs of women bend over giant baskets called *pweia*, which may stand more than a metre tall. Inside these baskets, and piled high on shallow trays made of coconut fronds called *sekunona*, are hundreds and hundreds of bundles of small, dry strips of banana leaves. One after another, women go to the centre of the *bukubaku* and call out a name, and more women, generally members of the deceased person's matrilineage, rush to throw their bundles—five here, 10 there, but always in increments of five—on the various piles. Each pile is designated as a sort of payment to those who have provided assistance to the now deceased while ill, and immediately following the death, and who are not members of the deceased's matriclan (Figure 6). At times, arguments arise over how these bundles, along with accompanying payments in colourful lengths of calico and notes and coins in kina,[1] are redistributed. Despite being instigated by a death, these

---

1   The official state currency of Papua New Guinea (PNG).

mortuary distributions, called *sagali* in the Kiriwina vernacular,[2] are more festive than mournful, and are a place where women direct and control resources that they have laboured to produce, in order to demonstrate the strength of their *dala* (matriclan).

The scene described above represents the general atmosphere of a *sagali* and, in my nearly two years in Kiriwina, I saw similar scenes played out dozens and dozens of times. Such events are, as Katherine Lepani (2012: 77) says, 'dazzling to the senses' but, more importantly, they represent embodied capacity and potential and generational fecundity. The importance of banana leaf textiles (*doba*) in Trobriand mortuary distributions is well documented, and has been the subject of considerable anthropological discussion (Bashkow 2011; Jolly 1992; Lepani 2012; Mosko 2000; Weiner 1974, 1976; see also Lepani this volume), though this 'sphere of exchange' (Bohannan and Bohannan 1968; Sillitoe 2006) has received far less attention, despite Annette Weiner's efforts, than *kula* transactions in subsequent analyses of the nature of exchange in a cross-cultural perspective. In her feminist-inspired restudy of Trobriand exchange in the 1970s, Weiner made influential contributions to anthropological theory with her examination of the importance of women's exchange practices. Banana leaf skirts and bundles, collectively referred to in the Kilivila language as *doba*, are produced by women from locally available materials. Of primary importance in the context of *sagali* are not, today, the beautiful, bright red skirts,[3] which remain an essential item in preparing oneself (*-katubayasi*) for Trobriand traditional dance (MacCarthy 2013), but rather the bundles of scraped and dried banana leaves called *nununiga*. Trobriand women often refer to the buying power of *nununiga* as 'like your *dimdim* money', as they may be exchanged— usually in the context of a *sagali*, in transactions called *valova*—for locally produced or externally manufactured goods (anything from a few betel nuts, a small portion of tobacco or salt, tapioca cakes and smoked fish to bubble gum, lollies or balloons [Lepani 2012: 75, 81; Weiner 1976: 78–80]). Whilst the manufacture of grass skirts is a specialised skill that

---

2   *Tok Pisin*, the pidgin language used commonly throughout much of PNG, is rarely used in the Trobriand Islands. While many educated Trobrianders speak English, the general language of communication is the vernacular language, referred to by Trobrianders as *biga yakidasi* (our language), and in the literature as Kiriwina or Kilivila, of which there are several mutually intelligible dialects.

3   Weiner (1976: 105–15) describes in detail the components of *sagali* during her fieldwork in the early 1970s, in which skirts—both in terms of the privilege of wearing the *sepwana* skirts (mourning skirts) and the role of skirts as prestations in the *sagali* distributions—appear to play a much greater role than I generally observed nearly 40 years later.

not all Trobriand women possess, the making of banana leaf bundles is a task that defines Trobriand womanhood. To lack the skills necessary to make bundles is to be *nakodana*—a term that literally means 'idle or lazy woman', but also implies a lack of essential knowledge

Figure 6. The frenzied activity of 'throwing' *doba* at *sagali*, Kabwaku village, Kiriwina
Source. Photographed by Michelle MacCarthy, 28 December 2009

In this chapter, I reassess the role of *doba* and its production as a defining aspect of proper Trobriand womanhood, as well as being central to maintaining social relationships through its distribution at *sagali*. Yet in recent years, amidst pressure from the leaders of several newly established evangelical churches in the Trobriands, and a well-established trend towards a focus on (western) education and increased engagement in the cash economy, some villages are choosing to abandon the production and exchange of *doba* in mortuary distributions (and, indeed, to curb or cease the practice of *sagali*) in favour of smaller exchanges, using cash and store goods instead of the locally produced banana leaf textiles. These changes mark a shift in the conception of the value of both the time and labour necessarily expended to produce *doba* and the value placed on the material properties of these bundles. This shift has been the subject of much local debate in recent years, as many women—and men—argue that *doba* exchange is of fundamental and defining importance to Trobriand identity and kinship obligations.

Value and values

Competing discourses are employed to justify a 'waste not, want not' attitude as espoused by the so-called 'revivalist' or evangelical churches. One argument characterises *doba* production as a poor use of women's time, which would be better spent in more 'productive' activity. The counter argument views *doba* production as constituting the unique identity of Trobriand Island women, who manufacture their own 'wealth', as well as the democratisation of labour independent of the formal economy, to which most people have limited access. I suggest that a fundamental tension lies at the base of these discourses, which is played out in various ways. On the one hand, there is a reflexive and determined effort to maintain 'culture', and the social obligations entailed therein, as part and parcel of a self-essentialised Trobriand identity looking to the past. On the other hand, there exists an equally reflexive but forward-looking discourse—'from darkness to light'— which emphasises modernity and a conscious move away from what some church officials and some Trobrianders characterise as their 'savage' past. But with revival forms of Christianity, I argue that the past becomes something to be broken from (Meyer 1998), not recirculated. What these competing discourses represent, I suggest, is a state of flux in conceptions of gendered personhood as instigated by tensions between Christianity and the ancestors, individual priorities as against inter- and intraclan obligations, and globalisation/modernity vis-à-vis regional specificity and a unique anthropological heritage. In response to this tension is a reevaluation and disjuncture in the perceived socioeconomic value of *doba*.

It may be useful to briefly reflect on the difference, and relatedness, of *values* and *value*. When I speak of objects having 'value', I do not, of course, mean only their use value and exchange or market value, as described by Karl Marx (1976). Instead, I refer also to less tangible, emotional ascriptions of meaning and importance, whether by individuals or communities. Chris Gregory calls value 'those invisible chains that link relations between things to relations between people' (1997: 12). David Graeber (2001: 40) asserts that value is only recognised in the eyes of another, the ascription of value rendering visible some social relationship: it is 'the way people represent the importance of their own actions to themselves' (Graeber 2001: 45). On the same lines, Michael Lambek (2013: 149) suggests that value is best understood expressly as a consequence of human activity and it circulates only through the actions of people. Values, on the other hand, might be considered as the ideal models of human behaviour, ethical ideas about virtue that are reflected in action and both individual and collective character (Cox and Macintyre 2014). Graeber (2001: 3), following Clyde Kluckhohn (1951: 395), points out that values are 'conceptions of the desirable', which are implicated in the choices people make about their actions—and, presumably, in how people judge both their own and others' actions. These ideas are inevitably gendered, and this is certainly true in the Trobriand case. I here invoke Louis Dumont's (1980) hierarchy of values in order to understand the relationship between the way Trobrianders value the church in relation to 'tradition' or *gulagula*, which might be described as the manners and customs associated with the ancestors (despite the fact that, as I shall show, the significance of *doba* as an exchange valuable is far from fixed). If the church, and the more individualistic discourses it advocates with respect to production and exchange, moves higher in the hierarchy than *gulagula*, the result is not only a change in the orientation of values—at least for those adopting revivalist rhetoric—but also a change in how both objects and actions are assigned value (in the more economic and absolute sense). Thus, the work needed to produce *doba,* the act of exchanging it, and the bundles themselves as a kind of currency or means of payment lose relative value in comparison to work for cash or food crops, exchange of more 'useful' goods, and money, and industrially produced goods as objects whose value outranks *doba* in a more modern, forward-looking, capitalist-individualist and Christian hierarchy of values. In the process, the role of women as producers and the guardians of the matrilineage is altered. It is not, I think, foregone though, as this value transformation is far from total, and these tensions are reflected in the debates and discomforts in the local context as individuals, clans and whole villages consider or embrace the eradication of *doba* as a means of exchange.

Gendering wealth

In her encounter with a young, educated Trobriand man she called Joshua, Weiner (1980: 273–77) was surprised to hear the man suggest that *doba* was wasteful and drained resources from men. Its use, Joshua thought should be discouraged. She states:

> To take away women's wealth and to alter the procedures of mortuary distributions and payments would force the most drastic changes in the status and roles of women *and* also in the status and roles of men. Not only would women become economically disadvantaged, but Kiriwina men would lose their base of political power [i.e. the link of yam production (men's work) and exchange to women] (Weiner 1980: 274, emphasis in original).

Similarly, my initial instinct, upon hearing that some villages had abandoned the practice of exchanging *doba*, was that the declining use of 'women's wealth', as Weiner calls banana leaf textiles, would have negative implications for the power and agency of women. On the contrary, my ethnographic research[4] indicates that by releasing themselves from the work of making and maintaining *doba*, many women have found new avenues to express their productivity and to generate new forms of wealth, such as weaving baskets that are sold in high volume at the Kiriwina airstrip. It has neither significantly reduced women's sociopolitical and economic position, nor has it altered men's base of power. Though locally generated forms of 'wealth' have in many cases been supplanted by western ones (currency and industrially manufactured goods), the extent to which such changes have fundamentally altered Trobriand social structure and gendered personhood remains somewhat ambiguous—even to Trobrianders themselves.

The sundry ceremonial transactions of Trobriand Islanders—from yams to *kula* shell valuables, stone axe blades and clay pots—have, of course, been a pivotal case study for theorising the nature of exchange practices cross-culturally from Bronisław Malinowski and Marcel Mauss through to the present day (e.g. Appadurai 1986; Damon 1980; Ekeh 1974; Gregory 1982, 1983; Hoenigman 2012; Jolly 1992; Leach and Leach 1983; Malinowski 1920a, 1920b, 1921; Mauss 1990; Mosko 2000; Sahlins 1965; Weiner 1974, 1976, 1980). *Kula* valuables are exchanged primarily in the interests of making a name for oneself, to gain status and prestige as a great 'player' of the *kula* game (Campbell 1983; Damon 2002; Kuehling 2005; Munn 1986). Other valuables may be exchanged alongside *kula* shells, but they are not the focus of exchanges. *Doba* (associated with women's work) and yams, clay pots[5] and stone axe blades (associated with men's work) are essential exchange goods that comprise requisite 'payments' (*mapula*) in the wake of a death—a process that 'ensures regeneration in the cosmic realm … The ephemeral bundles of

---

4   I spent approximately 18 months in 2009–10 on Kiriwina to undertake my doctoral research on cultural tourism in the Trobriands, during which time I became aware that some villages had stopped using *doba*. A return trip of three-and-a-half months in 2013, and a shorter visit in 2016, were undertaken as a postdoctoral fellow under the project 'Gender and Pentecostal Christianity', headed by Annelin Eriksen and funded by the Norwegian Research Council (Norges forskningsråd [NFR]) to more directly focus on this phenomenon. The ethnographic details described here reflect both periods of fieldwork, and the changes and developments noted over the eight years that I have been working in the Trobriand Islands.

5   While women may manufacture and exchange clay pots at their point of origin in the Amphlett Islands, which provides clay pots to islands like the Trobriands where clay to make such pots is lacking, in the Trobriands these valuable items are primarily exchanged by men.

dried banana leaves are the durable material of cultural resilience and continuity' (Lepani 2012: 75). Descent in the Trobriands is matrilineal. All Trobrianders identify with one of four clans (*kumila*), as well as with a matriline that has a common founding ancestor (*dala*). Weiner has theorised the 'density' or symbolic significance of Trobriand bundles and skirts, suggesting that their importance lies less with their specific biographies or power relating to chiefly rank—as with *kula* valuables for example—but rather the symbolic density of *doba* is linked generally to the primacy of matrilineal identity (Weiner 1994: 400).

Some scholars suggest that *kula* is a fairly recent institution, emerging in the last 500 years or so, and that it has changed considerably in orientation and execution since European contact (Keesing 1990; Schram 2013: 70–71; Van Heekeren 2014). Anecdotal evidence suggests that the same can be said for the manufacture and exchange of *doba*, both in terms of skirts and bundles. The brief report of a *lisaladabu sagali*, written by Assistant Resident Magistrate Alex Rentoul in 1929 (Bashkow 2011), makes clear that women's role in the manufacture and exchange of banana leaf bundles in mortuary distributions has a long history. However, there is evidence to suggest that, indeed, the use of *doba* has increased in volume over the past century. Changing technology (from shell to metal scrapers, from incising designs by hand to using carved wooden boards to quickly imprint designs) has made production of *nununiga* faster, and this seems to have resulted in an 'inflation' in the amount of bundles used in *sagali*, according to my informants (see also Weiner 1980: 276). Women told me that in the 'old days' (*tukunibogwa*), the baskets that were used to hold and carry the bundles (*pweia*) were much smaller, and that fewer bundles were exchanged. Weiner may well have arrived in the Trobriands when these textiles were in the peak of their popularity; since the mid-1980s, some villages that previously participated in these transactions began a collective movement to abolish their use, as I shall describe below. This also coincides with an increase in the use of calico, lengths of which are cut from bolts of brightly patterned Chinese-made cloth, as an essential exchange item in *sagali*, and women's move away from wearing grass skirts for daily apparel (as was still the case in Weiner's time) to skirts and dresses sewn of calico or second-hand clothing imported from overseas. I include this brief exegesis on the historical fluctuation in the importance and significance of *doba* to contextualise my own argument, demonstrating that changes in the use of *doba* in ceremonial transactions are not abrupt and specifically linked to Christian revival movements, but are rather a recent manifestation of a long history of adjustments to exchange practices.

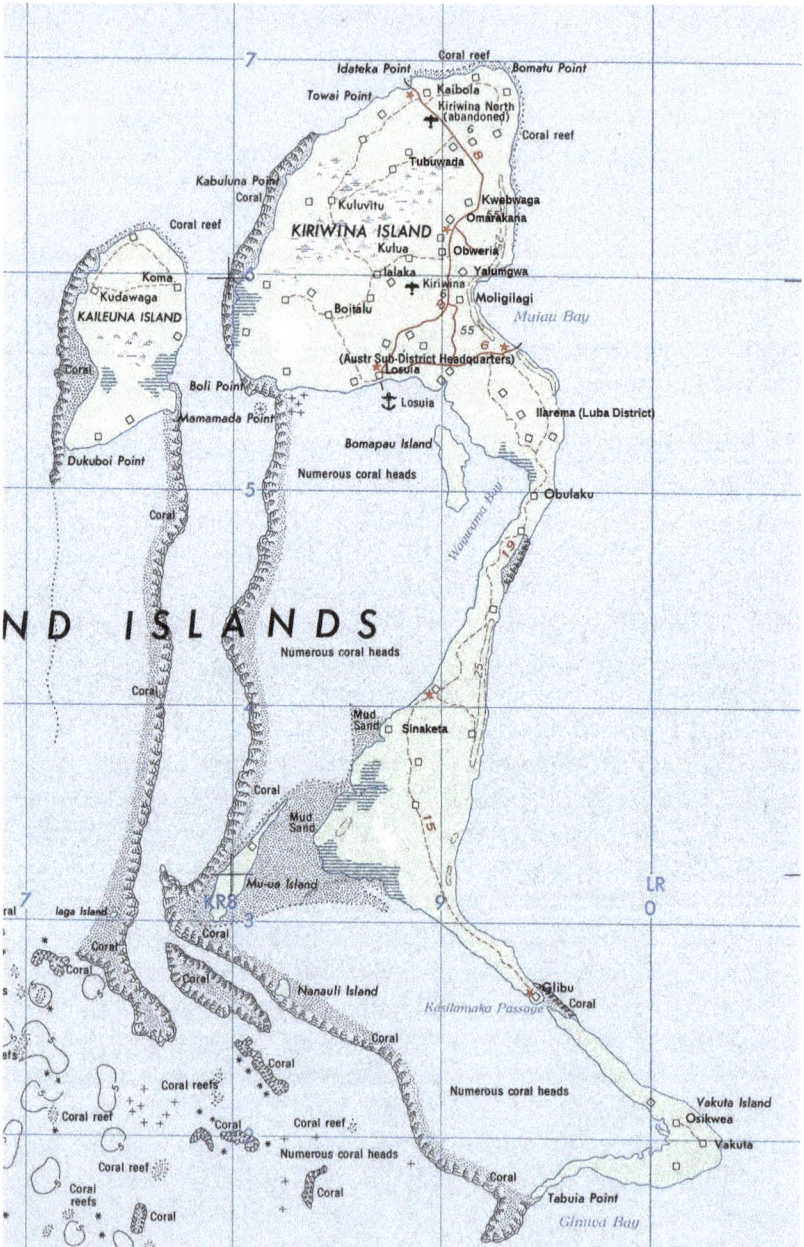

Map 1. Kiriwina, Trobriand Islands, Papua New Guinea

Source. Courtesy of the University of Texas Libraries, the University of Texas at Austin and modified by Michelle MacCarthy

Generating gendered wealth: The manufacture of *doba*

Weiner's cursory description of the production of *nununiga* (1976, Appendix 2) does not do justice to the process. It often begins with an excursion of a group of women, all preparing for an impending *sagali*, who may walk several hours to areas of the island where leaves from the particular banana tree called *wakaya* are plentiful. This process was exemplified for me in an excursion I made with several women to the village of Ilarema, in the area called Luba (see Map 1). Departing from Yalumgwa, our village of residence, the walk took about 90 minutes. We carried with us articles of clothing, lengths of cloth and kina notes to exchange with the Luba women, who gave us bundles of fresh *wakaya* leaves in return. The rate of exchange was a *kaupatala doba* (one parcel of fresh leaves) per piece of clothing, length of cloth or two kina note. This is approximately enough leaves to make one small girl's grass skirt, or some dozens of bundles.[6] In this case, the woman who organised the excursion also paid for a truck to collect the fresh leaves, and each woman who wanted to transport her haul (though not herself—the truck would be full of fresh *doba*, leaving no room for passengers) would pay 20 *nununiga* (finished bundles). While it would be possible, if strenuous, to *gebila* (carry on one's head) one or two of these stacks of leaves through the narrow garden paths and rough coral roads back home, more than this would be virtually impossible. The women mark their bundles, and are very concerned that each retrieves their own. The women I was with fairly ran back to their home village, in order that they would not to be too late to claim their 'raw' *doba* from the returned truck—they did not want to risk losing their designated piles. Having left our own village shortly after daybreak, it was dusk by the time we returned.

Once the fresh leaves are acquired, they must be scraped. Each leaf is torn into strips and, with deft, rhythmic movements, young girls, married women, divorcées and elderly widows all work to remove the outer fibres of the leaves by running a metal scraper over them. The leaves are placed one by one on a sheet of glass or, for *nununiga*, a carved wooden board that creates patterns on the lower third of each strip (Figure 7). One bundle of fresh leaves will take several hours to scrape. The scraped leaves are

---

6   When I asked women how many *nununiga* they could make from *kaupatala ya'udila* (one stack or bundle of fresh leaves), they could not give me an answer. It is highly variable, because if conditions are poor (e.g. it rains when the leaves are set out to dry) the yield will be lower, and some leaves may have defects that will render part or all of them unusable.

soaked in water overnight, and laid out to dry in the sun in neat rows weighted down with sticks, which must be moved periodically to prevent discolouration (Figure 8). In good conditions, the leaves might be dry in two to three days; heavy rains will slow the process, and may even render the leaves unusable, negating all preceding efforts.

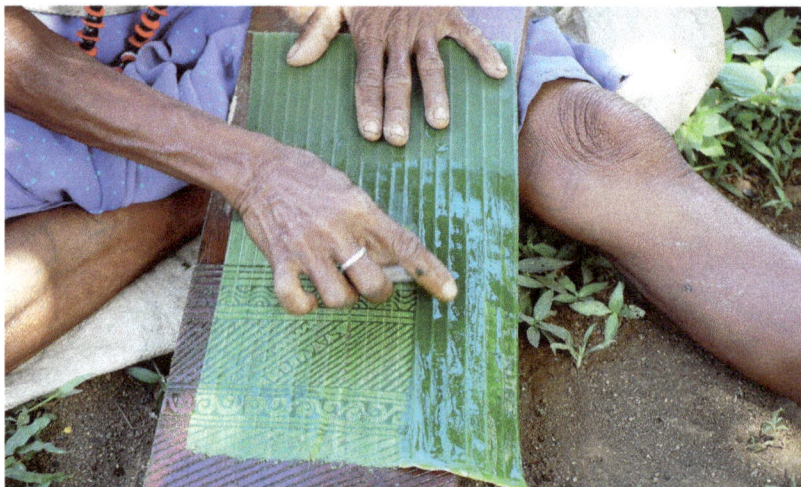

Figure 7. Fresh banana leaf scraped over carved wooden board to incise pattern, Yalumgwa village, Kiriwina

Source. Photographed by Michelle MacCarthy, 17 December 2009

Figure 8. Freshly scraped *doba* leaves drying in the sun, Yalumgwa village, Kiriwina

Source. Photographed by Michelle MacCarthy, 27 July 2009

Figure 9. Veronica Matadoya making new bundles of *nununiga*, Yalumgwa village, Kiriwina

Source. Photographed by Michelle MacCarthy, 17 December 2009, and used with Veronica's permission

If fine weather prevails, and the leaves dry quickly and cleanly, the making of new bundles can proceed. This task begins by recycling existing *nununiga*: those that have become mouldy, wet or dirty (*yapupagatu*) or are just too old (*yabogwa*). New leaves are added to the outside, to freshen up the bundles and make them look new (*yavau*) and clean (*yamigileu*) (Figure 9). Trying to give away old, dirty *nununiga* as payment in *sagali*, or in exchange for goods in the transactions called *valova* (explained above) can lead to arguments and bad feelings, as well as gossip about the woman at fault. In sum, the process of making fresh *doba* requires many days' work, and maintaining the bundles, which are subject to rot, mould and insect and rodent predation, is a neverending task. Further, men contribute their own resources to provide their wives with items that can be exchanged for *nununiga* in the *valova* exchanges such that, as Joshua noted, 'they [women] take our [men's] money' (Weiner 1980: 274). Thus, Joshua and other Trobriand men sometimes complain that the kind of wealth they value more (cash) is inefficiently transformed into a kind of valuable, in a separate (female) sphere, which they value less. In reality, women are only concerned with acquiring *doba* when the death of a member of one's own (or one's father's) clan occurs, so it is not necessarily a daily preoccupation. But, in preparation for a *sagali*, women can work for weeks or even months to amass sufficient stores of *nununiga* to demonstrate the strength of her *dala* (matriclan) and to ensure her good name as *nayo'udila* (a hard-working woman) and *na'esaesa* (woman of wealth).

Changing values: Instability in banana leaves

In Kiriwina, the largest and most densely populated of the Trobriand Islands, the bundles—along with other essential goods, both locally produced items like woven mats and store goods such as lengths of brightly patterned calico cloth, as well as coins and notes in kina—are essential exchange items that pass from clan to clan in the distributions following a death. While men and their yams, stone axe blades and clay pots also have their role to play in these exchanges, it is women's wealth and women's exchanges, as Weiner notes, that are the most visible in these complex mortuary distributions known collectively as *sagali*. Women gain status, respect and a good name by amassing vast quantities of bundles to give away after the death of a relative. For some urban Trobriand Islanders who return home after the death of a close relative, no amount of store-bought calico or kina notes can replace the symbolic value of *nununiga* to give away at *sagali*, and even some of the most cosmopolitan of Trobriand women will work to find ways of acquiring *doba* when they hear of a relative's death. In 2013, I was present for the *sagali* of a young woman of my adoptive mother's clan. The girl, and many close family members, lived in Port Moresby, but the burial and *sagali* were (as is the custom) held on Kiriwina. Ruth,[7] who works at a hotel in the nation's capital, felt so strongly that she must have *doba* to throw for her niece that she sent my adoptive father off with 30 kina to *valova* (she deliberately refrained from using a term that would connote a straight commodity transaction) for as much *doba* as he could get with the cash. This is the closest I have seen to the direct purchase of *doba*.

The exchange of *doba* at *sagali* is essential for meeting obligations to people from other matrilineages after a death and is the means for women to demonstrate the prosperity, power and strength of their matrilineage (Weiner 1988: 117; Lepani this volume). It is thus all the more significant that there is now, in some circles, a push to eradicate the practice. Missions and the church have had a strong presence in the Trobriands for a very long time—the Methodist church arrived in 1894, Catholic missions were established in the 1930s—but in the past 20 years or so, evangelical churches have begun to establish themselves in the islands. While not all the early churches actively discouraged women from making and exchanging *doba*, and those that tried were not, over the long term, very successful, in recent years evangelical churches such as Four Square, Rhema and the Christian Revival Church (CRC), as well as a few United Church leaders, have advocated that Trobriand women should stop 'wasting their time' making *doba* and instead focus on more so-called 'useful' activities such as church fellowship, caring for the family and striving for material and economic success.

Weiner wrote much about the economic and symbolic importance of banana leaf textiles, and the ways in which they mediated relationships between men and women (Weiner 1974, 1976, 1994; see also Hermkens 2013). Weiner stressed their stability, both in terms of the historical continuity of the volume and scale of *sagali* distributions (an assertion I challenged above), and in terms of their role as a 'buffer to Western economic intrusions' (1980: 276). According to Weiner's analysis, it is nearly unthinkable that *doba* should cease to underpin the complex distributions following a death. And yet, in several villages in Kiriwina, this is already the case—although exchanges continue, albeit in modified form.

---

7   I always asked the people with whom I did extensive work whether they preferred me to use their own name or a pseudonym if I should write about them. Their wishes have been reflected in each case.

While I do not wish to overstate the relationship between the arrival of Pentecostal forms of Christianity and the trend in some villages towards doing away with *doba*, the discourses espoused by evangelical church leaders are representative of the ways in which ideas about the value of banana leaves are changing, and the moral imperatives in reorienting productive activities towards less 'wasteful' endeavours.

Pentecostalism in the Trobriands

The arrival of Pentecostalism, or Revival Christianity (Trobrianders use these terms interchangeably), in the Trobriand Islands began in the mid-1980s. According to Kulaleku, the ward councillor for Kwebwaga (the first village on Kiriwina to embrace and build a Pentecostal church, and the village in which Annette Weiner was based), a need for a new and stronger faith had been locally identified in part because of the number of sorcery deaths. My informants in Kwebwaga told me that people were ready to embrace a change and bring relief to villagers who lived in fear of *bwagau* (black magic, sorcery). When a few Kwebwaga men went to Port Moresby, they were introduced to the CRC and Rhema churches, and felt that this 'strong' faith (*peula tapwaroru*) was needed back at home. An American pastor came to preach in 1986, and those suspected of being sorcerers were encouraged to pray and join the new church, and to renounce old ways. Sylvester, a Kwebwaga man, went to Bible College in Port Moresby and returned as the new CRC's first pastor in 1989. People quickly joined the new church in great numbers. Kulaleku estimates that 80–85 per cent of the village's population left the United Church to join CRC, while the current pastor of the church, Rodney, suggests that the number is over 90 per cent. This caused a rift between the two churches, but I was told that because the sorcery deaths were seen to diminish rapidly with the arrival of the new revivalist church, people believed in the efficacy of the new faith and the church remained strong. As part of their general message about the ways in which *gulagula Kilivila* (Trobriand custom) does not fit well with *tapwaroru* (Christian faith, prayer), since the late 1990s the practice of *sagali* has also changed in Kwebwaga. *Doba* plays only a small role in distributions, which have been reduced in size and scale to minimise the financial burden, as well as the time required, to work for *sagali*. Rodney told me, '*Isakemasi mwau okaukweda* (It gives us a hard time in our households). Now, we look for school fees, for clothes for our children, instead of wasting time looking for *doba*' (Discussion with Rodney, 11 August 2013, Kwebwanga village).

Once the Pentecostal churches were established on the island, there was a good deal of movement back and forth, in which people tried out the new churches, and in some cases returned to the longer-established United or Catholic congregations. Even today, marriages or disputes with church leaders can encourage people to begin attending services of a different denomination. This is not seen as problematic, since, my informants consistently told me, '*komwedodasi tadubumisa yaubada tetala*' (we all believe in one God). While the Catholic Church continues to be set apart in its highly hierarchical structure and more sedate hymns and prayers, most United Churches now practice a revival form of Christianity, which is scantly differentiable from Pentecostal beliefs and styles of worship (see, for example, Van Heekeren 2014: 5; see also Gooren 2010). It is perhaps no coincidence that none of the predominately Catholic villages have made significant movements towards eradicating *doba*,[8] while those villages that have are home to Pentecostal churches, 'revived' United churches or both.

Women rejecting women's wealth

Thelma, a young unmarried woman from Kwebwaga village, exemplifies the changes in attitudes and behaviour that devout Pentecostal women espouse, in direct opposition to custom. A healthy-looking girl of about 22 years of age, Thelma has a slight gap in her front teeth and, on the day I spoke with her, her hair was pinned up in braids, giving her a girlish look. While she is softly spoken and of gentle demeanour, she is all the same determined, self-assured and single-minded in her dedication to the church. She is a youth leader, and I first became aware of Thelma when I attended a CRC service in Kwebwaga, and was impressed with the power and leadership she demonstrated when leading the singalong and prayer that precedes the sermon. While most women her age are married with children, or else are on other islands or the mainland to study, Thelma told me she sees it as 'God's plan' that she should wait to marry and start a family. What is more, she has told her parents and members of her

---

8   While *doba* has not been eliminated in any Catholic villages thus far, the issue has been raised and debated within several Catholic congregations, including the village where I did the bulk of my fieldwork, Yalumgwa, as well as nearby Bawai village. Thus far, though, women have been reluctant to give up *doba* in these communities, and the parish priest at Wapipi (serving the northern half of Kiriwina Island Catholic parishes), who hails from Columbia and has worked in indigenous communities in South America, not only supports but participates in *sagali* distributions, in stark contrast to many (indigenous) leaders in the revival movement.

community that she will not participate in *sagali* in any capacity, because '*sagali gala yaubada lapaisewa*' (*sagali* is not God's work). Instead, she told me, the work she does must be to the glory of God, as she sees her future in God's hands. She says she provides 'living testimony' of how a woman can dedicate her life to God, and forego traditional obligations. She worries that '*gulagula bibiyusa tomota*' (custom/tradition will pull people), and distract them from the work of God: praying, evangelising and toiling in the garden or at 'productive' tasks to give tithes and offerings to the church (Interview with Thelma, Kwebwaga village, 14 August 2013).

Figure 10. Singalong preceding Sunday church service at Obweria United Church, Obweria village

Source. Photographed by Michelle MacCarthy, 28 July 2013

Thelma has made a personal decision to remove herself from the obligations of *sagali*. In some cases, clans or villages have made collective decisions to continue to practice *sagali* but without using *doba*, only cash and store goods. Others continue to use *doba* but significantly reduce the scale of *sagali* by eradicating the huge *lisaladabu* distributions held six months to a year after a death, once the family and *dala* members have had sufficient time to amass the store of resources they will then have to give away. During my fieldwork in Kiriwina, it was brought to my attention early on that there were several villages in which a decision had been made (collectively, by both men and women), and was generally abided by, that women would cease production of *doba* and forego the complex exchanges of banana leaf textiles at *sagali*. Instead, they practice only a small distribution immediately following the death, using primarily kina notes (that is, cash), calico cloth and store goods, possibly with the inclusion of some woven mats. *Lisaladabu*, is no longer held in some villages, while others retain the spirit of *lisaladabu* but have replaced *doba* as an object of exchange entirely with calico, store goods and cash. The villages most notable for their rejection of *doba* are Tubuwada (and the nearby villages of Kaulikwau and Bwaitavaia, within Tubuwada Ward) in the north of Kiriwina Island; Obweria,[9] to the south of Tubuwada but still in the Kilivila region; Ilarema in the middle of the island in the area called Luba; and Sinaketa in the south, in the region known as Kebwagina (see Map 1). As Map 1 makes clear, these areas are geographically dispersed across the entire island of Kiriwina.[10]

The people of Obweria village, which is about a 15-minute walk from my home village of Yalumgwa, have rejected the use of *doba* in *sagali* for over 20 years. Several individuals told me the story about this transformation. As early as 1994, the story goes, Darubuguyau, an old man from Obweria (one informant described him as a 'rascal fellow'), had a vision of God appear before him. God told him that Trobriand people should stop doing *sagali* because it was causing people to 'waste their time' in pointless endeavours. The old man explained to everyone that if they heeded God's edict, there would be no more sorcery deaths—sorcery being the causal explanation for most deaths in Kiriwina. After his vision, Darubuguyau made a personal transformation and joined a revivalist congregation of the United Church.

When news spread about Darubuguyau's vision and subsequent conversion, the residents of Obweria agreed to cease the production, exchange and storage of *doba*. When I asked people why this was seen as

---

9 Alternatively spelled 'Obwelia' in some publications, which reflects the fact that 'l' and 'r' are only sometimes phonemic in Kilivila, but are sometimes interchangeable, or pronounced differently depending on dialect.

10 The other, smaller Trobriand Islands such as Kitava, Vakuta, Kaileuna, Kuyawa and Munuwata have somewhat different ways of practicing *sagali*, which have also changed in recent years, in some cases hand in hand with the arrival of new churches, but a full description of how practices differ on the other islands is beyond the scope of this paper. Islands such as Kitava, however, which has a very strong revival church presence, present interesting case studies in their own right.

a good reason to change practices that had been carried out from the time of the ancestors, they explained that it was because people believed 'it was God's will'.

The broader historical context for the story of Darubuguyau's vision involves a split within the United Church in Obwelia village, which happened a decade earlier. One faction of the congregation remained associated with the mainline United Church and its regional and national hierarchy; the other faction began to practice a revivalist version of the faith (Figure 10). In the breakaway congregation, the use of guitars and tambourines was accepted and encouraged, songs were livelier, people engaged in worship more kinetically by clapping, waving arms and other actions, and the church hierarchy was less pronounced. Thus, people were already familiar with Pentecostal faith practices even before the first Pentecostal church was formally established in the village in the late 1990s, under the banner of the CRC Freedom Worship Centre (although a permanent church building was not erected until 2009). Incidentally, I was told that Darubuguyau's daughter was married to a pastor of the Rhema church, a Pentecostal denomination. The arrival of the new form of evangelical worship, and its accompanying ideals about the path to prosperity and salvation, seem to have given further impetus to the decision in Obweria to cease using *doba* in *sagali*.

When I asked women in Obweria why they had thoroughly given up the use of *doba* in exchanges, they told me that they had come to see the manufacture and exchange of *doba* as a waste of resources. They saw it as 'too time consuming, too pointless'. They said that they prefer to put efforts to more practical ends. 'We prefer to concentrate on the living, not the dead', one informant told me (13 May 2007, Obweria village). They stressed the need to focus on feeding and clothing their children, paying for school fees, and supplementing their garden food–based diet with trade store items such as rice and tinned fish. By giving up *doba* and the expensive practice of *sagali,* they were free to concentrate their resources on meeting the immediate monetary needs of the household, which they felt should be prioritised over the old practices that, to them, no longer held currency. Indeed, economic terminology predominated in these discussions, with the use of words like 'waste' and 'profit'. The emphasis, my Obweria informants told me, should be on providing for one's nuclear household rather than the extended family, and acquiring money over acquiring other forms of wealth or worrying about proficiency in performing 'traditional' Trobriand identity. The anthropology of Christianity literature is replete with examples of the increased individualism and discordant ideas of personhood that Christian conversion often entails (for example, Jolly, Stewart and Brewer 2012; Lutkehaus and Roscoe 2013; Robbins 2004, 2007; Tomlinson 2012). In this case, we see a second conversion from an earlier, highly syncretised Christianity, which allows greater flexibility to incorporate traditional ideas of sociality, to a second wave of conversion with far more overt discourses of modernity, prosperity and individual responsibility.

George, an erudite and well-travelled Trobriand man from Obweria village, also pointed out that Pentecostal churches discourage Trobriand women from making and wearing grass skirts, which are considered sexually provocative and hence sinful. Even those Obweria residents who have stayed as members of the United Church congregation in this village have taken up the call to abandon the practice of *sagali* and rarely wear the grass skirts elsewhere considered essential to doing 'proper' traditional Trobriand dance. Evoking Arjun Appadurai (1986), I argue that evangelical church preachings that discourage the use of *doba* (that is, both skirts and bundles), operate under an incommensurate regime of value than that espoused by those who stress the importance of so-called traditional exchange practices entailed in *sagali*. Ideas about 'productivity' in Pentecostal religious movements, as well as some more radical United Church factions, are fundamentally at odds with the kinds of exchanges that *sagali* and the mass distributions of *doba* represent. As one Obweria woman told me, 'Christianity is growing stronger than culture' (Mary, 13 May 2009, Obweria village).

A correlation is often made by Trobrianders between *doba*, in the form of bundles, and cash, as I pointed out earlier. Weiner noted this analogy as it was made to her 30 years ago (1986: 109; 1988: 120), and the same analogy was made to me by both women and men on numerous occasions. However, today, the value of *nununiga* relative to money is, in the eyes of some Trobriand people, slipping. For example, Steven Milamala, the pastor of the CRC in Obweria village, told me:

> *Doba* is legal tender here. It was valued by the original Kiriwina people. They [women] put their sweat into it, they invested their resources to get it. It's good, we [in the Pentecostal church] don't say *doba* is demonic. But it's *pupagatu* [dirty]. *Tomota gala bisikamsi, kikoni bimesa bikamsi, bimeyasi maena gaga* [People can't wear it, rats will come and eat it, it smells bad]. And a lot of time is consumed in this process. *Laplap boimeyasi dimdim* [White people already brought cloth pieces], and with this we can sew it, wear it, make pillowcases, or what—not like *doba*.

> *Doba* is a waste. It's better we just switch it out with *karekwa* [calico cloth] (Field notes, interview with Steven Milamala in a mix of English and Kilivila, translations mine where necessary, 5 June 2013, Obweria village).

There is an echo, here, of the words spoken by Joshua, as I discussed above, who comments negatively on the way *doba* manipulates resources and aims them towards women's economic activities, at the expense of men who work to create wealth for their wives, mothers and sisters.

It should be noted that not all Pentecostal churches have been successful in discouraging the continued practice of *sagali*, and the impetus for changing exchange practices does not come from the Pentecostal churches only. It is part of a broader trend in which many people wish to lessen the obligations entailed in *sagali* and concentrate more time and energy on endeavours that are likely to bring monetary profit. In the hamlet of Modawosi, where I was based for my fieldwork from 2009 to 2013, the Four Square church, another Pentecostal denomination, had been very recently established—in about 2006 or 2007. While in my section of the hamlet, fully 75 per cent of the households had left the Catholic congregation to attend the new church, there had been no consensus to move away from *doba* production and exchange, although the matter was discussed and debated at a community meeting (welcoming members of both the Catholic and Four Square congregations) that I attended in February 2010. While most in attendance agreed that the competitive and escalating nature of *sagali* was placing great economic burdens on both village residents and their wage-earning relatives in town, the idea of actually doing away with *doba* was an anathema to most at the meeting. While all acknowledged that now is the time of *tapwaroru* (church), the reasons given for maintaining the use of *doba* were many. Some stressed the importance of this form of wealth, which women can produce with their own labour, in helping Trobrianders to acquire things for which they would otherwise require cash to obtain. Others pointed to the need for *doba* as the appropriate way to thank those who have helped their relatives when they were old and sick. Still others commented on the importance of *sagali* for strengthening the *dala* or matriclan, and to ensure good relationships with affines and friends. While most felt there should be some limits on the volume of objects exchanged at *sagali*, most of the attendees (both men and women) saw the decision as one that should be made by the family of each dead person, rather than trying to do as Obweria village had done and make decisions that the entire community would be expected to abide by. Thus, ideas about which values should guide actions and, accordingly, which actions and things should be valued are in a state of flux as 'tradition' battles it out with 'modernity'—as many Trobrianders themselves see it.

Conclusions: Why *doba* matters—and what happens if it doesn't?

Following Mauss, in his 1938 essay 'A Category of the Human Mind: The Notion of Person; The Notion of Self' (though he was speaking of North American Indian societies), the women who in the Trobriands represent their clan can be seen to reflect the *personnage*: a set of names and peoples who represent the reincarnated soul of an ancestor who defines an individual's place in society and her role in rituals such as *sagali*. The dead person's kinswomen have a responsibility to make payments to members of other clans, as a show of both her own personal wealth and power and the strength of her matrilineage. The importance of *doba* in Trobriand exchange, as Weiner discusses in her 1976 monograph and in numerous articles, follows from women's importance as regenerators of their lineage. If we take a Marxian approach, the value of *doba* is derived from the labour of women who manufacture it. Taking a step further, we might say that when exchanged in *valova*, *doba* works as a classic commodity, while when given away at mortuary distributions, it carries many of the characteristics ascribed to the gift. As a gift, the distribution of *doba* is much more about the relationships between people, and the obligations both met and recreated, than it is about the bundles themselves. It does not matter if a woman manufactured the particular bundles she gives away; they are not individually inalienable in this sense. People do not speak of women who make *better doba* than other women, but they *do* commend women who amass *more doba* or, more specifically, who can give away the most *doba* at *sagali*. What matters is that women work to make and acquire *doba* (as well as other essential exchange goods), which represents their matrilineage. Thus, value itself is vested in the matrilineage. This works in much the same way, it seems to me, as men's production of yams, which likewise reflect their physical labour, their knowledge both in terms of the physical (which seeds to plant in which place at what time, when and how to thin and harvest the yams) and the supernatural (which magic spells to use, and how to perform them correctly), which are similarly used in essential reciprocal exchanges. Women, likewise, need to have the right knowledge and be able to perform the actual physical work required to produce *doba* (though, notably, as far as I know, magic is never used in the process of making it). Unlike other products of Trobriand labour, whether created by men (especially wood carvings, but also *kula* shells and other ornaments) or women (mostly woven handbags and sometimes mats), those that have the most dense values in obligatory exchanges at marriage and death (yams, *doba*) are perishable, and must constantly be regenerated. This may account for both their symbolic importance within Trobriand sociality, and for their *lack* of importance as objects exchanged with foreigners who cannot appreciate their symbolic weight. Thus imbued with symbolic cultural meaning as representing matrilineal identity and strength, the substitution of calico, store goods and cash should fall short (Figure 11). So, what are the implications when villages like Obweria get rid of *doba*? Do calico or other store-bought goods become imbued with comparable value when used in *sagali*, as Lepani has argued in this volume, or are they mere commodities? Perhaps both? There are conflicting moralities reflected in the sometimes disparaging, sometimes envious discourses of people in the communities that have abandoned *doba* in favour of *lakeda tapwaroru* (the way of the church), and those who cling tenaciously to the practice as essential to demonstrating the 'right' way of being a Trobriand woman who meets her exchange obligations in the 'proper' way.

Figure 11. *Sagali* with calico cloth and store goods, Wapipi village, Kiriwina

Source. Photographed by Michelle MacCarthy, 30 December 2010

Doba continues to have (at least in some villages) economic value, and can be exchanged like a commodity for goods at a set rate of exchange in *valova*, as I described at the beginning of this paper. However, much more importantly, it has social or symbolic value as being representative of a woman's work, knowledge and ability to reproduce the matrilineage. Without it, even when substituted by calico, cash or store goods, an important aspect of the transactions disappears. Nonetheless, for some Trobriand communities, this is the way forward; a means of becoming more 'modern', and of leading truly Godly lives. Yet for some Trobrianders of other faiths (especially Catholics), revival Christianity and the discourses about 'productivity' espoused may be viewed as an 'excuse' or way out of the hard work and time needed to acquire *doba*. Instead of pouring time, energy and money into *sagali*, women can work to make money for their families, pay their tithes and offerings to the church, contribute to school and church activities, and guarantee their place in heaven. Not all Trobrianders agree on whether doing away with *doba* represents a turning point in Trobriand identity and gendered personhood, or is proof that Trobriand Islanders are good Christians with their priorities in order. It is a truism that Trobrianders have long found various ways of incorporating new ideas into a cosmology that remains distinctly Trobriand; perhaps in the context of *sagali*, manufactured objects from soccer balls to underpants might gain density as substitutes for *doba*. As the process of shifting value and values away from *doba* continues, the enduring importance of intergenerational and wide-ranging kinship obligations remains to be seen. Neither values, nor value, are fixed, either independently or to one another.

References

Appadurai, Arjun (ed.). 1986. *The Social Life of Things: Commodities in Cultural Perspective*. Cambridge: Cambridge University Press.

Banton, Michael (ed.). 1965. *The Relevance of Models for Social Anthropology*. London: Tavistock.

Bashkow, Ira. 2011. 'Old Light on a New Controversy: Alex Rentoul's Account of the Trobriand Women's Sagali'. *History of Anthropology Newsletter* 38(2): 9–18.

Bohannan, Pau and Laura Bohannan. 1968. *Tiv Economy*. Evanston, IL: Northwestern University Press.

Campbell, Shirley F. 1983. 'Attaining Rank: A Classification of Shell Valuables'. In *The Kula: New Perspectives on Massim Exchange*, ed. Jerry W. Leach and Edmund Leach, pp. 229–248. Cambridge: Cambridge University Press.

Carrier, James (ed.). 1992. *History and Tradition in Melanesian Anthropology*. Berkeley: University of California Press.

Cox, John and Martha Macintyre. 2014. 'Christian Marriage, Money Scams and Melanesian Social Imaginaries'. *Oceania* 84(2): 138–157. DOI: 10.1002/ocea.5048.

Damon, Fred H. 1980. 'The Kula and Generalized Exchange: Considering Some Unconsidered Aspects of the Elementary Structures of Kinship'. *Man* (n.s.) 15(2): 267–293. DOI: 10.2307/2801671.

———. 2002. 'Kula Valuables: The Problem of Value and the Production of Names'. *L'Homme* 162: 107–136. DOI: 10.2307/25133533.

Dumont, Louis. 1980. *Homo Hierarchus: The Caste System and its Implications*. Complete revised English edition. Chicago: University of Chicago Press.

Ekeh, Peter. 1974. *Social Exchange Theory: The Two Traditions*. Cambridge, MA: Harvard University Press.

Gooren, Henri. 2010. 'The Pentecostalization of Religion and Society in Latin America'. *Exchange* 39(4): 355–376. DOI: 10.1163/157254310X537025.

Graeber, David. 2001. *Toward an Anthropological Theory of Value: The False Coin of our Own Dreams*. New York: Palgrave.

Gregory, Chris. 1982. *Gifts and Commodities*. London: Academic Press.

———. 1983. 'Kula Gift Exchange and Capitalist Commodity Exchange'. In *The Kula: New Perspectives on Massim Exchange*, ed. Jerry W. Leach and Edmund Leach, pp. 103–117. Cambridge: Cambridge University Press.

———. 1997. *Savage Money: The Anthropology and Politics of Commodity Exchange*. Amsterdam: Harwood Academic Publishers.

Hermkens, Anna-Karina. 2012. 'Becoming Mary: Marian Devotion as a Solution to Gender-based Violence in Urban PNG'. In *Engendering Violence in Papua New Guinea*, ed. Margaret Jolly, Christine Stewart and Carolyn Brewer, pp. 137–161. Canberra: ANU E Press. Online: press-files.anu.edu.au/downloads/press/p182671/pdf/ch04.pdf (accessed 26 January 2017).

———. 2013. *Engendering Objects: Dynamics of Barkcloth and Gender among the Maisin of Papua New Guinea*. Leiden: Sidestone Press.

Hoenigman, Darja. 2012. 'A Battle of Languages: Spirit Possession and Changing Linguistic Ideologies in a Sepik Society, Papua New Guinea'. *The Australian Journal of Anthropology* 23(3): 290–317. DOI: 10.1111/taja.12002.

Jolly, Margaret. 1992. 'Banana Leaf Bundles and Skirts: A Pacific Penelope's Web?' In *History and Tradition in Melanesian Anthropology*, ed. James Carrier, pp. 38–63. Berkeley: University of California Press.

Jolly, Margaret, Christine Stewart and Carolyn Brewer (eds). 2012. *Engendering Violence in Papua New Guinea*. Canberra: ANU E Press. Online: press.anu.edu.au?p=182671 (accessed 27 June 2015).

Keesing, Roger M. 1990. 'New Lessons from Old Shells: Changing Perspectives on the Kula'. In *Culture and History in the Pacific*, ed. Jukka Siikala, pp. 139–163. Helsinki: the Finnish Anthropological Society.

Kluckhohn, Clyde. 1951. 'Values and Value-orientations in the Theory of Action: An Exploration in Definition and Classification'. In *Towards a General Theory of Action*, ed. Talcott Parsons and Edward Albert Shils, pp. 388–433. Cambridge: Harvard University Press.

Kuehling, Susanne. 2005. *Dobu: The Ethics of Exchange on a Massim Island, Papua New Guinea*. Honolulu: University of Hawai'i Press.

Lambek, Michael. 2013. 'The Value of (Performative) Acts'. *HAU: Journal of Ethnographic Theory* 3(2): 141–160. DOI: 10.14318/hau3.2.009.

Leach, Jerry W. and Edmund Leach (eds). 1983. *The Kula: New Perspectives on Massim Exchange*. Cambridge: Cambridge University Press.

Lepani, Katherine. 2012. *Islands of Love, Islands of Risk: Culture and HIV in the Trobriands*. Nashville, TN: Vanderbilt University Press.

Lutkehaus, Nancy C. and Paul B. Roscoe (eds). 2013. *Gender Rituals: Female Initiation in Melanesia*. New York: Routledge.

MacCarthy, Michelle. 2013. '"More than Grass Skirts and Feathers": Negotiating Culture in the Trobriand Islands'. *International Journal of Heritage Studies* 19(1): 62–77. DOI: 10.1080/13527258.2011. 637946.

———. 2016. 'The Morality of *Mweki:* Performing Sexuality in the "Islands of Love"'. In *Gender and Christianity in Melanesia: Towards a Unified Analysis*, ed. Michelle MacCarthy and Annelin Eriksen. Special issue of *The Australian Journal of Anthropology* 27(2): 149–167. DOI: 10.1111/ taja.12191.

Malinowski, Bronisław. 1920a. 'The Economic Pursuits of the Trobriand Islanders'. *Nature* 105: 564–565. DOI:10.1038/105564a0.

———. 1920b. 'Kula: The Circulating Exchanges of Valuables in the Archipelagoes of Eastern New Guinea'. *Man* 51: 97–105.

———. 1921. 'The Primitive Economics of the Trobriand Islanders'. *The Economic Journal* 31(121): 1–16. DOI: 10.2307/2223283.

Marx, Karl. 1976 [1867]. *Capital: A Critique of Political Economy*, vol. 1, trans. B. Fowkes. London: Penguin Books.

Mauss, Marcel. 1985 [1938]. 'A Category of the Human Mind: The Notion of Person; the Notion of Self'. W.D. Halls, trans. In *The Category of the Person: Anthropology, Philosophy, History*, ed. Michael Carrithers, Steven Collins and Steven Lukes, pp. 1–25. Cambridge: Cambridge University Press.

Mauss, Marcel. 1990. *The Gift: The Form and Reason for Exchange in Archaic Societies*, trans. W.D. Halls. New York: W.W. Norton. Original edition, *Essai sur le don*, first published 1950 by Presses Universitaires de France en Sociologie et Anthropologie.

Meyer, Birgit. 1998. '"Make a Complete Break with the Past." Memory and Post-colonial Modernity in Ghanaian Pentecostalist Discourse'. *Journal of Religion in Africa* 28(3): 316–349. DOI: 10.2307/1581573.

Mosko, Mark. 2000. 'Inalienable Ethnography: Keeping-While-Giving and the Trobriand Case'. *The Journal of the Royal Anthropological Institute* 6(3): 377–396. DOI: 10.1111/1467-9655.00022.

Munn, Nancy. 1986. *The Fame of Gawa: A Symbolic Study of Value Transformation in a Massim (Papua New Guinea) Society*. Cambridge: Cambridge University Press.

Parsons, Talcott and Edward A. Shils (eds). 1951. *Towards a General Theory of Action: Theoretical Foundations for the Social Sciences*. Cambridge: Harvard University Press.

Robbins, Joel. 2004. *Becoming Sinners: Christianity and Moral Torment in a Papua New Guinea Society*. Berkeley, CA: University of California Press.

——. 2007. 'Afterword: Possessive Individualism and Cultural Change in the Western Pacific'. *Anthropological Forum* 17(3): 299–308. DOI: 10.1080/00664670701637750.

Sahlins, Marshall. 1965. 'On the Sociology of Primitive Exchange'. In *The Relevance of Models for Social Anthropology*, ed. Michael Banton, pp. 139–236. London: Tavistock.

Schram, Ryan. 2013. 'One Mind: Enacting the Christian Congregation among the Auhelawa, Papua New Guinea'. *The Australian Journal of Anthropology* 24(1): 30–47. DOI: 10.1111/taja.12019.

Siikala, Jukka (ed.). 1990. *Culture and History in the Pacific*. Helsinki: the Finnish Anthropological Society.

Sillitoe, Paul. 2006. 'Why Spheres of Exchange?' *Ethnology* 45(1): 1–23. DOI: 10.2307/4617561.

Tomlinson, Matt. 2012. 'God Speaking to God: Translation and Unintelligibility at a Fijian Pentecostal Crusade'. *The Australian Journal of Anthropology* 23(3): 274–289. DOI: 10.1111/taja.12001.

Van Heekeren, Deborah. 2014. 'Why Alewai Village Needed a Church: Some Reflections on Christianity, Conversion, and Male Leadership in South-East Papua New Guinea'. *The Australian Journal of Anthropology* 25(1): 91–111. DOI: 10.1111/taja.12069.

Weiner, Annette B. 1974. 'Women of Value: The Main Road of Exchange in Kiriwina, Trobriand Islands'. PhD thesis. Bryn Mawr College.

——. 1976. *Women of Value, Men of Renown: New Perspectives in Trobriand Exchange*. Austin, TX: University of Texas Press.

——. 1980. 'Stability in Banana Leaves: Colonialism, Economics and Trobriand Women'. In *Women and Colonization: Anthropological Perspectives*, ed. Mona Etienne and Eleanor Burke Leacock, pp. 270–293. New York: J.F. Bergin.

——. 1986. 'Inalienable Wealth'. *American Ethnologist* 12(2): 178–183. DOI: 10.1525/ae.1985.12.2.02a00020.

——. 1988. *The Trobrianders of Papua New Guinea*. New York: Holt, Rinehart and Winston.

——. 1994. 'Cultural Difference and the Density of Objects'. *American Ethnologist* 21(2): 391–403. DOI: 10.1525/ae.1994.21.2.02a00090.

Poem: *Doba*—Trobriand Skirts

Katherine Lepani

Sun-bleached banana leaves
split down to fibres, layered
and fringed. Plant life transformed,
woven on human loom. Women's
hands work fibres into skirts,
valuables in matrilineal exchange.

Continuity through exchange
of one form for another. Leaves
rustle in island breeze, skirts
flutter like sunspots through layers
of green, whispering the motion of women,
the lore of nature transformed.

Skirts tell of clan life transformed,
chart history through reciprocal exchange.
From death to rebirth, children of women
move in a spiral. From leaves
to skirts, life becomes layered
with meaning. Feathered skirts

of deep seed powder red, skirts
made in mourning when death transforms
the living into spirits at sea. Layers
of skirts piled high for exchange,
passed from one clan to another, leave
behind the sorrowful keen as women's

voices are lifted of grief. Women
dance in full plumage, skirts

flared from their hips. Leaves
shimmer in motion, transformed
by colour, jubilation, by the exchange
of tears for a feast; by layers

of colour—purple, green, yellow; layers
of voices in harmonious song. Women
gather together to exchange
news and stories, wearing hand-sewn skirts
of calico and ribbon. Spirit transformed,
life renewed, sorrow mutely leaves.

Layers of fibres woven into colourful skirts
by women whose work tells of life transformed
in exchange, in the breath of banana leaves.

1991

3

Women's Wealth and Moral Economies among the Maisin in Collingwood Bay, Papua New Guinea

Anna-Karina Hermkens

Introduction

The repetitive beat of the *kundu* drums, carrying the men's chanting, echoes through the hills and fjords of Tufi as Maisin dancers, dressed up in their colourful regalia, make their way to the mission station field. The audience's gaze moves between the strikingly vivid display of red and black designs that are painted on the white tapa loincloths that both male and female dancers wear, and the elaborate male headdresses swaying back and forth to the beat of the music (Figure 12). While the men's long and narrow strip of tapa loincloth (*koefi*) allows them to move freely and sway their entire bodies back and forth, women's movement is restricted and confined by their rectangular-shaped tapa loincloths (*embobi*), which are tightly wrapped around their hips, covering their thighs and knees. In contrast to the men, they keep their upper bodies still and with great subtlety move their hips while shuffling their naked feet forwards and backwards. Although dancing as a group, or rather as a tribe, the dancers actually dance together in multiple sets of same-sex pairs, with each individual dancer's gender and clan identity being visualised and embodied through the designs painted on their tapa loincloths and the specific shells and feathers they wear (Figure 13). Dancing in utter concentration for hours and hours, the repetitive movements and the monotone music induce an almost trance-like state. The dancers transcend time and place as they address their ancestors, their ancestors' journeys, wars, land claims, as well as past loves and romances, through the tapa designs, dances and songs. By means of their clothing, the dancers have transformed from ordinary men and women into withdrawn ancestral figures of splendour, beauty and restraint (Hermkens 2007; see also Schieffelin 1976: 1–25).[1] At the same time this performance is a performative act (Lambek 2013) that conveys, embodies and constitutes an overabundance of values that are both ethical and economical, and related to the production or making of tapa, and its uses as a garment, gift and commodity.

Figure 12. Maisin dancers wearing their tapa loincloths at a church festival held near Tufi

Source. Photographed by Anna-Karina Hermkens, 30 September 2001

---

1   But it's not only for the wearers that the performance of tapa and their decorated body brings about an experiential dimension. The audience is likewise drawn into this powerful display of concentration, strength and beauty. However, originating from different tribes, they repeatedly try to lift the invocation by drawing the dancers back to the present, eliciting loss of concentration and thereby mistakes through joking and insulting comments.

Figure 13. Maisin dancers wearing their regalia and tapa cloths decorated with clan designs

Source. Photographed by Anna-Karina Hermkens, 30 September 2001

The tapa cloths worn by the male and female Maisin dancers are not just used as garments during Anglican Church festivals as the one described above. Tapa, which is made and painted by Maisin women, features in Maisin economic, political, social and spiritual life as an object of wealth that is both 'alienable' and 'inalienable' (Weiner 1992). In the past, tapa was used as a blanket, wrapped around sago in order to transport it from the gardens to the village, and deceased people were first wrapped in mats and subsequently covered with a piece of tapa before being buried.[2] More recently, sold at national and international markets as an object of ethnic art, tapa contributes significantly to Maisin livelihood. This alienable tapa cloth is also used in barter and ceremonial exchanges. Today, Maisin women are the main producers of tapa in the region and beyond; many neighbouring and more distant cultural groups who have stopped manufacturing barkcloth, but also groups who have lost or have no tradition of wearing barkcloth, wear Maisin tapa as a 'traditional' garment during festivities and cultural performances (see also Bonshek this volume). In addition to local, regional and international transactions with this alienable tapa cloth, tapa, decorated with clan designs, features as inalienable clan property. Unless it is utilised as a way to cement relationships, it may not be given away outside the clan, or sold. This inalienable cloth is often used as festive and ceremonial dress, playing an important role in church festivals and life-cycle rituals, such as marriage and mourning. In these contexts, the wearing and giving of tapa are embodied performances (Hermkens 2010) that convey and, at the same time, constitute beliefs and values about gender relations and identity, mediating relations between the individual and the social, and connecting the living with the ancestors, God and the Church.

These various properties, meanings and values of tapa are also discernible in the eastern Pacific, where tapa is equally made by women, and features as a garment and gift during various ceremonies and rituals (Addo 2007, 2013, this volume; Jolly 2008; Veys this volume; and Young Leslie and Addo 2007). As the editors of a special volume on Pacific textiles point out, Pacific textiles are surprisingly durable in their sociality. 'Through their production, deployment, and malleable physical form, they lend themselves to metaphor', and they are wonderful mediums for pragmatic creativity (Young Leslie and Addo 2007: 16). Strikingly, most of the anthropological studies on tapa deal with tapa from the eastern Pacific

---

2   Today pieces of cotton cloth have replaced the tapa used to cover the deceased's body.

or, when focusing on Melanesia, barkcloth made by men, or tapa that is used in male-dominated rituals (for example, Fajans 1997; Meyer 1992; Williams 1928, 1940). It seems that tapa produced by Papua New Guinean women has been neglected by anthropological scholars, despite the fact that Annette Weiner (1992: 47) already elucidated the importance of cloth as an essential form of material wealth and the locus of women's strategies, power and agency. In this chapter, I add to this knowledge and deal with the relationship between Melanesian tapa as a form of 'women's wealth', and its use in gift and commodity exchanges among the Maisin of Oro province in Papua New Guinea (Map 2).

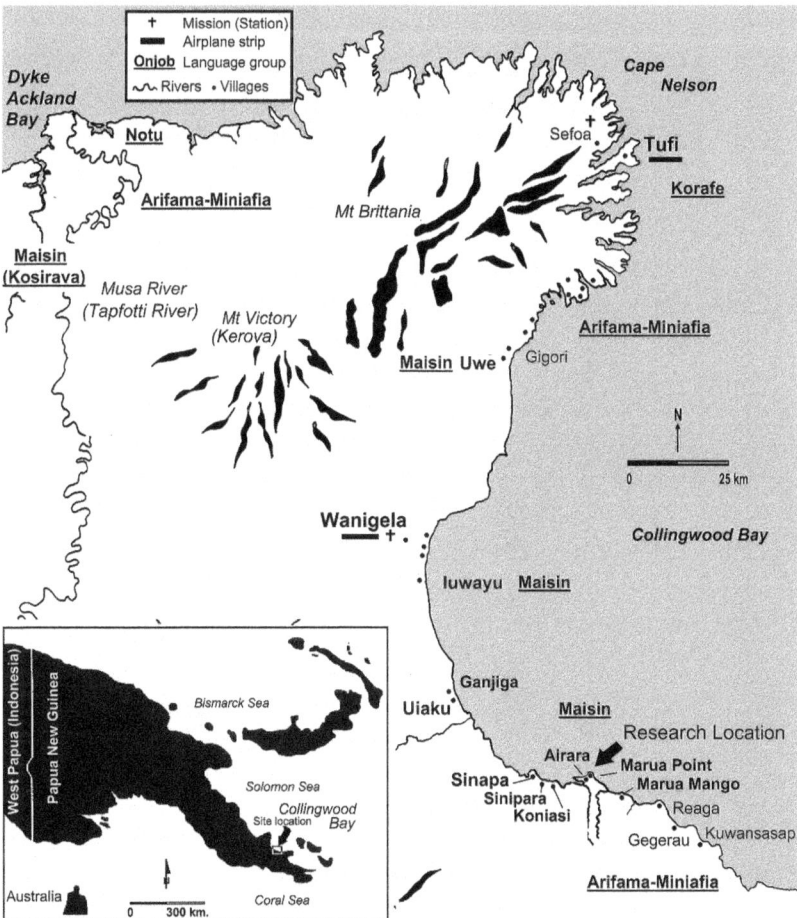

Map 2. Collingwood Bay, Oro Province, Papua New Guinea

Source. Drawn by Anna-Karina Hermkens

Among the Maisin people, as elsewhere in the Pacific, practices of decorating and performing the body during rituals and festivals, such as the one described earlier, are intertwined with practices of giving. In fact, the presentation of the decorated body and the presentation of tapa as a gift, are performances that engender personhood and social (kinship) identities, as well as relationships. Maisin dancers embody and display their gendered clan and Maisin identity, at the same time as they impart a bit of themselves through their performance and the tapa they give in return for the food and hospitality they receive from their hosts. Also in ceremonies, such as in marriage and mourning rituals, the intimate connection between decorating and performing the body, the exchange of objects like tapa, and the establishment of social personhood and the nurturing of relationality is profound (Hermkens 2010). In these instances, the main purpose of tapa, both as dress and as gift, is the establishment and maintenance of social relationships. This implies that people's identities are not only relational, but also 'distributed' in both their social and material surroundings. The constitutive outside encompasses other people, ancestors (see also Knauft 2002: 27) and materialities such as tapa. This concurs with Marilyn Strathern's observation that objects circulate within relationships in order to make relations in which objects can circulate (1990: 221). Inspired by the influential work of Marcel Mauss and Karl Marx, Chris Gregory advocated a firm relationship between personhood and modes of exchange, arguing that things and people assume the social form of persons in a gift economy, while they assume the social form of objects in a commodity economy (Gregory 1982: 41). Gregory acknowledged that reality is much more complex and diverse and that, for example, a single object can assume different social forms depending upon the context (see also Godelier 1973: 128; 1999). Drawing on the work of James Carrier (1995) and Edward LiPuma (1998), Rachel Morgain and John Taylor in an edited volume on *Gender and Person in Oceania* (Hermkens, Taylor and Morgain 2015) remind us that this copresence of gift and commodity exchange demands 'careful revelation of how these forms of exchange mutually articulate and how they crystallise and engender different dynamics of sociality and agency' (Morgain and Taylor 2015: 3). The copresence of gift and commodity exchange is visible among the Maisin, who use tapa both as a gift and a commodity in various types of exchanges and transactions. Margaret Jolly (2015) argues that we should better understand and appreciate this copresence and, what she terms, the creolisation of gifts and commodities.

I will build upon these insights by focusing on how value is created in exchanging tapa as a gift and commodity. But I will first unravel how value is created in the processes of making, as this shows how value, gendered personhood, relationality and action are interlinked, not just in the exchange of objects, but also in their creation and their use in performances such as church festivals and exchanges. As has been argued by Thomas Widlok (2013: 13) and others (for example, Graeber 2001: 4; Lambek 2013), action, performativity and agency are very much part of how value is created. I will start by briefly elucidating the intimate correspondence between Maisin women and tapa, and how they are part of each other's substance. This will be followed by an overview of Maisin exchanges and an analysis of what happens when these imbued or saturated cloths are exchanged during life-cycle rituals, and bartered or sold as commodities.

Women making tapa

Among Maisin, women are traditionally responsible for both the manufacture of barkcloth and the application of black designs and red pigment on the tapa surface. The importance of tapa for Maisin people is reflected in the statement 'Maisin is tapa'. Moreover, because of its importance for Maisin livelihood and identification, everybody agrees that all women, even those married into Maisin from the outside, have to learn how to make and design it. Although each woman has her own style of design, Maisin tapa is always clearly identifiable, as women remain within the boundaries of what is regarded as good Maisin tapa. Aesthetic concepts of what makes a good tapa and a good design are mainly confined to the texture of the tapa and the structure of the design—it must consist of at least four lines—and care is taken not to spill red pigment outside the black lines. Individual preferences for the work of particular women do exist, but both men and women will always stress that all Maisin women are capable tapa makers, drawers and painters.

However, the intricacy of making, designing and painting tapa becomes clear when adult women married into Maisin, or visitors like me, start learning to make tapa. As I witnessed and experienced, making and designing Maisin tapa requires technical and creative skills (*seraman*), strength, as well as knowledge (*mon*), which are part of Maisin personhood and sociality, and thus not easily or quickly learned.[3] In fact, these skills, attributes and knowledge are most efficacious when embodied from a young age onwards. The particular way of beating the inner bark of the paper mulberry tree (Broussonetia papyrifera, locally called *wuwusi*) into pliable tapa cloth; the techniques associated with designing the meandering black lines and their intricate application on, and correspondence with, the rough tapa surface; and, finally, the intimate connection between the red pigment (*dun*) with women's bodies and blood, all require and at the same time produce what Marcel Mauss (1979: 97–123) referred to as 'gendered body techniques'. As I argue and show elsewhere (Hermkens 2013, 2015: 13), these body techniques, and the way tapa continues to shape and constrain female bodies when worn, show how the gendered roles women are expected to perform, and are continuously inscribed and embodied through the reiteration of nondiscursive practices such as beating, designing and wearing tapa. These practices do not just interact with but correspond to the tapa surface. According to Tim Ingold (2013: 105), correspondence implies a sentient back and forth movement in time that creates something else. The rather coarse fibrous texture of the barkcloth influences how the lines can be applied, resisting some movements and facilitating others. The whole practice of making and drawing tapa is thus part of a process in which the women artists are participants (see also Ingold 2013: 21). In addition to the physical correspondence between women and tapa in acts of making and wearing, making tapa has specific cosmological associations and is related to notions about reproduction, childbirth and creation, which are important in defining womanhood (Hermkens 2015; see also Schneider 1987: 413). This interplay between cosmology, gender and cloth has also been noted in other parts of Oceania (for example, Colchester 2003: 9; Young Leslie and Addo 2007: 19). In many contexts, cloth production and utilisation are closely associated with mothers and the love and responsibilities that they devote to their children and extended families (Addo 2007, 2013, this volume; Young Leslie and Addo 2007: 18).

Monica Taniova, at the time of my fieldwork a cheerful 35-year-old mother of five children with a beautifully tattooed face (Figure 14),[4] was one of the younger, acknowledged good tapa makers among the Maisin.

---

3   Personhood among Maisin is referred to as *mon seraman*, just as the skills and attributes needed to make Maisin tapa. In a recent article (Hermkens 2015), I analyse in more detail this intimate connection between Maisin tapa, womanhood and notions of the person and self.
4   Fieldwork among the Maisin people took place between 2001 and 2002 and in 2004.

Her proficiency with the *nasa* brush surpassed the skills of many other women, drawing straight and almost perfectly symmetrical designs on the fibrous and somewhat rough tapa surface. Monica loved drawing barkcloth designs. While other women sometimes tended to make quick drawings because of the monetary necessity to make tapa, Monica always placed much effort and imagination into her designs. If it were up to her, she would spend even more time making tapa. As she said, 'I really like drawing and painting, and I would like to do this the whole day. In fact, I used to do that, but now I have plenty work to do for my parents-in-law, husband and children' (interview with Monica, Airara village, 2001). This statement reveals the impact of virilocal residency as well as the many responsibilities tapa makers like Monica face. Monica cannot depend on her brothers and sisters to provide her with help or foodstuffs. Because she was born in Ganjiga village, her parents and brothers are two hours' sailing distance from her current residence in Airara, where she lives with her husband, her children and her parents-in-law in a large house on the edge of the village, which is part of her husband's clan. Being responsible for the maintenance of the house and her husband's garden, and especially for the feeding of both her own family and her in-laws, she has little time to spend on making tapa. In fact, she has to carefully balance her time and activities to be able to make, design and finally paint the cloth.

Monica always prepared and beat her tapa bark on the platform underneath her husband Clifford's house, which is in fact her working area. While her in-laws, and sometimes her children and husband, often rested in the large elevated shelter (*barè-barè*) next to the house, I would frequently find Monica working in 'her area', where she would also do the cooking. Monica's youngest child, Christina, would often sit with her underneath the house or play with other children in the area while her older sisters and brother were at school. Watching her mother making and designing tapa means that Christina is socialised in the intricacies of making tapa from a very young age, just as Monica was. As the latter recalls:

> My mother Stella taught me how to beat and design tapa. First, I learned how to beat tapa; the drawing of the designs, I learned somewhat later. When I was about 14 years old, I wanted to try it, so I got a small piece of tapa and printed a design on it, just like my mother made them. My mother saw it and said it was not bad but I had to try it again. She showed me where to put the dots and how to apply the red paint (Interview with Monica, Airara village, 2001).

Figure 14. Monica patching holes in a piece of barkcloth
Source. Photographed by Anna-Karina Hermkens, 15 July 2004

According to Monica, Maisin women have to make tapa. As she put it, 'It is our custom, we grew up with it, and nowadays tapa is our living. We make tapa, sell it, and get money with which we can buy things from the trade store' (Interview with Monica, Airara village, 2001). She insists that her daughters must learn the techniques of beating tapa and drawing designs. Linda, her second-eldest child, already knows how to beat tapa, although she does not do it as frequently as her mother.

Since I lived close to her, I often witnessed Monica drawing on her platform underneath the house, or occasionally on the elevated shelter. Maisin women make two types of designs: alienable designs and inalienable clan designs (*evovi*). Alienable designs are created in the mind before applying them, although women would also first draw their designs in the sand, trying them out without spoiling valuable barkcloth. Before setting out to make a new design, Monica would think about it and then 'draw' the design with four fingers on the white surface of the cloth. In this way, she would visualise her mental image of the design. The four fingers represent the four black lines that will meander and curve parallel to each other, creating three 'veins', of which the central one will be left white and the outer two filled with red dun. If satisfied, she would apply the design with black pigment, called *mi*. This implies that Monica already knew in advance what she was going to draw. This is very different from working without preconceived notions about the eventual outcome. As Monica explained, 'If I don't think about the design properly, I will make a mistake and spoil the design and the tapa' (Interview with Monica, Airara village, 2001). In addition to these alienable designs that result from women's imagination and creativity, sometimes inspired by designs in magazines, each of the 36 Maisin patrilineal clans has its own tapa designs, called *evovi*.

Maisin believe that when emerging from a hole in the Musa area, each clan ancestor brought his clan emblems (*kawo*). Clan emblems can vary from types of magic, social conduct and fire, to drums, dancing gear and tapa designs (*evovi*). The tapa clan designs are named and are often figurative, representing mountains, animals or specific artefacts that relate to the clan ancestor's travels and his claims on land, animals and artefacts. As such, clan tapa contains information about ancestral journeys, land claims and relationships between specific clans (see further Hermkens 2013).

While especially men control the narratives dealing with the journeys associated with particular landmarks, the knowledge concerning the manufacturing of clan designs is in the hands of women, who transfer this knowledge and craft from mother to daughter and from mother-in-law to daughter-in-law. In designing a clan's identity, women are crucial. They control the knowledge of the designs and their manufacture through which the clan itself is reproduced. Gendered forms of knowledge, power, affiliation, differentiation and identity are not only intertwined and expressed through particular types of tapa, they are also manipulated through tapa. The prohibition on wearing another person's clan design exemplifies this, since to do so would simultaneously denote a claim to land.

Both types of designs are drawn in black and coloured in with red pigment. Among the Maisin, the manufacturing of pigment was, as in other Pacific cultures, 'a magico-symbolic process' (Teilhet 1983: 49). In the past, the manufacturing and use of the red pigment (called *dun*) was bound by rules and taboos. Unlike the black pigment, the red dye was mixed and boiled inside the house in a separate clay pot, which was not used for cooking food. Small children and men were not allowed to look at it or come near it. The view was that men's external bodily substances would 'spoil' the paint by causing it to 'dry up' or making it 'less red' and thus contaminate the dye because their substances are 'matters out of place' (Douglas 2004: 50). While working with the dye, women were secluded from the rest of society, not allowed to eat and drink or have sexual intercourse (Barker 2008: 114). They also had to speak quietly and, out of respect and fear of 'spoiling' the paint, they would refer to the dye as *tambuta* or *taabuta*, meaning 'red blood'.[5] Since the ingredients of the dye have to be boiled and the resulting *dun* had to be applied when it is still warm, the association with living blood becomes more apparent (Figure 15). The ancestral clan designs depicted on tapa cloth can be seen as representing the male part in the conception of clan tapa; the red dye refers to the female blood that is necessary to complete it and make the design (and cloth) alive. Through the designing and painting process, a woman thus gives birth to an entity of cloth, thereby reproducing the patrilineal clan and its ancestral origins. This symbolised production of new life connects the ability to design and paint tapa with

---

5   *Taa* means blood, and *buta* is another word for *mu*, which means red or ripe. Today, the manufacturing of the red dye may be performed in public and children are allowed to sit with their mothers when applying it on the tapa cloth.

the character of womanhood. Only strong, initiated, mature and sexually active women were believed to be able to handle the paint. Although today, while men are entering the production of barkcloth, they still avoid processes involving *dun* (see also Forshee 2001: 32). Moreover, only women have the prerogative associated with drawing and painting clan designs. As such, the significance of women reproducing the clan by drawing and painting clan designs on barkcloth continues. This is striking, as it is generally believed that Melanesian women do not produce the important symbols of their community, as this is seen as the prerogative of men (Teilhet 1983: 47).

In short, the specific gendered time and space involved in making tapa and learning about tapa, the arduous beating and pounding of tapa, and women's posture while making, drawing and painting tapa—sitting for hours unsupported with the legs stretched out—are all strongly connected with notions about how women should physically behave, their work ethos and their responsibilities. Women who do not make tapa are considered lazy and sometimes even 'bad' housewives, as they do not provide for their families. In this way, tapa plays an important role in local sexual politics, in which both women and men depend upon each other.

Significantly, making tapa defines especially the female body, both spatially and physically. It is connected with women's bodies and their minds, at the same time producing Maisin women who produce and reenact Maisin sociality through the making of tapa. This performativity is embodied, with both cloth and women becoming and being part of each other's substance (Hermkens 2015). It may thus be tempting to argue that, due to women's production of and intimate connection with tapa, this 'cloth' can be considered as 'women's wealth' or as women's property (Weiner 1989). In the next section, I will elaborate on Maisin exchanges and in particular on objects like tapa and the values that are exchanged, followed by an analysis of the commodification of tapa and how this affects the intimate relationship between women and tapa cloth.

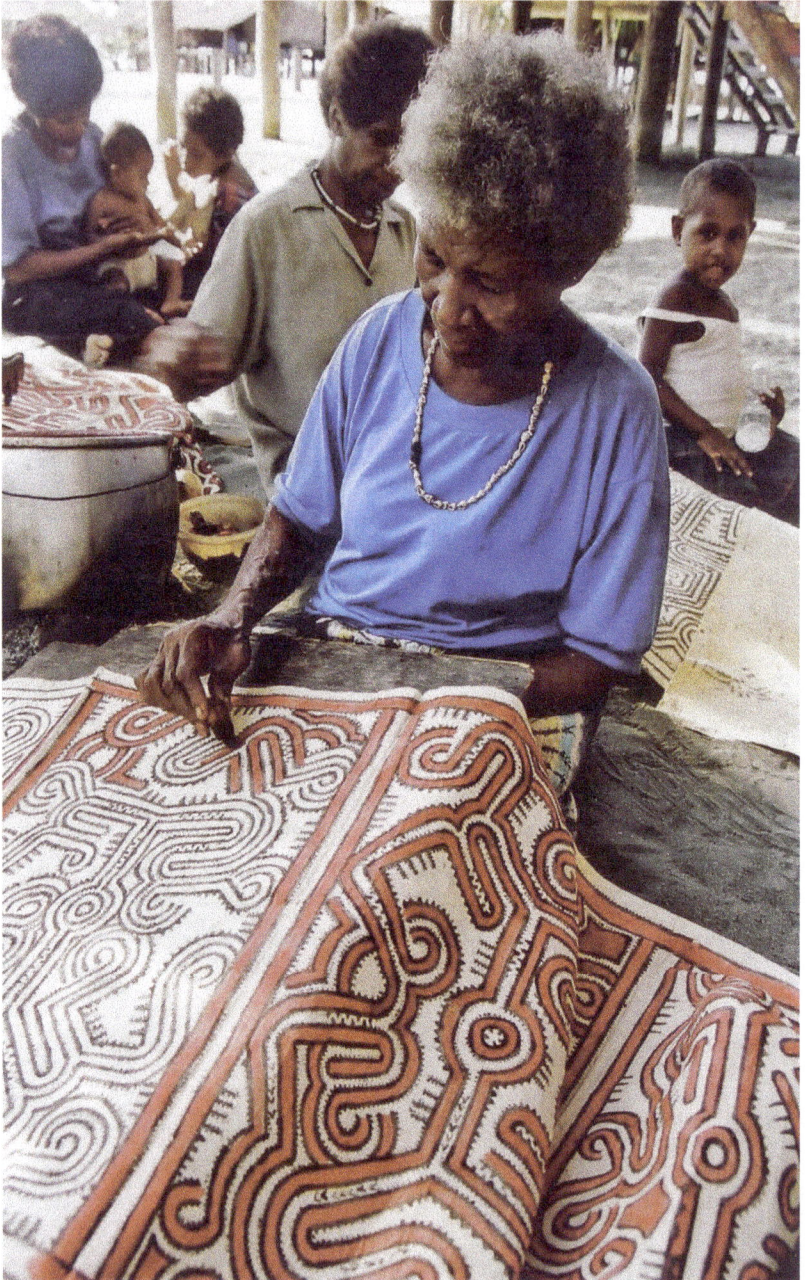

Figure 15. Mildred painting a piece of tapa with red pigment that is kept warm on a fire

Source. Photographed by Anna-Karina Hermkens, 17 April 2001

Objects and values of exchange

Among the Maisin, the necessity to give plays a paramount role in everyday life and is the core of the organisation of social relationships. The necessity to give is called *vina*, and is one of the most dominant concepts of Maisin ways of living and thinking. Maisin describe this principle of reciprocity as 'exchanging' and 'compensating', or 'paying back'. It means that if someone gives you something or helps you, you are obliged to give a return gift. This return gift has to at least equal the value of the received gift and ideally overtop it.

Each occasion has its proper *vina* response (see also Hermkens 2013). If a person helps you in the garden, you give him or her raw food. If, due to a death, an area has to be 'cleared', or made accessible again, women will cook food together and share it with the deceased's relatives. If a husband belts his wife, her uncles (her mother's brothers) may demand compensation (food or money), and her brothers may seek revenge on her husband. In the past, but also more recently, a daughter was sometimes given as *vina* to marry a young man if he had helped her father or her clan enormously. And if a person falls and his or her in-laws or affines show their respect by throwing themselves on the ground as well, this person will have to compensate the in-laws by giving them food (or money). After a person has received a great amount of help or respect from other people, relatives or in-laws, he or she is compelled to make a return gift or compensation, referred to as *vina*. If, for example, someone has fallen from a coconut tree and is carried back to the village, this person will have to compensate his carriers and prepare a 'washing shoulders' (*siva veyowi*) ceremony. He or she will raise a pig and prepare enough food for this occasion to feed the people and their clans who helped him or her. Enough pots of cooked food (containing vegetables, fish and pig meat) have to be prepared in order to be presented to the helpers. In the past, the helpers' shoulders' would be washed with pig fat, thereby symbolising the work they had done and the compensation they would receive. In short, *vina* exchanges take place every day and during various occasions. Moreover, it encompasses and exceeds the boundaries of the various anthropological analytical distinctions of exchange. For Maisin, *vina* encompasses all formal and informal exchanges between individuals, groups of people and clans. This means that both a bride-price payment, as well as the sharing of food to compensate someone for his or her aid, is referred to as *vina*.

Daily life exchanges

In daily life, exchanges or practices of sharing take place between husband and wife and the immediate family, the affines. For example, a woman will work on her husband's land, and in exchange he will give some goods to her family. In a similar way, she has to take care of his parents and provide them with the things they need. These exchanges are not always without comment. As many Maisin men will state, they prefer to get married to girls from a distant village, so they will not be burdened by having to provide their affines with gifts of food and money. In a similar way, a girl's parents will prefer her to marry within the neighbourhood so she, and her husband, can take care of them. Women preferably marry close to their father's clan as well. Such daily exchanges between family members also take place between the various households within one clan. Women bring food to their classificatory clan sisters or take care of their children while working in the garden. Both cooked and raw food is given, but also clothes and money. In addition, female clan members ask for goods like sugar and salt if present and, of course, betel nut is requested and shared within (and outside) the clan. They also help each other with making tapa, sharing the red pigment and giving tapa or *wuwusi* (tapa tree) to female clan members when they ask for it. Men within one clan may help each other when building a house or a garden fence. However, this kind of male exchange occurs far less frequently than the exchanges between women married into one clan.

In addition to exchanges that are part of the reciprocal relations established within groups due to marriage, there are also exchanges that exceed household and clan boundaries. Women often bring food or goods like clothes to relatives living in other clans, especially if they have been asked to do so. In addition, women exchange labour. If a woman helps a female friend or relative from another clan with an act such as making tapa, rolling up pandanus or working in the garden, she will receive food or other goods in return. Each time someone gives an item or gives help, this act of giving has to be balanced by the receiver and so on. This kind of daily sharing structures Maisin life and occurs especially between women. Men help each other as well, but this is predominantly within the clan. If outside help is needed, for example to build a house or to make a garden fence, a more formal and generous act of giving has to take place in order to 'pay them back' for their help. In general, this implies cooking food for the men (and women) who helped, or paying them with money.

Importantly, the informal daily exchanges seem to especially create relationships between women, both inside and outside their husbands' clans. The advantage of these transfers is that during times of food shortage, these additional gifts of food aid women and their families to get by, although one cannot depend upon them either, as these practices of sharing food are not necessarily reciprocal. Moreover, the disadvantage of the necessity to give is that, if asked for, people have to give not only goods like sugar and salt, but also personal belongings. In order to prevent having to give away belongings (even money) people hide the possessions they want to keep.

Thomas Widlock (2013) points out that some of the practices described above are not necessarily reciprocal, but should be regarded as sharing. Instead of viewing these exchanges as either a covert form of market behaviour or as an extended form of reciprocity in line with Marshall Sahlins' (1988) work, he argues that sharing is a complex social phenomenon that makes rather specific requirements in regard to bodily copresence, relatedness and interaction. The challenge of sharing, he argues:

> continues to be that people do share what they value, they share without receiving or even expecting returns, and they even—at times—value sharing itself. More specifically, they primarily value the sharing action by others while they themselves may avoid sharing by hiding things or at least by trying not to share at all times and under all circumstances (Widlock 2013: 12).

The daily exchanges I have described in the context of Maisin life have no format, but are the product of complex interactions that depend upon the relatedness of those involved and how they categorise each other, not just in terms of kinship but also in terms of amity (see also Widlock 2013: 20). Monica giving taro to a female friend without this person's asking, demanding a coconut from a relative, helping a neighbour to paint tapa without being asked to do so, and requesting a knife from a close friend are all part of daily complex interactions between people that inform how and what one may ask, demand and give, or not. When personal dynamics change, these practices of sharing will change too, while the more formal reciprocal exchanges between clans will continue as they were. This concurs with Widlock's observation that sharing is something different from reciprocity, as it requires 'particular actions by both provider and taker, accepting certain kin relations, responding to speech acts, and recognizing physical presence' (Widlock 2013: 21).

Barter and life-cycle exchanges

In addition to daily practices of reciprocity and sharing such as outlined above, Maisin also engage in more sporadic and, at the same time, more formal exchanges with acquaintances and strangers in order to obtain specific, highly valued objects. Maisin women always have to make sure that tapa, string bags, pandanus mats and clay pots are present in the house.[6] It is their responsibility to either make them or obtain them through barter. These female-produced objects are the major exchange items among and between the Maisin and neighbouring linguistic groups, and are used in daily practices of sharing, bartering, commodity and ceremonial exchanges. In the past, Maisin men would make engraved headrests, shell and bore-tusk necklaces, and they still make engraved lime sticks as well as the elaborate feather headdresses that visualise and embody patrilineal clan identity. Lime sticks, along with particular necklaces, are among the heirlooms cherished by both male and female clan members. Furthermore, men are responsible for organising formal exchanges and accumulating and distributing the objects in such exchanges. Along with money, pigs, raw and cooked food and store-bought goods, the main objects that are exchanged are tapa, pandanus mats and clay pots—objects that are all made by women. Unlike women, men do not produce things like tapa that embody and express the complementarity between men and women in constituting, personifying and expressing the patrilineal clan. What a man does is exchange his wife's (or wives') and female relatives' labour, which is embodied in the food they harvest and prepare, and in the objects they make or acquire through barter.

Maisin women predominantly give painted tapa in barter exchanges, which secures the acquisition of non-Maisin products like red shell necklaces (called *wakèki*) from Milne Bay, pottery from Wanigela women, and sometimes string bags from Biniguni women—objects

---

6   Maisin have always depended on the barter system with Ubir- and Onjob-speaking women living near Wanigela mission station to obtain the highly valued clay pots, which are only manufactured by these women (see Bonshek this volume). In the past, Wanigela women used to produce their own tapa, but at a certain point in time they started to rely on Maisin productions and the barter system. Maisin women use clay pots on various occasions. They are used as cooking pots at festivities and ceremonies, as ceremonial gifts, and at wedding ceremonies in which the bride has to break a clay pot from her groom's family. In addition, Maisin women use clay pots to barter with Biniguni women for string bags. They take second-hand clay pots up to the Biniguni mountain villages or Biniguni women take them back after having visited the coastal villages.

that are used in both daily and ceremonial exchanges.[7] Men make and sometimes barter for canoes with Miniafe or other people by giving tapa, which is made by their wives or other female relatives. Some of my male and female interlocutors stated that barter is *vina*, thereby making no distinctions between local and regional forms of exchange and between gift and barter exchange. However, not everybody included barter within the concept of *vina*, stating that barter was like 'buying' (*kumas*), because you know in advance what you are going to receive for your 'gift'. As one female interlocutor stated with regard to barter relationships with Wanigela women: '*Tapa tamème na wusu timènana*' (We give them tapa, and they will give clay pots in return) (Hermkens 2013: 208).

Bartering occurs both between people who know each other, as well as between strangers. Sometimes women will barter with distant relatives or female friends who married into other villages. On other occasions, when women travel around or visitors come to their village, they will equally take the opportunity to barter their goods. Especially between previous exchange partners, extended exchanges may take place (see also Bonshek this volume). This involves trust and respect towards each other, since one depends upon the other to make the return 'gift' of the barter somewhat later. I witnessed Maisin women giving tapa to Wanigela and Biniguni women in order to receive respectively a clay pot or a string bag. These latter items were sometimes given in return months after the initial barter agreement had been made. In a similar way, Maisin women received clay pots for which they were supposed to give tapa sometime in the near future.

Men and women state that bartering is mainly women's work, especially if it involves objects made by women. But, even with bartering for canoes, which are made by men and regarded as their property, a woman has to be involved because she has to agree to the amount of tapa that is given in exchange for the canoe. In some cases, women individually negotiate to obtain their own canoe by giving tapa to the man who wants to barter

---

7   *Wakèki* or *bagi* are small variants of the red spondylus necklaces that are part of the *kula* exchanges among the Massim in Milne Bay. In the past, they were obtained through trade with Goodenough Island via the Mukawa people. Since Maisin men were working on plantations in Milne Bay from the 1910s until World War II, they were also bought at trade stores on, for example, Samarai Island, or received as gifts from Milne Bay friends.

it. In other cases, the husband will seek support and agreement from his wife in order that she will make the agreed amount of tapa. It also occurs that deals to obtain a canoe are made between two men without any direct consultation with the wife who has to produce the counter (barter) gift. In these cases, especially when the amount of tapa is too big in relation to the size of the canoe, the wife's female relatives and friends help her design and paint it, at the same time criticising the deal made by her husband by gossiping about it.

Importantly, most of the objects used and obtained in barter are also part of life-cycle exchanges. In fact, barter makes these formal or ceremonial exchanges possible as it provides women and their households with the gifts to give. During life-cycle rituals, the giving of particular objects, such as tapa, mats and clay pots, are important in the 'objectification' of identities (Miller 1994). Gender and clan identities are constituted and relationships between groups are elucidated, revealing systems of respect and power. Especially a mother's brothers play an important part in these formal exchanges. They are responsible for the initiations of their sister's first-born child with whom they (the uncles) will develop a special relationship. And upon marriage, they will receive and distribute the bride price paid for their sister's daughter(s). The initiations, and the countergifts that have to follow, mark the special but also fragile relationship between the in-laws (for example, wife givers and wife takers). This relationship has to be maintained, and certain goods and respectful behaviour are expected and sometimes even enforced. A large part of the exchanges performed between Maisin are therefore performed between the wife-takers' and wife-givers' groups. During life-cycle rituals, tapa plays an important role as a garment that is given to wear to the child being initiated, the girl getting married (Figure 16) and the widow or widower ending her or his mourning period (Figure 17). But it also features as a gift to the affines, along with mats, clay pots, string bags and foods (Figure 18).

Figure 16. Georgina being dressed up in her father's regalia on her wedding day

Source. Photographed by Anna-Karina Hermkens, 31 December 2001, and used with Georgina's permission

Figure 17. Abraham undergoing his 'end of mourning' ritual

Source. Photographed by Anna-Karina Hermkens, 25 December 2001, and used with the permission of the participants

Figure 18. Pile of gifts for Georgina's in-laws, including pots, mats and tapa

Source. Photographed by Anna-Karina Hermkens, 31 December 2001

So what we see in life-cycle rituals is men exchanging women's objects in the ongoing cycle of initiating or opening and balancing (*marawawe*) relationships between groups of people (for example, between the wife-giver's and wife-taker's clan), and redefining relationships between the living and the deceased (Hermkens 2013). At the same time, exchanges performed during life-cycle rituals mark the establishment of the individual's social person, referred to as *mon seraman*. This is similar to Orokaiva ceremonial exchanges, which mark social relationships and construct an individual's *hamo* (Iteanu 1995: 139; see also Hermkens 2015). However, while among the Orokaiva, land, pigs, taro plants and ornaments are essential components and partners in ritual exchanges (Schwimmer 1973: 5, 85–186), among the Maisin, women's work is referred to as *buro seraman* (work for which *seraman* is needed), which taps into and, at the same time, constitutes women's *mon seraman*. This labour is materialised in objects such as tapa, pandanus mats and clay pots that are essential components in exchange, along with pigs, taro and other kinds of food. This significant role of women's labour or women's objects as mediators in exchange is more reminiscent of Trobiand mortuary exchanges (*sagali*) where women's banana leaf bundles (*doba*) reflect the continuing ideological concerns of matriliny and human reproduction in Trobiand society, ensuring intergenerational social stability (Lepani 2012; Weiner 1976). Among Maisin, women's objects, like tapa, and women's labour in general reflect human reproduction in relation to the patrilineal clans, as well as important patrilineal kin and affinal relations. As such, women's wealth lies in the ability to give tapa, string bags, mats and pottery as gifts—objects that embody women's affective labour. So what happens when these objects are turned into commodities?

Commodities, shifting values and gender relations

Since the 1930s, several attempts have been made to commercialise tapa, both by foreigners and Maisin people themselves. The most important and recent attempt was made in the context of the antilogging campaigns in the early 1990s (Barker 2008). With the aid of a variety of organisations, the Maisin launched a lawsuit in the National Court to rescind licences that had been granted to logging companies to deforest Maisin ancestral lands. Meanwhile, a Maisin Integrated Conservation and Development (MICAD) organisation was established to provide oversight and a form of governance across the Maisin villages. Supported by Greenpeace, who dubbed its campaign 'Painting a Sustainable Future', and a Peace Corps couple who were stationed in Uiaku for two years, MICAD was to become a viable tapa-producing cooperative. The reason why tapa cloth was so attractive for activists was twofold:

> First, it was a distinctive and attractive Indigenous art form that, with proper marketing, might provide Maisin with an alternative and sustainable source of income from selling off their ancestral lands. Second, it was made by women at a time when one of the few things international development and environmental agencies agreed on was the necessity to promote projects that improved both the economic lot and political clout of women in their communities (Barker and Hermkens 2016: 195).

Paradoxically, the commercialisation initiatives led to adverse effects on women's workloads, status and domestic situations. While some families and individual women benefited from tapa sales, in general, women's workloads increased dramatically. Tapa production increased considerably, while, at the same time, more food was needed to be grown and prepared for the waves of international and national visitors (Barker and Hermkens 2016: 196). In addition, the well-intended interventions by outsiders provoked much resentment among men, who claimed that they went against Maisin 'traditions'. A number of husbands even beat their wives in retaliation for participating in workshops and in overseas delegations (Barker and Hermkens 2016: 196). As a result, women's involvement in decision-making processes was limited. Moreover, the monopoly MICAD attempted to impose upon tapa production and purchases diminished women's control over the sales and proceeds of their production,[8] with much of the profit eaten up to fund the travel of male executive members to and from Port Moresby (Barker and Hermkens 2016: 196). After the Peace Corps couple and Greenpeace representatives left, the international tapa markets collapsed, while women's position in the tapa business remained more or less the same.

---

8   MICAD developed a formula in which the size of the design (not of the tapa) determines its monetary value. In 2001–02 and 2004, MICAD paid in general K1.25 per square inch (the equivalent of AU$1 at that time), while the Anglican Church managed to offer K2 or even more. The increase in tapa production at the time of the Greenpeace support also encouraged local people to set up a production line where some women would draw the designs while others would add the red pigment (Barker 2008).

Despite the decline in tapa markets, people are still eager to sell tapa as it is one of the few means for them to make money.[9] Regularly, groups of women can be seen painting stacks of tapa because one of their husbands suddenly decided to travel to the city in order to sell tapa. Female friends and relatives will help the wife with designing and/or painting in order to get the bulk of the tapa finished on time. On several occasions during my fieldwork in Airara, I witnessed Monica painting both day and night for a couple of days, desperately trying to finish the cloths in time for her husband, Clifford, to take them for sale on his regular trips to Alotau. Clifford would inform her about his intended 'business' trip some months in advance, urging her to make tapa for him to sell. During this time, Monica would alternate her duties as a mother and wife with beating tapa and drawing the alienable designs. But she would not yet apply the red pigment. In order to ensure the paint on the tapa is vibrantly red, which Maisin consider to be the norm as it signals vitality, she would only start painting a few days before Clifford was about to depart. This would happen as soon as word about the arrival of the cargo boat was heard. Monica then spent as much time as possible applying the red pigment to her pieces of tapa cloth. This always caused much stress, as it meant she had an enormous workload and had to continue painting during the night in order to get the pieces of tapa finished on time. Although he acknowledged his wife's workload and stress during these times, Clifford would never help her and she depended upon the goodwill of other women to help her finish the work in time. She would try to catch up on some much-needed sleep after Clifford's departure, which was difficult with five children and her elderly in-laws to take care of. Importantly, at the same time that Monica's and other women's responsibilities and work has intensified due to the ongoing commercialisation of tapa, they are losing their traditional control over tapa.

Maisin men are increasingly gaining control over tapa production, its destination and revenues, with tapa often no longer being considered part of its maker. While other objects made by women, such as string bags, mats and pottery, still belong to their female producers and barterers, tapa is gradually being alienated from the women who make and use it.

---

9   Tapa cloth has also been the chief means for churchwomen to raise funds to support their activities and the local church (see further Barker and Hermkens 2016).

Married women in particular have to consult with their husbands before giving tapa away at exchanges, use it in barter, or sell it (Hermkens 2013). As Clifford stated:

> My wife Monica cannot sell tapa without letting me know, but if I want to sell a finished tapa, I can do it without letting her know. She once gave three pieces to MICAD for them to sell, but they didn't pay her, and I am still angry with that. If she wants to give tapa to contribute to a mourning ceremony or bride-price payment, that's okay. But if I am here, we should talk about it (Interview with Clifford Taniova, Airara, 2001).

In short, the classification and value of tapa is changing.[10]

Arjun Appadurai's introduction to his edited volume *The Social Life of Things* (1986) already elucidated how things can move both within and between different classificatory categories. Maisin tapa exemplifies his thesis that it's more useful to think about 'things in a certain kind of situation' than about objects as being certain kinds of things (1986: 13). The commercialisation of tapa defines its value in economic terms, while as a gift in bride price or other ceremonial exchanges, it has value in social terms. However, the economic or commodity value of tapa seems to negatively impact various established 'regimes of value'—shared value standards (Appadurai 1986: 15) that facilitate the exchange of tapa. As Sylvester Moi, former chairman of MICAD, expressed:

> During the last MICAD meeting [in 2002], several board members expressed the view that few *tapa* trees had been planted because MICAD had given so few new orders. This signals the fact that the traditional value of *tapa* is changing towards a commercial value only. Before, people had heaps of *tapa* in their houses so that they could give them during initiations and other festivities. Now, little *tapa* is given during such occasions. Also, less *tapa* is being used in barter. I feel sorry about this, especially when I see the *tapa* hats and bags that are being made. People perceive *tapa* as a cash-crop, a way to make money. But *tapa* constitutes an important part of our traditions. This seems now to get lost (Interview with Sylvester Moi, Ganjiga village, 2001).

Wanigela women who want to barter their clay pots for Maisin tapa, share Sylvester Moi's concern that tapa is losing its traditional value in gift and barter exchange. Instead of the traditional 'one pot in exchange for one

---

10   Importantly, clay pots are also no longer regarded as a woman's individual property if they were bought with money. In these cases, male and female informants stated that the object belongs to the family.

tapa', their Maisin counterparts want more pots or even cash and, as such, Wanigela women are confronted with changed value standards on the Maisin's side. The result is that traditional regimes of value in the context of barter have turned into clashes of classification and incoherent value systems, resulting in tensed barter conditions and frustrations on the Wanigela side (see further Bonshek this volume).

Obviously, the shifting classifications and values of tapa in both gift and barter exchange imply a struggle over control. Following Appadurai on the interplay between politics and value (1986: 56–58), in her article on hierarchies of values at the Cambodian Angkor Wat temples, Lindsay French states, 'it is in the struggle to impose a particular system of classification … that hierarchies of value are established and the politics of classification and evaluation are revealed' (1999: 173). The struggle over the classification and value of tapa amongst Maisin foremost reveals the power relations between gendered persons with respect to objects like tapa.

As Renée Hirschon in her edited volume *Women and Property – Women as Property* argued, 'property is a crucial indicator of the balance of power between women and men' (1984: 1). The quote from Clifford with regard to his wife giving away and selling tapa shows how men increasingly seek to control the commodity value and the revenues of tapa, thereby alienating women from the tapa they make. This alienation also occurs at another level with Maisin elders refusing to commodify clan tapa and clan designs, and to commercialise the alienable general designs outside of Papua New Guinea. At several international occasions, such as the exhibition of tapa at the Berkeley Museum in 1995, and the experimentations of Monica and two other Maisin women with tapa designs at the Philadelphia Fabric Workshop and Museum in 1997 (Hermkens 2013: 304, 317–19), Maisin elders agreed that the individual artists should not be revealed to the public as tapa belongs collectively to the Maisin. In these instances, Maisin elders and the community at large were concerned that women like Monica may gain advantage through exposure and recognition of their individual work. At the same time, offers to commercialise tapa designs, by the outdoor company Patagonia, have been turned down as elders are afraid they will lose control over 'Maisin' designs. In these instances, where individual gain and the loss of control over Maisin tapa designs are to be averted, Maisin tapa is no longer regarded as a woman's individual, a family's or clan property, but as Maisin cultural property (Hermkens 2013: 325).

According to Strathern (1984: 165), objects such as tapa may be owned and therefore disposed of, but they are not alienable, as the labour that produced these objects remains part of the producer and, when given away, this labour has to be compensated for. As described earlier, women's objects like tapa in *vina* are not about exchanging wealth in an economic sense, instead they deal with exchanging and maintaining social life. The objects made and given by women are closely intertwined with all facets of Maisin life, and as such constitute vital and essential values related to daily life and birth, initiation, marriage and death. One could label tapa as 'women's wealth' (Weiner 1989), but in fact this would be too narrow a classification. Ultimately, it is about the complementarity of Maisin gender relations and the significance of women's work (*buro seraman*) in the procreation of each patrilineal clan as materialised in the making and wearing of clan tapa. Along the same lines, tapa is also not women's property, but the product of Maisin sociality as a whole. When alienable tapa becomes commodified, it is no longer valued *as* women's labour enmeshed in the social order achieved through long-term gift exchange, but valued as a product *of* women's labour. Although the revenues from tapa may be used for gifts, thus once again mediating relationships between people, it does seem that the commodification of tapa has changed its social value and its significance in creating and maintaining social balance through gift and barter exchange. From a Marxist perspective, this would also suggest that women's labour becomes objectified in tapa as a commodity. More fundamentally then, it is not tapa that is subjected to reification, but women themselves, 'whose own life-making activity, their labour power, is taken from them and represented in a coercive commodity form' (Haraway 2008: 175). Women thus become the commodity form (Haraway 2008: 175). In her reflection on Anglo-feminist theory, Donna Haraway points out that within particular streams of thought, women do not suffer reification in the way Marx describes the process for the worker. Instead they face a much worse fate.

> In masculinist sexual orders, woman is not a subject separated from the product of her life-shaping activity ... She *is* a projection of another's desire ... There is nothing of her own for her to reappropriate; she is an object in the sense of being another's project (Haraway 2008: 176).

This particular framing obviously takes away all agency women have as well as their desire. But Maisin women do have agency and desire in determining and influencing the barter and, perhaps more indirectly, the commodity value of tapa. Moreover, I think it is important to rethink materiality (both in objects and gendered bodies) beyond mere economy and capitalism, and acknowledge local epistemologies and value 'systems' while still being able to compare the material consequences of particular values and ethics (see also Alaimo and Hekman 2008: 7–8). Women like Monica are not just subjected to reification, they are also empowered through the responsibility, joy, love and sentient relationship they develop in the processes of making, wearing, giving, bartering and selling tapa. Contemplating a different, more intimate view of value reveals that perhaps the greatest value of tapa lies not in its conceptually bounded significance as a cultural artefact and object of exchange, but rather in its being a creative practice that nurtures both a woman's family and herself. This nurturing relates to a woman's ability to provide and care for her family via tapa, but also stems from the correspondence between tapa matter and her own mind and body. And perhaps, for women like Monica, this intimate correspondence between matter, body and mind, and the continuous drive to recreate this experience and create tapa, is at the heart of what is, and should be, valued most.

References

Addo, Ping-Ann. 2007. 'Commoner Tongan Women Authenticate "Ngatu Pepa" in Auckland'. In *Hybrid Textiles: Pragmatic Creativity and Authentic Innovations in Pacific Cloth*, ed. Heather E. Young Leslie, Ping-Ann Addo and Phyllis Herda. Special issue of *Journal of Pacific Arts* 3(5): 60–73.

——. 2013. *Creating a Nation with Cloth. Women, Wealth, and Tradition in the Tongan Diaspora*. Volume 4. Association for Social Anthropology in Oceania (ASAO) Studies in Pacific Anthropology. New York and Oxford: Berghahn.

Alaimo, Stacy and Susan J. Hekman (eds). 2008. *Material Feminisms*. Bloomington: Indiana University Press.

Appadurai, Arjun (ed.). 1986. *The Social Life of Things: Commodities in Cultural Perspective*. Cambridge: Cambridge University Press.

Barker, John. 2008. *Ancestral Lines: The Maisin of Papua New Guinea and the Fate of the Rainforest*. Toronto: Broadview Press.

Barker, John and Anna-Karina Hermkens. 2016. 'The Mothers Union Goes on Strike: Maisin Women, Tapa Cloth and Christianity'. In *Gender and Christianity in Melanesia: Towards a Unified Analysis*, ed. Michelle MacCarthy and Annelin Eriksen. Special issue of *The Australian Journal of Anthropology* 27(2): 185–205. DOI: 10.1111/taja.12193.

Carrier, James. 1995. *Gifts and Commodities: Exchange and Western Capitalism since 1700*. New York, London: Routledge.

Choi, Hyaeweol and Margaret Jolly (eds). 2014. *Divine Domesticities. Paradoxes of Christian Modernities in Asia and the Pacific*. Canberra: ANU Press. Online: press.anu.edu.au/publications/divine-domesticities (accessed 30 March 2017).

Colchester, Chloë (ed.). 2003. *Clothing the Pacific*. Oxford and New York: Berg Publishers.

Craig, Barry, Bernie Kernot and Christopher Anderson (eds). 1999. *Art and Performance in Oceania*. Bathurst: Crawford House Publishing.

Douglas, Mary. 2004 [1966]. *Purity and Danger: An Analysis of Concepts of Pollution and Taboo*. London and New York: Routledge.

Fajans, Jane. 1997. *They Make Themselves, Work and Play among the Baining of Papua New Guinea*. Chicago: The University of Chicago Press.

Forshee, Jill. 2001. *Between the Folds: Stories of Cloth, Lives and Travel from Sumba*. Honolulu: University of Hawai'i Press.

French, Lindsay. 1999. 'Hierarchies of Value at Angkor Wat'. *Ethnos: Journal of Anthropology* 64(2): 170–191. DOI: 10.1080/00141844.1999.9981597.

Godelier, Maurice. 1973. *Perspectives in Marxist Anthropology*. Cambridge: Cambridge University Press.

——. 1999 [1996]. *The Enigma of the Gift*. Chicago: University of Chicago Press. Trans from the French by Nora Scott. 1996. *L'Enigme du don*. Paris: Libraire Arthéme Fayard.

Graeber, David. 2001. *Toward an Anthropological Theory of Value: The False Coin of our own Dreams*. New York: Palgrave.

Gregory, C.A. 1982. *Gifts and Commodities*. London: Academic Press.

Haraway, Donna J. 2008. 'Otherworldly Conversations; Terran Topics; Local Terms'. In *Material Feminisms*, ed. Stacy Alaimo and Susan J. Hekman, pp. 157–187. Bloomington: Indiana University Press.

Hermkens, Anna-Karina. 2007. 'Church Festivals and the Visualization of Identity in Collingwood Bay, Papua New Guinea'. *Visual Anthropology* 20(5): 347–364. DOI: 10.1080/08949460701610589.

——. 2010. 'The Gendered Performance of Cloth, Ritual and Belief'. In *Religion and Material Culture: The Matter of Belief*, ed. David Morgan, pp. 231–246. London and New York: Routledge.

——. 2013. *Engendering Objects: Dynamics of Barkcloth and Gender among the Maisin of Papua New Guinea*. Leiden: Sidestone Press.

——. 2015. 'Mediations of Cloth: Tapa and Personhood among the Maisin in PNG'. *Gender and Person in Oceania*, ed. Anna-Karina Hermkens, John Taylor and Rachel Morgain. Special issue of *Oceania* 38(1): 10–23. DOI: 10.1002/ocea.5070.

Hermkens, Anna-Karina, John Taylor and Rachel Morgain (eds). 2015. *Gender and Person in Oceania*. Special issue of *Oceania* 85(1).

Hirschon, Renée (ed.). 1984. *Women and Property – Women as Property*. London and Canberra: Croom Helm.

Ingold, Tim. 2013. *Making: Anthropology, Archaeology, Art and Architecture*. Oxon and New York: Routledge.

Iteanu, André. 1995. 'Rituals and Ancestors'. In *Cosmos and Society in Oceania*, ed. Daniel de Coppet and André. Iteanu. Explorations in Anthropology, pp. 135–164. Herndon, VA: Berg.

Jolly, Margaret. 1991. 'Gifts, Commodities and Corporeality: Food and Gender in South Pentecost, Vanuatu'. *Canberra Anthropology* 14(1): 45–66. DOI: 10.1080/03149099109508475.

——. 2008. 'Of the Same Cloth: Oceanic Anthropologies of Gender, Textiles and Christianities'. Invited Distinguished Keynote Lecture for the Association of Social Anthropology in Oceania, The Australian National University, Canberra, 14 February 2008.

——. 2014. 'A Saturated History of Christianity and Cloth in Oceania'. In *Divine Domesticities: Christian Paradoxes in Asia and the Pacific*, ed. Hyaeweol Choi and Margaret Jolly, pp. 429–454. Canberra: ANU Press. Online: press-files.anu.edu.au/downloads/press/p298891/pdf/ch162.pdf (accessed 31 January 2017).

——. 2015. '*Braed Praes* in Vanuatu: Beyond the Binaries of Gifts and Commodities'. In *Gender and Person in Oceania*, ed. Anna-Karina Hermkens, John Taylor and Rachel Morgain. Special issue of *Oceania* 85(1): 63–78. DOI: 10.1002/ocea.5074.

Knauft, Bruce. 2002 [1999]. *From Primitive to Post-colonial in Melanesia and Anthropology*. Ann Arbor: University of Michigan Press.

Lambek, Michael. 2013. 'The Value of (Performative) Acts'. *HAU: Journal of Ethnographic Theory* 3(2): 141–160. DOI: 10.14318/hau3.2.009.

Lepani, Katherine. 2012. *Islands of Love, Islands of Risk. Culture and HIV in the Trobiands*. Nashville, TN: Vanderbilt University Press.

LiPuma, Edward. 1998. 'Modernity and Forms of Personhood in Melanesia'. In *Bodies and Persons: Comparative Perspectives from Africa and Melanesia*, ed. Michael Lambek and Andrew Strathern, pp. 53–80. Cambridge: Cambridge University Press.

Mauss, Marcel. 1979 [1950]. *Sociology and Psychology: Essays*. London: Routledge & Kegan Paul.

——. 1990. *The Gift. The Form and Reason for Exchange in Archaic Societies*. New York, London: W.W. Norton. Original edition, *Essai sur le don*, first published 1950 by Presses Universitaires de France en *Sociologie et Anthropologie*.

Meyer, Anthony J.P. 1992. *The Funerary Tapa-Cloths of the Nakanai from New Britain*. Series: Océanie-Oceania, No. 11. Paris: Galerie Meyer.

Morgan, David (ed.). 2010. *Religion and Material Culture: The Matter of Belief*. London and New York: Routledge.

Morgain, Rachel and John Taylor. 2015. 'Transforming Relations of Gender, Person, and Agency in Oceania'. In *Gender and Person in Oceania*, ed. Anna-Karina Hermkens, John Taylor and Rachel Morgain. Special issue of *Oceania* 85(1): 1–9. DOI: 10.1002/ocea.5069.

Miller, Daniel. 1994 [1987]. *Material Culture and Mass Consumption*. Oxford: Blackwell.

Sahlins, Marshall. 1988. *Stone Age Economics*. London: Routledge.

Schieffelin, Edward L. 1976. *The Sorrow of the Lonely and the Burning of the Dancers*. New York: St Martin's Press.

Schneider, Jane. 1987. 'The Anthropology of Cloth'. *Annual Review of Anthropology* 16: 409–448. DOI: 10.1146/annurev.an.16.100187. 002205.

——. 2006. 'Cloth and Clothing'. In *Handbook of Material Culture*, ed. Christopher Tilley, Webb Keane, Susanne Kuechler-Fogden, Mike Rowlands and Patricia Spyer, pp. 203–220. London: Sage.

Schwimmer, Erik. 1973. *Exchange in the Social Structure of the Orokaiva: Traditional and Emergent Ideologies in the Northern District of Papua*. London: C. Hurst & Company.

Strathern, Marilyn. 1984. 'Subject or Object? Women and the Circulation of Valuables in Highlands New Guinea'. In *Women and Property – Women as Property*, ed. Renée Hirschon, pp. 158–175. London and Canberra: Croom Helm.

——. 1990 [1988]. *The Gender of the Gift: Problems with Women and Problems with Society in Melanesia*. Berkeley: University of California Press.

Teilhet, Jehanne. 1983. 'The Role of Women Artists in Polynesia and Melanesia'. In *Art and Artists of Oceania*, ed. Sidney M. Mead and Bernie Kernot, pp. 45–56. Palmerston North: Dunmore Press.

Weiner, Annette B. 1976. *Women of Value, Men of Renown: New Perspectives in Trobriand Exchange*. Austin: University of Texas Press.

——. 1989. 'Why Cloth? Wealth, Gender and Power in Oceania'. In *Cloth and Human Experience*, ed. Annette B. Weiner and Jane Schneider, pp. 33–72. Washington DC: Smithsonian Institution Press.

——. 1992. *Inalienable Possessions: The Paradox of Keeping-While-Giving*. Berkeley: University of California Press.

Weiner, Annette B. and Jane Schneider (eds). 1989. *Cloth and Human Experience*. Smithsonian Institution Press.

Widlok, Thomas. 2013. 'Sharing: Allowing Others to Take What is Valued'. *HAU: Journal of Ethnographic Theory* 3(2): 11–31. www.haujournal.org/index.php/hau/article/view/hau3.2.003/383.

Williams, Francis E. 1928. *Orokaiva Magic*. London: Humphrey Milford.

———. 1940. *Drama of Orokolo. The Social and Ceremonial Life of the Elema*. Oxford: Clarendon Press.

Young Leslie, Heather E. and Ping-Ann Addo. 2007. 'Introduction. Pacific Textiles, Pacific Cultures: Hybridity and Pragmatic Creativity'. In *Hybrid Textiles: Pragmatic Creativity and Authentic Innovations in Pacific Cloth*, ed. Heather E. Young Leslie, Ping-Ann Addo and Phyllis Herda. Special issue of *Journal of Pacific Arts* 3(5): 12–21.

4

Revaluing Pots: Wanigela Women and Regional Exchange

Elizabeth Bonshek

Revaluing pots: Wanigela women and regional exchange

The women of Wanigela are known throughout Collingwood Bay, Papua New Guinea (PNG), for making cooking pots (*baitab nokwat*) that are exchanged widely within the region.[1] The clay pots have a distinctive design: as a minimum, a series of applied lines arranged in undulating patterns located around the rim or, more extensively, over the body of the pot, depending on its type. *Baitab nokwat,* the form used in exchanges, characteristically carry incised designs on the body with the applied wavy line motif confined to the rim. In the past, girls would have grown up watching their mothers skilfully manipulate the clay they had collected to make the vessels needed to carry and store water (*simon*); to eat or serve with (*sewaf, ramo*); to participate in ceremonial feasting (*sabed*); to cook with (*baitab nokwat*), or use as objects of exchange.

---

1   There are four local languages (*tok ples*) spoken in Wanigela: Ubir and Oyan are Austronesian languages; Onjob and Aisor are non-Austronesian. Ubir is the lingua franca of Wanigela. However, it is not unusual for Wanigelans to speak Maisin, the *tok ples* of their southern and northern neighbours, as well as Korafe (spoken in Tufi) and Miniafi (also to the north). Most men also speak Tok Pisin, Papua New Guinea's national language. However, Tok Pisin is not spoken widely by many of the senior women, who speak English instead (also a national language, along with Motu). Henceforth Ubir language words will be used in the text unless indicated otherwise.

While most Wanigela women today have replaced clay pots for aluminium ones made in China and purchased from trade stores, *baitab nokwat* remain in use in longstanding regional exchanges within Collingwood Bay for canoes, hunting dogs, string bags, mats and barkcloth—the latter required by Wanigela women for festive dancing. *Baitab nokwat* feed into secondary exchanges and have been recorded at Agaon on the inland border of Milne Bay Province and Central Province (Busse, Araho and Baiva 1991; see also Hermkens this volume).

In the past, *baitab nokwat* were essential to the acquisition of *nunug*, shell necklaces of great symbolic value. Drawing upon their marital and kinship relationships with potters, men traded *baitab nokwat* for *nunug*, which were only obtainable as a result of long canoe voyages beyond Collingwood Bay to the south. Today, *nunug* expeditions have dropped out of Wanigela social memory: only the oldest men and women can remember them having occurred or have heard about them. And while the manufacture of pots for exchange within the Collingwood Bay region continues, the use of pots in all their forms within the Wanigelan home has reduced significantly, together with a marked reduction in the number of women who make pots (Bonshek 2008). This circumstance contrasts with a continued use of *baitab nokwat* by people from outside Wanigela seeking pots to maintain their social and ceremonial obligations.

Today, potters are mostly women aged 50 and over. They told me that they made pots because 'that is what Wanigelans do' (Bonshek 2008). For them, making pots manifested a unique aspect of their cultural production, although this was never directly articulated by them (or by their husbands and male relatives). In the past, learning to make pots was a part of a girl's upbringing (boys did not learn how to make pots).[2] A vigorous potter would have stored up a supply of pots ready for exchanges or for other demands. But in the 1960s, as Wanigela women began to marry men who resided outside of the villages in town, their parents decided daughters who left Wanigela did not need to learn to make pots (Egloff 1974: 74). Perhaps as a result of this shift in practice, together with the availability of metal alternatives, the younger generation of Wanigela women associate pottery making with the activities of the senior

---

2   While this is still the case, in 2007 one man had begun to make pots in flower shapes and to sell these at the dive resort in Tufi. He told me that he could not make the traditional forms, which belonged to the women only, but that it was OK for him to create new forms. His wife, who was a potter, was supportive and helped him.

women of their villages, although a small number of young women now see a potential to earn cash through pottery making. Thus the dynamics surrounding the continuing, if reduced, production of pots has been subject to changing circumstances as the result of interaction with global forces impacting upon local economies for some time (see Patterson and Macintyre 2011 for the critique of the nature of definitions of 'globalisation' and 'modernity'). However, in recent decades, further changes occurring outside of Wanigela, but from within the region, and stemming from new developments in the sustainable production of objects that Wanigelans exchange for, are contributing to the revaluing by Wanigelans of their pottery production. An insight into some of these changes was revealed in a pot exchange expedition made in 2002.

An exchange expedition

In 2002, I accompanied five potters from the villages of Wanigela on a pot-trading expedition. Phyliss, probably in her 60s, was regarded as a very experienced potter, having learnt her skills as a young girl.[3] She had undertaken her last exchange trip about a year previously. On this trip, she had three pots she wanted to exchange. Carol, in her mid-50s, had started making pots only a couple of years prior to this trip, but was more than competent. She had four pots to exchange. Her last exchange trip, to the Maisin market in Uiaku some four hours' canoe trip south of Wanigela, occurred about three to four years previously; before she became a potter. She had travelled to Uiaku with her classificatory sister, and her sister's mother who had made the pots for that trip. Sarah had exchanged pots more recently, travelling with her husband to Uiaku to exchange 10 pots for barkcloth, which she then took to Port Moresby and sold for K50.[4] Pim, a woman in her 60s, had not travelled away from Wanigela to exchange pots since she was a young girl. She remembered clearly that she had gone to Airara (a Maisin village to the south) with her sister (her father's sister's daughter), taking four pots to exchange for barkcloth. The last member of the group, Sharon, took two pots with her. She told me that she had not exchanged pots for 'many years'. Her last opportunity had been with her husband, who at the time had been a medical officer, which required him to go on patrol to various outstations in the region. She had accompanied him to Airara, and exchanged four

---

3   Real names are not used in this account.
4   Papua New Guinea's currency is the Kina (K).

pots for barkcloth, which she had then given to Sister Helen Roberts, head of the medical clinic at Wanigela, who sent them on to Australia for sale. This was some time prior to 1991.[5] Sharon had wanted the money to pay for her first-born daughter's school fees. The five women were active members of the Anglican Church and members of the Mothers' Union.

Figure 19. A woman with *baitab nokwat* packed ready for transport (1967). Each pack contains four pots wrapped and secured for carriage suspended from the head. On the 2002 expedition, the women did not use this carrying method, simply placing their pots packed inside string bags directly into the canoe

Source. Photographed by Brian Egloff, 1967, and used with his permission[6]

---

5   The date of this trip is uncertain: Sister Roberts died in 1991 but had been based in Wanigela since 1949.
6   My thanks to Brian Egloff for permission to use his photograph.

The trip was organised for my benefit as well as theirs. I accompanied them as a newly arrived researcher interested in pottery and pot making. For them, the trip was a demonstration of the way to do things: how Wanigela women exchange pots.[7] We climbed aboard a motor dinghy and set off for Airara, roughly 90 minutes to the south of Wanigela.[8] Phyliss's son accompanied us, acting as escort for his mother and her companions. Ordinarily such a trip would have been undertaken by outrigger canoe or by walking, making the journey unachievable in a single day (Figure 19). On this occasion, the women walked from their homes inland in the bush, a two-hour walk for some of them, and stayed with relatives on the beach overnight, rising at dawn to commence the trip to Airara.

A note had been sent ahead of us through the Mothers' Union to announce our visit. When we arrived, we were met by six Airara women—one of whom was related to Carol (the women were related through their great-grandmothers and they addressed themselves as 'cousin-sister' when using English). Sarah also knew one of the Airara women who had 'married into' Wanigela.

Having disembarked from the dinghy, we all sat on the 'visitors' platform' of the house belonging to one of the hosts, and the women chatted to one another for some time and we drank coconut juice. Then the Wanigela women placed their pots in front of where they were sitting. An Airara woman interested in a particular pot walked around the seated potter, and asked what the potter would like in exchange. The potters told their hosts whether they wanted *ara* (a man's barkcloth) or *beber* (a woman's barkcloth). These interactions continued, accompanied by earnest conversation.

Carol put out all four of her pots, and said that she wanted one *ara* for a large pot (which measured 28 cm wide x 22 cm high); changing to Maisin language, she added that she wanted one *embobi* (a woman's barkcloth) for a smaller pot. Pim also wanted one *ara* for her pot, and completed an exchange with a woman she knew, but to whom she was not related. Carol exchanged one large pot (36 cm wide x 20 cm high) for two

---

7   I carried out fieldwork between 2001 and 2003 as a doctoral candidate at The Australian National University, Canberra; fieldwork in 2007 was undertaken as a research fellow on the Melanesia Art Project 2005–10, a joint project between the University of Cambridge and the British Museum, London, funded by the Arts and Humanities Research Council, UK. Subsequent research was undertaken as Assistant Professor, University of Canberra (2010–15).

8   I financed the motor boat for the trip.

men's barkcloths. Sarah exchanged one pot for one *ara* with a woman with whom she was friends, but not related. Another woman took two of Sarah's pots, and agreed to give two women's barkcloths in exchange. At this point, the Wanigela women had not seen any of the barkcloth offered to them.

When the barkcloth was produced, there was consternation. It was not finished: the cloth had not been painted. This became a matter of great concern to the Wanigela women. The cloth shown to them had an outline of a design marked out in black but the red infill colour had not yet been applied. Carol became quite insistent that the 'Wanigela women' wanted finished barkcloth, which they needed for Lady Day some 18 days away.[9] She said that she did not want to leave her pots without taking the barkcloth, and that she could not come back for them later. After about an hour, dealings appeared to be coming to a halt. And then someone suggested travelling on to Murua, the next village. But we all stayed where we were, betel nut arrived, and the women continued to sit around and chew.

Carol recommenced her negotiations for her barkcloth. She spoke to the mother of the woman who had made some of the barkcloth she was interested in, who, it transpired, was negotiating on the daughter's behalf. They agreed to exchange two pots for one *ara* and one *beber*, and Carol agreed to the cloth being sent up to Wanigela the following Thursday. Before we all moved on to Murua, Phyliss clinched her transaction, exchanging a *beber* for one pot with a Wanigela-born relation (husband's sister's daughter) and exchanged a second pot with an Airara woman she did not know.

At Murua, the exchanges were carried out on the platform of a canoe pulled up on the beach. Carol exchanged one pot with a relative (her cousin's wife) in exchange for one *beber*. At midday, we left Murua and went further south to Sinapara. Carol made enquiries here in Maisin, and we were directed to move on to Sinapa, a village further along. We left the dinghy and walked, heading for the house belonging to a woman called Violet. Carol and Violet were related: their great-great-grandfathers had been brothers. From here, word that Wanigela women had arrived and wanted to exchange pots for cloth was sent out to Koniasi, a small village to the south.

---

9   Lady Day falls in association with Easter in the Anglican Church calendar and is celebrated by members of the Mothers' Union.

We sat around on Violet's visiting platform, waiting for the Koniasi people. Violet explained that it was a difficult time to get barkcloth because the drought had affected the growth of the mulberry trees (see Barker 2008 and Hermkens 2013 for barkcloth manufacture). As she spoke, she brought out a piece of barkcloth that she had tried to sell through the Maisin Integrated Conservation and Development project (MICAD, see Barker 2004, 2008; Hermkens 2013). MICAD exported Maisin barkcloth for sale to Port Moresby, the nation's capital, to provincial capitals, as well as internationally. She told us that MICAD had priced the piece at K44 and that she would accept two pots for this piece. No one took up the offer.

Sharon exchanged one pot for one *beber* with 'old Petra' who was an old friend of Carol's, but who did not know Sharon. Pim exchanged one pot for a barkcloth, and a second for a string bag with a woman called Polly, whom she did not know. Carol also exchanged a pot for a *beber* with Polly, who was a friend. Carol rejected another cloth because it was too small and would not fit around her waist, it did not have the proper edging and it was not painted. When the exchanges at Violet's house were concluded, we returned to the dinghy and headed back to Wanigela, arriving some two hours later.

A continuing tradition

The women on the expedition were amongst a small group in Wanigela for whom making pots continues to be a part of village life (Bonshek 2008). Their organisation and participation in the exchange expedition continued a tradition partially recorded by the first European arrivals to Wanigela in 1899, who observed not only how pots were made, but that pots were used in exchange with neighbouring villagers for barkcloth (Bonshek 1989). Pots continue to be made using the same method, a coiling technique that is distinctive to Wanigela (May and Tuckson 2000).

Only women make pots. They dig up the raw clay from the source, which is located on village land (*wasa motob*). Being on *wasa motob*, not clan land, anyone who is from Wanigela can access the clay, and having done so take it to a potter for the production of pots. Traditionally, the task of collecting clay was done early in the morning, at a time when the activity would be unlikely to be witnessed. While the removal of stones and debris from the clay in preparation for working and the construction of the pot itself might be carried out in view of family members, perhaps on the house verandah or in a purpose-built pot house, the firing of the vessels was a secretive affair to be undertaken in silence. It is at this time that the pots are in most danger. Cracking can take place during firing, so the potter 'cooks' the vessels in a secluded area where no one can see her working and where inadvertent speech presents no risk.

Figure 20. Potter applying design elements to her pot with a shell
Source. Photographed by Elizabeth Bonshek, 2002

All pots are made in the same way. Clay is rolled into a solid cylindrical shape, the dimensions of which determine the size of the final *nokwat* (pot).[10] The cylinder shape is placed on its end, and the potter pushes the sides of the clay downward, forming a shape similar to an upside down mushroom. The sides of the upturned mushroom head are made firm, and the potter then removes portions from the 'stem', which she rolls into coils and then applies to the rim of the upturned 'mushroom'. The potter continues to take clay from the centre of the stem to build up the sides of the pot until the stem is used up, at which point the rudimentary shape of the pot has been achieved.[11] Once the form she desires is achieved, the potter leaves the pot to dry and then refines its shape using a paddle, and scrapes it to thin out the sides. When ready, the distinctive design is applied by pressing tiny coils into the surface of the pot, creating a series of wavy lines in curvilinear patterns. The body of the pot may be decorated in this way too, or if destined for exchange, have incised patterns on the body rather than applied motifs. Potters often stand while making their pots (although elderly potters may choose to sit) and this is a distinctive feature of Wanigela women's technique (Figures 20 and 21).

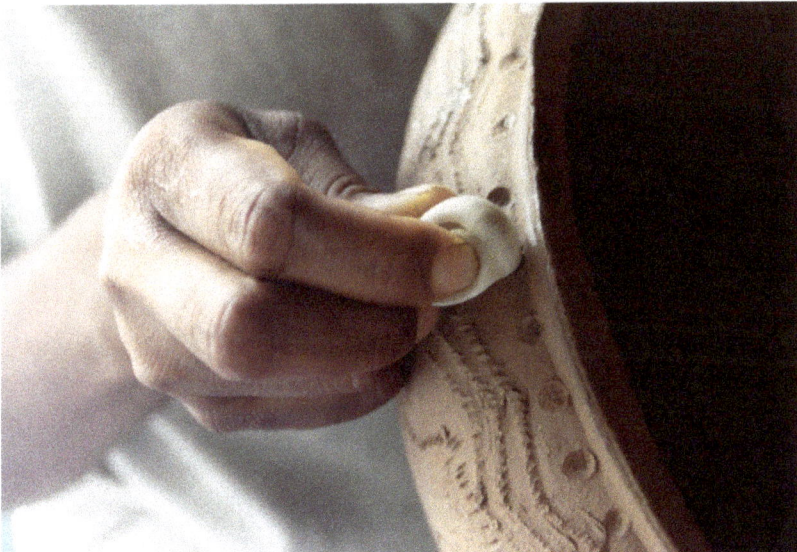

Figure 21. Application of designs while seated
Source. Photographed by Elizabeth Bonshek, 2002

10   *Nokwat* is the word for both a pottery vessel as well as the 'clay', the material it is made from.
11   Margaret Tuckson comments that this method 'has the advantage of keeping the clay in the centre at an even dampness for easy rolling of coils' (Specht, May and Tuckson 2001, n.p.).

While all pots are made in the same way, they are not all destined for exchange. Pots with intricate applied patterns covering the body are kept out of the exchange network, although they might be given away as gifts. Such highly decorated pots are not readily visible in people's houses, but they may be brought out with some pride if interest is shown in them. These 'heirloom' pots often carry clan designs, and as such they manifest a connection between the pot, its owner and his or her clan identity. At the turn of the twentieth century, Percy Money, based at the Anglican Mission, photographed clan pots placed next to burial sites. In 2002, pots continued to mark grave sites in the cemetery (Figure 22), but in some cases the design has been replaced by the name of the deceased.[12]

Figure 22. A 'flower pot' placed beside a grave in the cemetery at Wanigela. The potter has written 'JESUS' on one side. In former times, a clan design was used. The white stones in the foreground mark the perimeter of the grave. Bright plastic flowers cover the grave

Source. Photographed by Elizabeth Bonshek, 2002

---

12 This is perhaps an incidence of the 'graphicalization of meaning' in contemporary Wanigela. For a comparison see Michael O'Hanlon's work (O'Hanlon 1995).

A changing tradition

In former times, men exchanged *baitab nokwat* for feathers with people inland, and for obsidian flakes and shell valuables with people living on the coast at Cape Vogel (Egloff 1974, 1979: 77; May and Tuckson 2000; Schwimmer 1967, 1979). Men travelled southwards towards Milne Bay on long-distance expeditions, which lasted for weeks, organised along clan lines. They went to exchange *baitab nokwat* for strings of ground shell disks known as *nunug* (one *baitab nokwat* was exchanged for 20 *nunug*). *Nunug* formed a part of bride-price payments, which all Wanigela families needed, and also body decoration for particular clans (Bonshek 2005, 2008). *Nunug* were bestowed upon both young men and women at 'first-born' initiations (*aabo*), in which the mother's brother decorated his niece or nephew. The wearing of *nunug*, or their possession, was therefore associated with attaining adult status. Once decorated, a boy or girl was able to participate in dances, the prelude to amorous relationships and 'marriage'. Men and women needed *baitab nokwat* to obtain the necklaces required for their first-born sons and daughters to move into a marriageable status within society, and to celebrate their passage into a new stage of life. The first-born children performed this rite of passage for their younger siblings.

I met only two men who had memories of *nunug* expeditions, one of whom had taken part in such an event. He had been about 14 years old at the time, and thought it was the last of his clan's *nunug* expeditions. (He thought it must have occurred around 1947 to 1950 because the event followed shortly after the conclusion of World War II.) He also thought this was possibly the last *nunug* expedition made by any of the 50 or so clans living in Wanigela.

The acquisition of *nunug* brought renown to the men who acquired them. Participation by a young man in *nunug* expeditions was a mark of his adult status (boys did not go on such expeditions). Wanigela men, therefore, depended upon the skills of their wives, mothers and grandmothers in making the pots used to obtain *nunug*. Women's work in the form of *baitab nokwat* was therefore essential for the acquisition of *nunug* and formed an essential part of the family's cultural capital and a requirement for cultural reproduction in Wanigela (see also Weiner 1977).[13]

---

13 Alongside the transaction of *baitab nokwat* for *nunug*, Wangelan men exchanged sago for pigs, and a particular type of banana (*ogi darag*).

However, there is no longer a common understanding of the value of pottery making and pot use throughout the community regarding pots used in the home, for ceremonies or for exchange. While the process of commodification of pots for cash has an unclear history, it is certain that prior to independence, and continuing into the mid-1990s, the Anglican Mission assisted in the export of pottery (both *baitab nokwat* and 'flower pots') for sale in Port Moresby and Popondetta. Today, this outlet is no longer viable, nor is there government infrastructure to facilitate moving pottery out of Wanigela for sale. But potters do sell *baitab nokwat* and 'flower pots' when they can. They take *baitab nokwat* to the market in the Maisin village, Uiaku (11 kilometres away) or to the Korafe village market in Tufi. Getting pots to the provincial capital Popondetta or to the national capital, Port Moresby, is an attractive idea: a *baitab nokwat* that might possibly sell in Wanigela for K5 (at the market held at the airstrip) can be sold for K20 'in town'. However, the potter must have the opportunity to get the pots out of Wanigela first, and this generally means having family networks living away from the village. At K20 a piece, plus the cost of getting pots to the external markets, pottery sales do not constitute a reliable or significant income (Bonshek 2008). Nonetheless, some women see such sales as an opportunity that provides much wanted income.

In 2000–03 very few elderly women still produced pots in large numbers for themselves or their family members, or as commissions (Bonshek 2008). In contrast to past practice, novice potters were mostly married women, not young girls. Residing with their husband's family, they looked to their mothers-in-law and grandmothers, not their mothers, for instruction. The contemporary mode of transmission of pottery knowledge has implications for the continued transmission of clan designs, as daughters are no longer exposed to clan knowledge pertinent to the designs of their natal clan. For the men and women of senior generations, while knowledge about pot making and designs was not articulated as wealth, clearly pots manifest economic, cultural and social value (in Bourdieu's [2000] sense of 'value'; and Weiner 1977).

While men's exchanges for *nunug* are a thing of the past, some Wanigela women do continue to exchange *baitab nokwat,* sometimes in large numbers. While barkcloth, string bags and mats are exchanged one for one, in 2002, 30 pots were exchanged for a small canoe, and 60 pots for a pig needed for a church celebration. In both these cases, women negotiated these exchanges themselves. But it is quite acceptable for a family member to transact pots on a woman's behalf and, equally, a woman might supply pots for her family members to transact on their own account. As the expedition illustrated, most exchanges occur through already established social relations or in conjunction with these. However, as demonstrated through the negotiations on Violet's verandah, it appears that the nature of the social relations of exchange might be on the verge of transformation. These transformations became apparent via the expectations surrounding the exchanges that occurred on the expedition, which in turn reflected 'shifting regimes of value' (Appadarai 1986). The changes encountered on the expedition, occurring at the local level, have their origins in regional and international conservation movements, and are manifest in the reconstitution of 'artefacts' into 'art' from the perspective of international non-government organisations and prospective art buyers and dealers.

Shifting regimes of value

Arjun Appadurai (1986) uses the concept of a commodity's trajectory to describe the potential uses an object (commodity) might have in any given social context. Using this framework, I propose that pots move along a number of different trajectories: they may be kept for domestic use for cooking; they may appear at ceremonial occasions such as feasting when they are used in presentations of cooked food; they may serve to display clan identity; they may be treasured as material connections with deceased family members; they may be given away as gifts; and they may enter the exchange network. In the last case, *baitab nokwat* form important components in the extensive regional exchange network operating in the Collingwood Bay area. But what is the nature of their value in regional exchange?

Appadurai argues that 'economic exchange creates value' and that 'value is embodied in the commodities that are exchanged … rather than in the forms or functions of exchange' (1986: 3). Adopting this position, it is the social context of the exchange of *baitab nokwat* in which Wanigelan women engage (their 'commodity situation' [Appadurai 1986: 13]) that is important. In the following discussion, attention to the commodity candidacy of *baitab nokwat* emerges through the example of the pot exchange expedition, especially in relation to an interpretation of the suggestion that a pot be sold for K44 as a 'diversion'. Here, as Appadurai suggests, a 'diversion' is a departure from usual practice, thus carrying with it the possible development of a new standard.

For Appadurai, the commodity candidacy of a thing refers to the 'standards and criteria (symbolic, classificatory, and moral) that define the exchangeability of things in any particular social and historical context' (1986: 14). Furthermore, objects might circulate through or across differing 'regimes of value' in space and time (4). For Appadurai, the attractiveness of this phrase lies in its flexibility—it need not presuppose 'a complete cultural sharing of assumptions' concerning the transaction of 'commodities', but 'such regimes of value account for the constant transcendence of cultural boundaries by the flow of commodities, where culture is understood as a bounded and localized system of meanings' (1986: 15).

The interactions between the potters and their Maisin counterparts in this case is interesting because they display an overlapping, or overlaying, of 'boundaries'. As suppliers of pottery, the potters are Wanigelans: Wanigelans have sole access to the clay and pottery making is unique to the Wanigela villages. As such, all potters are Wanigelans (although not all Wanigelans are potters). But as Wanigelans, potters also identify themselves as belonging to what is in fact one of a number of discrete villages, as speakers of one of four *tok ples* languages and belonging to one of the 50 or so clans that reside there.[14] As the suppliers of pots within a regional network of exchange, Wanigelans also claim a place in a broader regional stage: they are from Collingwood Bay and they participate in exchanges of some antiquity with their neighbours. Depending on historical connections, specific events and the agents involved, potters continuously shift their alliances. They might identify with specific *tok ples* speakers and have particular village affiliations, but also identify as being Wanigelan or being part of a wider Collingwood Bay-wide exchange network (Bonshek 2005). Within Wanigela, the idea of a 'bounded' cultural group is highly problematic, as people differentiate themselves on the basis of language and clan within the context of any specific activity.

Disregarding for a moment the problematic associations of positioning oneself within a local (language and village) context and subsequently in regard to the outward-moving ripples of connection (from village to region constituted by history and the passage of time), the transactions during the expedition took place within existing social networks. The women who exchanged with one another on this occasion could trace family

---

14   Each of the 50 or so clans have their own histories of origin and migration into Wanigela.

connections through intermarriage, descent and residence. In addition to these kinship connections, as active members of the Wanigela Mothers' Union and the Airara Women's Union, the women were connected via the structural organisation of the Anglican Church. Two of the women at least had also previously lived in Airara: one when her husband had been posted to the area as a teacher, and the other when her husband was stationed at the medical outstation there. 'Strangers' were introduced through these pre-existing social links and networks (Strathern 1988; Weiner 1977).

The potters entered into their transactions with a number of expectations revolving around the attributes they felt constituted an acceptable piece of barkcloth for exchange. At the first village, the women entered into negotiations without seeing the barkcloth on offer. Their expectations became clear (to the outsider) when the unexpected occurred: the cloth was not completed—it had not been painted. Further, in one case the size was not big enough to accommodate an adult man or woman. A woman's barkcloth must be a large rectangle, worn wrapped around the waist one-and-a-half times, and allowing room for trimming the fringe (the customisation of the cloth with an individual's clan design). A man's barkcloth must be long and narrow, proportioned so as to be worn as a loincloth, with plenty of room at either end to allow for fringes to be cut. (The potters did not judge the barkcloth on the basis of the designs they carried.)

The Wanigela women were unhappy about accepting unfinished cloth because they were anxious about whether it would be completed on time: they wanted to leave Airara with their barkcloth in hand. Coming back to Airara was not an option for them as they did not have ready access to a canoe in which to return. The Wanigela ladies would be reliant upon the Airara women to bring the barkcloth to Wanigela. But at the same time, while worried about these matters, Carol explained to me (as much as to reassure herself it seemed to me at the time) that the Airara women knew how the 'bush ladies' lived. They (the Airara women) had visited in 2001, so 'the Airara women knew that the Bush ladies did not have canoes'. So the rationale for proceeding with accepting unfinished cloth was presented to me as one based on the Airara women's familiarity and prior knowledge of Wanigela's women's circumstances. And, in fact, the barkcloth did arrive the following week.

In Appadurai's terms, the Wanigela women can be understood as viewing the barkcloth and pots as being in a standard relationship with one another—a relationship built upon precedent. From the Wanigela women's point of view, there were common assumptions about what constituted an appropriate exchange regardless of the specific difficulties that arose.

Using Appadurai's framework, the *baitab nokwat* were 'commodities by destination': they were objects made by potters with the intention of using them in exchanges (1986: 15). Their circulation in the specific case related here reflected 'a shifting compromise between socially regulated paths and competitively inspired diversions' (Appadurai 1986: 17). The interaction on Violet's verandah, through which arose the possibility of selling instead of exchanging a barkcloth, represented such a 'diversion': for the potters it introduced altered assumptions about what the exchange of pots for barkcloth constituted. Violet's offer lay beyond the Wanigela women's anticipations; it originated outside the then current regimes of value (the exchange of one pot for one barkcloth). In this case, the Wanigela women responded to the diversion by ignoring it.

However, it is important to recognise that the establishment of a cash value is not, of itself, unacceptable to the potters; as mentioned, Wanigela women do sell their *baitab nokwat*. Of all the pot transactions I recorded between 2001 and 2003, 25 per cent were concerned with pots made for a cash sale. While this appears a sizeable percentage (a quarter of all the transactions), in fact only a small number of pots (10.6 per cent of the total number of pots transacted) were sold or earmarked for sale. They were sold at markets in Wanigela, Tufi or Uiaku. The highest price for one pot was K20, which was considered a very good price, and not a price that a 'local' would be expected (or asked) to pay. It was the outsider's price. Pots appeared for sale only rarely in the Wanigela market during 2001 to 2003, and I inadvertently caused confusion amongst the potters I knew by buying one at K20.

At the time I did not know the potters very well, and I had simply thought the pot on sale was very beautiful. After I purchased it, two potters I knew visited me and quizzed me on why I had made the purchase. They were very perplexed by what I had done—all that was necessary to get such a pot was to ask one of the potters I knew to make it. The acquisition of pots from someone I was not connected to, and the payment of such a large sum, was not compatible with the social networks and obligations that were developing around me (and of which I was obviously unaware until then). Also, for them, the pot was simply a pot. While I had particularly liked the pot I bought (the design on it was especially to my liking) my inquisitors were not concerned with what I saw as 'quality' or my aesthetic sense regarding pots and the motifs they carried. Any potter could supply me with a *baitab nokwat*, but a potter I was connected with should be the woman to make it for me (Bonshek 2015).

I suggest that there are two aspects that might be considered in unravelling the impact of a request for a cash price. First, as demonstrated, from the Wanigelan perspective, a cash value belongs in another regime of values— that of sales to outsiders, not exchanges between people in Collingwood Bay. So, when Violet asked for a cash price while sitting on her verandah, for the Wanigela women her offer was outside the regime of value associated with the regional exchange network: the cash value disrupted the values attendant upon exchange (a standard size of a pot, for an appropriately sized barkcloth). In Appadurai's terms, the existing social relationship that constituted the exchange was altered.

Second, while not verbally corroborated by Wanigelans, it is, I think, suggestive that all exchanges concerning pots that I encountered comprised exchanges of either one for one, or exchanges of pots in multiples of five with 20 as a base. In the Ubir counting system, five is termed 'one hand', 10 is 'two hands', 15 is 'two hands and a foot', and 20 is a 'man' (*orot*). Thus the numbers one to 20 may be conceived of as a unity or the completion of a whole: 'one man'.[15] Other exchange equivalences involving pots are recorded in Table 1.

Table 1. Exchange equivalence of pots with other items in 2001–03

Baitab nokwat		Exchanged for
1 *baitab nokwat*	=	1 barkcloth
1 *baitab nokwat*	=	1 string bag
1 *baitab nokwat*	=	1 pandanus mat
1 *baitab nokwat*	=	20 shell necklaces
30 *baitab nokwat* (or 1½ men)	=	1 canoe
60 *baitab nokwat* (or 3 men)	=	1 pig
1 *baitab nokwat*	=	K20 at the 'town price'
20 *baitab nokwat* (or 1 man)	=	gift (of 20 pots) associated with bride price (but not itself constituting bride price)

---

15   The expression for a singular thing is *kaitomom*, and 20 is *kaitomom orot* (one man).

So while Wanigela women do sell pots, Violet might have moved into unrecognised 'numerical territory' when she asked for K44. I suggest that, from a Wanigelan perspective, the sum itself was odd, as well as entering contentious territory in terms of transforming an existing regime of value into something else. The price of her barkcloth had been set by MICAD. But in asking the MICAD price, she opened up the possibility of denying the value associated with longstanding historical exchanges and, in doing so, potentially denying the social nature of the exchange itself. The request for cash in this context compromised both the quality of social relations surrounding exchange, and disturbed established regimes of value. In Appadurai's terms (1986: 29–41), the exchange of what were once commensurate 'desires' became, on this occasion at least, incommensurate, as one partner's expectations shifted.

This investigation is constrained to the potter's viewpoint. The 'diversion' originating from the Maisin end of the exchange reflected changes caused by an 'aid project' initiated by Greenpeace. For my purposes, Greenpeace is viewed simply as a globalised organisation, whose aims are targeted to its own interests (specifically the prevention of logging in the region). The operations of Greenpeace in Collingwood Bay have been detailed elsewhere (Barker 2008; and Hermkens 2013) and are not of central importance to this chapter, except for the flow-on effect experienced by the potters as exemplified during the expedition. But it must also be remembered that the case presents the responses of older women in the community, who may not represent the views of younger women. The senior women were demonstrating how pottery exchange works, but in so doing their encounter with local incursions of global forces revealed insights into changing perceptions of wealth and value.

The events also present a dilemma for those who are confronted with serious challenges in their acquisition of cash. The senior potters were not disconnected from, or undesiring of, cash. But their own avenues for earning cash through pottery production had not been developed either by themselves or outsiders. Some felt that the developments in barkcloth production, as a result of Greenpeace's activities in Collingwood Bay to create a sustainable industry for the Maisin (see Hermkens this volume), ignored them.

Global impacts—transforming artefacts into art

Prior to PNG's independence, Sister Helen Roberts, the nursing sister who had been running the Anglican Church's medical centre in Wanigela for a considerable number of years, provided an irregular outlet for the sale of both barkcloth and pots (Barker 2007: 77). These exports of 'artefacts' from Collingwood Bay to outsiders is not well documented, but follows from the supply of ethnographic items to museum collections in Australia, England, Scotland and elsewhere dating to the turn of the twentieth century (Beran and Aguire 2009; Bonshek 1989; and Hermkens 2013). An early assessment of the potential for commercial sales of barkcloth and pots in the 1960s did not view the situation for pots very favourably when compared to barkcloth—pots were relatively heavy and also fragile (Schwimmer 1967, 1979).

Since 1996, as a result largely from the work of Greenpeace International, Maisin barkcloth has been commoditised for western audiences as 'art' and sold through MICAD (see further Hermkens this volume). As John Barker comments, barkcloth was attractive to the conservation movement in a number of ways: it was 'sustainable', easy to ship, a symbol of continuity of tradition, iconic of Oceanic art forms, and importantly it represented women's work (Barker 2008: 191). During this period, MICAD collected barkcloth from all the Maisin villages, set a price according to size, and sold the cloth in towns within PNG as well as overseas. It is one of these pieces of barkcloth that had not been sold via MICAD that Violet was trying to move on.

Perhaps a victim of the 'West's' ideological distinction between art and craft, Wanigela pottery has not made the transformation into art, from the 'art world' point of view (but see Beran and Aguire 2009). Pots remain largely objects of 'material culture' that provide museums with evidence of how cultural practices and contemporary cultural values might have changed or continue over time. My own acquisition of 13 Wanigela pots for the Australian Museum, Sydney, in 2003 was destined for a natural history museum holding extensive anthropological collections that provided the potential to analyse continuity and change (Bonshek 2015). Under their contemporary collection development policies, these pots are now conceived of primarily as 'cultural heritage' and 'cultural collections' rather than as 'art' (Australian Museum 2014).

To my knowledge, Wanigela pots have been exhibited as 'art' on two occasions only, but not promoted as artwork in terms of sales. First during the 1960s, at the time that artist Patricia May and potter Margaret Tuckson made a substantial collection of pottery from PNG (May and Tuckson 2000) for the Australian Museum, Sydney, and some 40 years later, in 2001, at the Djamu Gallery, a former art gallery venue at Australian Museum's Customs House site (Specht, May and Tuckson 2001). Both exhibitions drew upon the same collections held at the museum. The Wanigela component was comprised of pots collected between 1904 and 1910 by Percy Money—a lay missionary with the Anglican Church who made an extensive collection of a broad range of material culture from Wanigela (Bonshek 1989)—and some 50 years later from the collection made by May and Tuckson. The second exhibition promoted an artistic interpretation in its display method. However, such transformations of the objects' status (art vs artefact [Myers 2001]) were played out within the museum's field of cultural production with no direct effect or involvement of the Wanigela potters.

In contrast, in the 1990s, barkcloth was subject to a differing trajectory on the global stage. Maisin barkcloth has been displayed as art in exhibitions in the United States of America (Barker 2008), and has been produced and, importantly, priced for sale and display in international exhibitions. Since 2006, barkcloth from neighbouring areas to the north have been sold as 'art'[16] and exhibited in private and public galleries.[17]

The success, or otherwise, of sustainable barkcloth production for Maisin villages is discussed elsewhere (Barker 2008; Hermkens this volume); however, within Wanigela, where there is a history of exchange relationships of some continuity documented in European records over 100 years ago, the changes in barkcloth production and pricing by MICAD have had disrupting flow-on effects. While barkcloth production has been placed centre stage in the transformations of objects from items of material culture to art through both national and international exposure, pottery remains largely embedded within local regimes of value and as a 'craft' to any potential 'art' buyer.

---

16   For example, Ömie Artists (Inc.). Online: www.omieartists.com (accessed 28 June 2015).
17   For instance see *Wisdom of the Mountain*. Art of the Ömie exhibition held at National Gallery of Victoria, 27 November – 21 March 2010. Online: www.ngv.vic.gov.au/exhibition/wisdom-of-the-mountain (accessed 28 June 2015).

The development of a mechanism for Maisin to earn cash through the sales of barkcloth has not gone without notice in Wanigela. While most women in Wanigela do not understand the details of how MICAD barkcloth sales operated at the time, or the connection with Greenpeace, they saw Maisin women making money, and they experienced through Violet a preference for cash rather than exchange. But Wanigela women too want to have cash, and consequently some viewed developments in Maisin barkcloth sales with envy. This unhappiness spilt out in comments that 'Wanigelans own barkcloth too', that 'the Maisin stole barkcloth making from Wanigela using sorcery'. I was told that during the 1950s, Maisin sorcery had caused all the mulberry trees in Wanigela to die, and that the designs that are applied to the barkcloth 'belong to Collingwood Bay, not just to the Maisin'. These women drew upon regional identities, not village affiliations, to express their frustration.

Violet's offering of her barkcloth for sale at the MICAD price of K44 not only took barkcloth outside the regional network of a one-to-one relationship between Wanigela pots, Maisin barkcloth, Miniafia string bags and mats in which the women customarily operated, but strayed into an avenue of cash generation from which Wanigela women felt excluded.

Conclusion

Between 2001 and 2003, the production and circulation of *baitab nokwat* by senior women in Wanigela represented a continuity of tradition, in terms of both a manufacturing technique and in the social relations in which these processes are enmeshed. Pots were not traded for food, which Wanigelans do not need to import (cf. Arifin 1991: 375; May and Tuckson 2000; Welsch and Terrell 1998). Women's production of pottery was not connected solely to utilitarian needs (where 'demand' and 'desire' are understood as natural, fixed and transcultural states or needs [Appadurai 1986: 29]). According to both senior men and women, making pots was emblematic of being Wanigelan.

In the past, both men and women needed *baitab nokwat* to fulfil social obligations. These pots were essential components for exchange expeditions made by men to obtain valuable *nunug* (shell necklaces) essential for *aabo* (first-born ceremonies) and *kekes* (bride price). Special pots (*sabed*) were also used in feasting that took place between clan groups. The latter are no longer made, and the men's voyages for exchange terminated in the mid-1940s. It appears that further change is also on the horizon for the women's use of pottery. Women increasingly want to sell pots for cash, but have no real market to sell through: they do not have easy access to provincial towns and, since independence, tourists no longer visit Wanigela. But while women may want to, and do, sell pots for cash in some contexts (pots may be commissioned, or taken to market and sold), their replacement for cash in exchanges with local neighbours is not welcomed by older Wanigela women.

For these women, it is exchange with the Maisin women that is of value (Appadurai 1986: 28). The transfer of MICAD prices by the Maisin women to the sphere of exchange holds the potential to undermine what have long been commensurate values. For the Wanigela women on the trip, what Appadurai would call the 'commodity candidacy' of the pots holds the potential for being altered and the very possibility of this being the case is disruptive. In Appadurai's terms, the Wanigelan's view of the 'cultural framework' of the exchange, the conventions that govern the exchangeability of things (one-for-one exchange; or a calculation based on 20), were being attenuated as one party to the exchange appeared to be on the verge of withdrawing from this convention; hence values were in danger of becoming 'unyoked' (1986).

The commoditisation of Maisin barkcloth therefore poses a real problem for Wanigela women. It remains to be seen whether the Maisin will push further down the path of commoditisation in their exchange transactions with their Collingwood Bay neighbours, or whether commoditisation will be confined to sales within MICAD operations outside the region. A crucial factor will be how desirable Wanigela pots remain for Maisin, and whether Wanigela potters will set their price in cash.

For now, older women are happy supplying pots for their relatives to sell. But younger women, who have begun to consider making pots as a means to improve their economic standing through earning cash, may not wish to give away their labour for the benefit of extended family members or for the maintenance of the social relations deemed so important by the potters on the expedition. Since 2003, there has been one pot-making project in Wanigela, based in the Onjob village of Koreaf, which has attempted to revalue pot making. The instigator of the project articulates the promotion of pottery manufacture as something that defines Koreaf women's identity, and as a practice that supports Onjob tradition. He makes a distinction between Onjob identity and Wanigela identity in his promotion of pot making, and was inspired by his own observations of how MICAD has worked with the Maisin in developing barkcloth for commercial production. But his project reveals a different kind of transformation: the objectification of pot making as a cultural practice bound to an expression of cultural identity (Miller 1987).

The manufacture and exchange of *baitab nokwat* in Wanigela is not yet a dying tradition, but it is in a fragile state. It might be recontextualised as an economic activity providing access to the cash economy and thus move away from an exchange economy; or it may be revalued as an objectified product of Wanigelan tradition, or indeed both. For now, while unchanged in visual appearance, *baitab nokwat* conceal fluctuations in the social relations surrounding the production and use of these distinctive, and regionally important, objects of women's wealth.

References

Appadurai, Arjun (ed.). 1986. *The Social Life of Things: Commodities in Cultural Perspective*. Cambridge: Cambridge University Press.

Arifin, Karina. 1991. 'Social Aspects of Pottery Manufacture in Boera, Papua New Guinea'. *Bulletin of the Indo-Pacific Prehistory Association* 11: 373-387. DOI: 10.7152/bippa.v11i0.11401.

Australian Museum. 2014. *Cultural Collections Acquisition Policy 2014–2017*. Online: www.australianmuseum.net.au/Our-policies (accessed September 2014).

Barker, John. 2004. 'Between Heaven and Earth: Missionaries, Environmentalists, and the Maisin'. *In Globalization and Culture. Change in the Pacific Islands*, ed. Victoria Lockwood, pp. 439–459. Upper Saddle River, NJ: Pearson, Prentice Hall.

—— (ed.). 2007. *The Anthropology of Morality in Melanesia and Beyond*. Aldershot: Ashgate.

——. 2008. *Ancestral Lines: The Maisin of Papua New Guinea and the Fate of the Rainforest*. Peterborough, Ontario: Broadview Press.

Beran, Harry and Edward Aguire. 2009. *The Art of Oro Province. A Preliminary Typology*. Sydney: The Oceanic Art Society.

Bonshek, Elizabeth. 1989. *Money, Pots and Patterns: The Percy Money Collection of Bark Cloth and Pottery held at the Australian Museum.* MA thesis. St Lucia: University of Queensland.

——. 2005. 'The Struggle for Wanigela: Representing Social Space in a Rural Community in Collingwood Bay, Oro Province, Papua New Guinea'. PhD thesis. Canberra: The Australian National University.

——. 2008. 'When Speaking is a Risky Business: Understanding Silence and Interpreting the Power of the Past in Wanigela, Oro Province, Papua New Guinea'. *Journal of Material Culture* 13(1): 85–105. DOI: 10.1177/1359183507086220.

——. 2015. 'Ethics and Collecting in the "Postmodern" Museum: A Papua New Guinea Example'. In *The Ethics of Cultural Heritage*, ed. Tracy Ireland and John Schofield, pp. 145–164. New York: Springer Press.

Bourdieu, Pierre. 2000. *Pascalian Meditations.* Stanford, CA: Stanford University Press.

Busse, Mark, Nick Araho and Ivuyo Baiva. 1991. *Traditional Trade and Migration among the Daga: Report of a Research Trip through the Owen Stanley Mountains of Central and Milne Bay Provinces.* Port Moresby: National Museum of Papua New Guinea.

Egloff, Brian. 1974. 'Contemporary Wanigela Pottery'. *Occasional Papers No.2, Anthropology Museum*, pp. 67–79. St Lucia: University of Queensland.

——. 1979. *Recent Prehistory in South East Papua.* Canberra: The Australian National University Press.

Hermkens, Anna-Karina. 2013. *Engendering Objects. Dynamics of Barkcloth and Gender among the Maisin of Papua New Guinea.* Leiden: Sidestone Press.

Ireland, Tracy and John Schofield (eds). 2015. *The Ethics of Cultural Heritage.* New York: Springer Press.

Lockwood, Victoria (ed.). 2004. *Globalization and Culture. Change in the Pacific Islands.* Upper Saddle River, NJ: Pearson, Prentice Hall.

May, Patricia and Margaret Tuckson. 2000 [1986]. *The Traditional Pottery of Papua New Guinea*. Adelaide: Crawford House Publishing.

Miller, Daniel. 1987. *Material Culture and Mass Consumption*. New York: Basil Blackwell.

Myers, Fred (ed.). 2001. *The Empire of Things: Regimes of Value and Material Culture*. Santa Fe: School of American Research Press.

O'Hanlon, Michael. 1995. 'Modernity and the "Graphicalization" of Meaning: New Guinea Highland Shield Design in Historical Perspective'. *The Journal of the Royal Anthropological Institute* 1(3): 469–493. DOI: 10.2307/3034571.

Patterson, Mary and Martha Macintyre (eds). 2011. *Managing Modernity in the Western Pacific*. St Lucia: University of Queensland Press.

Schwimmer, Ziska. 1967. *Report on Handcrafts of the Northern District*. Port Moresby: Department of Business Development.

——. 1979. 'Tapa Cloths of the Northern District'. *Pacific Arts Newsletter* 9: 6–11.

Specht, Jim, Patricia May and Margaret Tuckson. 2001. *Sospen Graoun. Pottery from Papua New Guinea*. Exhibition catalogue, Sydney: Australian Museum.

Stark, Miriam T. (ed.). 1998. *The Archaeology of Social Boundaries*. Washington, DC: Smithsonian Institution Scholarly Press.

Strathern, Marilyn. 1988. *The Gender of the Gift: Problems with Women and Problems with Society in Melanesia*. Berkeley: University of California Press.

Weiner, Annette. 1977. *Women of Value, Men of Renown: New Perspectives in Trobriand Exchange*. Brisbane: University of Queensland Press.

Welsch, Robert and John Terrell. 1998. 'Material Culture, Social Fields, and Social Boundaries on the Sepik Coast of New Guinea'. In *The Archaeology of Social Boundaries*, ed. Miriam T. Stark, pp. 50–77. Washington, DC: Smithsonian Institution Scholarly Press.

5

The Extraordinary Values of Ordinary Objects: String Bags and Pandanus Mats as Korafe Women's Wealth?

Elisabetta Gnecchi-Ruscone

Introduction

Korafe women, like the neighbouring Maisin, Miniafe and Ubir women, have long been recognised in regional and national contexts as coming from the Cape Nelson/Collingwood Bay area of Papua New Guinea because of their distinctive facial tattoos and barkcloth. Beyond this 'ethnic' or regional identity, these items of body adornment are also constitutive of the gender identity of the village women who wear and produce them (Barker 2008; Hermkens 2013). Like many other aspects of villagers' lives, the practices and significance linked to tattoos and barkcloths have been transformed in the years since the incorporation of villagers into the colonial national and global worlds (Gnecchi-Ruscone and Hasselberg 2012). While tattoos have mostly been relinquished in recent years, barkcloths have retained their importance as women's valuables and as markers of local identity, particularly in the context of struggles for self-determination by Collingwood Bay people in the face of unscrupulous deforestation plans (Barker 2008). Anna-Karina Hermkens (2013) has carefully documented the performative aspects of barkcloth production, use and exchange as gift and as commodity by Maisin women; drawing out the links between the objects' life histories and the material side of people's identities (see also Hermkens this volume).

I am interested in exploring two objects that may be less distinctive, but that are used daily by women in Collingwood Bay—namely string bags and mats. Pierre Lemmonier rightly calls us to consider the involvement of mundane objects in different aspects of a group's social life, and the nonverbal communication they participate in as 'revealed when we regard them as things to make, manipulate and act upon, and not—or not only—something to look at, decipher, exchange, or discuss' (2012: 134). I want to explore the ways in which string bags and mats, 'render tangible or actualise in a performative way important aspects of social organisation, culture, systems of thought, or actions' (14).

Following Hermkens' example, I will consider these two items of women's wealth to have different biographies pertaining to different realms (technical, ritual and social). 'Within these biographies each object is expected to follow a desirable ... life path' (Hermkens 2013: 331). These paths intersect with different fields of action such as marriage, exchange, identity and brother–sister relationships. Of particular relevance here are the concepts of 'affordances' and 'mapping' as applied to Melanesian contexts by Graeme Were, who argues for a locally shared logic that 'emphasizes a focus on material thinking, not just on the properties of materials, but also on how these properties—through transformation—connect to the social world' (2013: 585). Simply stated, affordances are the possibilities that people, the makers of things, can perceive in the different materials available in their environment—guiding their choice of material, and influencing the structure and form of the final object. Conversely, mapping is a 'logical property of affordance', which allows us to consider the intersubjectively shared logic by which the transformation of material through the intentions, choices and design of men or women connects its intrinsic physical properties to the expression of social realities.

The technical life of objects involves the process of transforming raw materials into valuable items, which occurs through women's specific intentional actions. These actions entail processes of how the required know-how and skills are obtained, as well as the changes in technology that have been incorporated by women in the manufacturing of string bags and mats. Ludovic Coupaye affirms that the values, qualities and properties of artefacts are not given characteristics of the objects, but result from technical processes of production; they are 'capacities intentionally placed within, ingrained, embodied or materialised in the artefact' (2013: 92). Tim Ingold's reflection that things are not finished at the end of their production process but are 'carried on in their use' (2013: 85–100) suggests that such properties flow into their ensuing life paths.

Applying the concepts of affordance and mapping to the study of Nalik pandanus mats, Were is able to associate the use of two distinct types of pandanus leaves to produce different types of mats expressing different social relations. *Amotmot* pandanus leaves are used to make stitched mats; concomitant with their protective function during life-cycle ritual is their association to more traditional, short-term local relationships. *Awoiwoi* pandanus leaves, however, are used in the production of more durable plaited mats, of imported design, and they are used in more mundane situations and associated with a wider network of individualised relations (Were 2013: 596), thus confirming Lemmonier's (2012) claims concerning the performative properties of material goods in expressing social relations.

In the following pages, I will follow the biographies of string bags and mats made by Korafe women, showing their life histories and entanglements with diverse fields of action and thought. Like the Nalik, Korafe use different pandanus leaves to produce stitched and plaited mats and, like them, they privilege the more local stitched mats in ceremonial occasions. String bags can also be made with different materials: natural fibre, now reserved for special string bags that signal the wearer's commitment to traditional values; and the more practical, versatile and durable artificial string, used for more ordinary string bags. However, objects too have a life history. In life-cycle rituals, things that are commonly used in mundane situations follow a ritual path. As such, their social life comprises the transactional dimension of valuables and how women use them in life-cycle exchanges to establish and maintain relations. Developing Arjun Appadurai's (1986) argument that things move between social contexts, both Maureen MacKenzie (1991) and Hermkens (2013) have demonstrated that objects made by women acquire different meanings and values in the course of their lives. Following on their insights, I will show that string bags and pandanus mats are valuable in that they are indispensable items of daily work and life, embodying the labour of their makers, and that they acquire ritual value when they are used in life-cycle ceremonies. In fact, these items objectify particular women's work and intentions in creating and sustaining relations through informal exchanges.

The question that remains open, then, relates to the introduction of string bags and pandanus mats into formal exchange networks between clans. Annette Weiner launched the debate on women's wealth with her ground-breaking ethnography *Women of Value, Men of Renown: New Perspectives in Trobriand Exchange* (1976). She described *sagali* exchanges in which Trobriand women ceremonially exchange banana leaf bundles and skirts as 'women's wealth'. Here, women compete to gain power and prestige for themselves and their matrilinear subclans (*dala*) within a context that is separate from, yet interdependent with men's exchanges. Weiner concludes that the *sagali* exchanges are pivotal in the reproduction of each *dala* and of Trobriand society as a whole (see also Lepani, and MacCarthy this volume). My question, therefore, is whether string bags and mats, when given by women in the context of ceremonial exchanges, can be said to become women's wealth.

Making string bags

There is a constant need for string bags (*áti*), and women of all ages are continuously making new ones. Girls and women who are not busy with other tasks, such as gardening or cooking, are often looping string bags. Deft women can also continue looping while walking. Often young girls sit next to more expert women—their sisters, mothers and grandmothers—in order to draw on their skills and knowledge when they run into difficulty, or when they start a new kind of stitch. Making a string bag is considered to be a very time-consuming task, it can take weeks, but then a good quality *áti* can withstand several years of heavy-duty, daily use.

The majority of string bags are now made from synthetic string. Both women and girls enjoy experimenting with the possibilities offered by colourful store-bought strings. The front side of the string bag—the one that is seen when it is carried hanging over one's back—is decorated by alternating sections resulting from the use of different elaborate stitches within and between rows of loops. The resulting textured appearance, combined with the alternating colours, allows women to create their own distinctive patterns, which personalises their string bags. The back part is made using plain stitches (*binóno*) only; whatever colour thread was being used at the end of the row at the front runs into the back part until it is used up, thus the pattern of colours on the rear is casual.

Some women elect certain colours and patterns as their preferred designs, and become associated with them. For example, Jessette Ikirima, a senior woman from Goodenough village, uses red, black and white strings; she says that the particular combination of colours and stitches that she employs is her own distinctive personal mark. Both times I left the village after a period of fieldwork (in 1988 and then 2014), she retrieved a string bag stored inside her house to give to me as a farewell gift. Although 27 years had passed between the two occasions, the bags she gave me were virtually identical (Figure 23).

Figure 23. Jessette presents a newly unfurled string bag

Source. Photographed by Elisabetta Gnecchi-Ruscone, 19 January 2014 and used with Jessette's permission[1]

Some looping styles 'belong' to specific clans. Women from the Jávosa clan, for example, make the base of the string bag using a stitch, called *kóke*, resembling the footprints of *kóke* bowerbirds (Farr et al. 2008: 313). Other types of stitch are peculiar to different parts of the bag: closer-knit loops (*sokifa*) are used to fashion the base; others are used to finish the bag, forming and strengthening its mouth (*bondìba* and *rùvi*, respectively); yet other stitches make up the strap (*tino*) by which it is carried.

---

1   Permission to publish the photographs used in this paper, as well as the names of the people in them, was given on 25 August 2015.

Before nylon string became available, string bags were made with fibres from the inner bark of the *siria* tree (Gnetum gnemon [Gnetaceae]).[2] The women would strip the bark off the plant, remove the outer layer and beat the softer fibres before leaving them in the sun to dry. They would then tear the fibres (*vìjari*) and use the palm of their open hands to make a three-ply string *kàina* by rolling the fibre up and down their calf (*avàri*). The string could be left undyed (*ésa*), be steeped in black dye produced by burning the resin from the *banìngu* tree, or dyed red by boiling it with the bark of a type of mangrove (*fofóra*). Today, women use a combination of bush and store-bought dyes.

Because of the considerable extra work involved, women only occasionally make string bags with *kàina*: usually to give to someone or for sale to tourists. Jessette had been asked by her classificatory brother to make him a personal string bag using bush string and the customary combination of white, black and red colours. This was a long-term project, involving many hours of work, which she fitted into her busy routine over a period of several weeks when she had the time to spare. Recognising this, her brother had harvested the fibres himself, saving her a trip into the bush.

Using string bags

Once she has completed a string bag, a woman turns it inside out and rolls it up for storing. *Áti jojegári* refers to the action of unfurling it and turning it back to the right side, when it is to be used for the first time. Knowing how to store and preserve a string bag, and the gesture involved in giving it to someone to use is as important as knowing how to make it.

String bags are essentially containers for carrying useful, valuable and precious things. Women always carry them hanging against their backs, suspended by the strap from their foreheads. When the load is particularly heavy, women use a padding of leaves or cloth to protect their shoulders. Similarly, a smaller padding may be placed between the strap and the woman's forehead to prevent it from biting into her skin. There are several types of string bags of varying sizes for carrying different kinds of things. The larger ones (*áti yabámara*) are specifically intended for carrying mats, pillows, blankets, clothes or other voluminous but not too heavy items needed by the woman and her family on trading trips to other villages.

---

2   For scientific names of natural species I refer to Farr et al. (2008).

Large amounts of tubers and other produce are carried in the coarser *gámo áti*. These string bags stretch to accommodate heavy loads, to the point that a woman might ask someone to help her haul it up into position. Once in place, she is able to walk long distances carrying produce to her village, the market or to the venue of a feast.

Mothers have a further string bag (*tatáu*), in which they carry their last-born baby. These string bags are beautifully manufactured using different coloured strings. The baby lies on a pillow within the womb-like netbag, it can be shaded from strong sunlight with a piece of cloth draped over the mouth of the bag. The *tatáu* allows the mother to work while cradling the child, or to hang it in a nearby shady spot. A fretful infant can be pacified by swinging the string bag backwards and forwards or by walking with a bouncing step (*boinboinghari*). Usually, however, a baby is placed inside the string bag once it has fallen asleep, and when it awakes it is peeled out of the *tatáu* to be changed or fed. Although fathers participate in many aspects of their children's rearing—they play, clean and even rock them to sleep by swinging a hanging *tatáu*—I have never seen a man carrying one on his back as a woman would.

Finally, every woman owns a smaller string bag, called *túmo áti*. This is a woman's personal string bag in which she carries tobacco, betel, money and her small knife. Men also use small personal string bags. Unlike women, they sling the strap over their shoulder. A man's string bag is called *jávo*, the same term used for 'personal name', and is closely linked to its owner's identity. A man's *jávo* contains his most personal and precious possessions, such as his personal cutlery, a mirror and comb, his tobacco, as well as betel, pepper and a lime pot. These items are associated with a man's powers and they are also vulnerable to sorcery attacks, therefore it is considered extremely bad mannered and dangerous to touch another man's string bag. A powerful man's *jávo* is also out of bounds to his wife and children, who will not touch it unless expressly instructed by the owner. At his death, a man's widow packs his *jávo* with all those items that he used to carry with him on a journey. This is buried with him to accompany him on his last journey (Gnecchi-Ruscone 2007).

Significantly, a man's *jávo* is made by a female relative—generally his mother, sister or wife. The owner's clan emblems that are part of the bag's stitching pattern are made by the women, but other emblems such as shells or feathers are applied subsequently by the *jávo* owner himself. MacKenzie (1991: 157–60) has argued that when Telefol women give their male relatives string bags that they have looped, and to which men apply feathers, the resulting feathered bilums are the product of multiple authorship (Strathern 1988) and a metonym of the relation between women and men, giver and receiver. Hermkens too, commenting on Maisin women's production of barkcloth painted with clan emblems, makes the point that while women are reenacting notions of gender and gender relations, they are also responsible for the creation, reproduction and transmission of an important kind of their patrilineal clans' emblems and, as such, clan identity (2013: 27, 86, 116, 139, 145–46).

Beyond their utilitarian function, then, string bags are also articles of personal adornment. In the everyday context, string bags are perhaps the most recognisably 'traditional' element of contemporary dress, regardless of the creative incorporation of new materials, colours and looping techniques. Indeed, this very flexibility permits wearers to express diverse aspects of their identity, such as gender, age, marital status, clan identity and aesthetic taste. Carrying a string bag made with bush material displaying the conventional red, white and black pattern is a statement of ethnic identity, and adherence to customary values. This choice is often made by senior men, who also add clan emblems to their *jávo*, communicating a further layer of identity. In contrast, younger men are more likely to adopt western-style bags, expressing adherence to modern or cosmopolitan values. Attachment to traditional values is also implied by women who make *áti* with bush string, whether they make them for themselves, to give to men or for the tourist market, where the traditional aesthetic is translated into monetary value.

Exchanging string bags

Women often make string bags to give in different types of transactions, which are invested with different meanings and significance: little girls were encouraged to make miniature *áti* to give me to take home to Italy, but sisters and cousins, grandmothers and granddaughters, and girlfriends all regularly made string bags to give each other informally; the recipient discussing the colours and patterns with the maker. The significance of these informal exchanges is that of consolidating the kind of habitual and expected reciprocity among friends and kin sharing close relations. Similarly, the gifts of *jávo* made by women for the men to whom they are related—their brothers, husbands and sons—are expressions of love and attachment, and establish or confirm long-term relationships. At the same time, though, the *jávo* given by a woman to a man is a reminder of the cross-clan relationships for which women are responsible and which, in their multiple roles as wives/mothers and daughters/sisters, they mediate. The maker of this string bag, from the point of view of the recipient, is in every case the representative of the 'other' clan to which she belongs.

There are several ceremonial occasions on which women make formal gifts of string bags. Since a woman is expected to participate in the gifts made by her husband's clan as well as that of her brothers', a farsighted woman will have a few spare string bags (as well as other items such as clay pots,[3] mats and barkcloths) to contribute to exchanges occurring at first-born child 'decoration' (*vujári*), marriage exchanges (Figure 24) and the ceremonies in which a widow is released from mourning obligations and decorated with new clothes and a new string bag (also called *vujári*, see Gnecchi-Ruscone 2007).

Figure 24. Women belonging to the groom's support group retrieving their string bags

Source. Photographed by Elisabetta Gnecchi-Ruscone, 15 January 2014

---

3   Clay pots are also made by women. They are now used mainly on festive occasions, exchanged at marriage and during *vujári*. They are not considered in this paper because they are not produced by Korafe women, but obtained by exchange with Ubir women from the Wanigela area (see Bonshek this volume).

While some string bags are gifts in their own right, others are filled with cloth or barkcloth and then given, acting as both vessel and gift. These are called *áti ghayáfa*, the same term being used for wealth exchange goods. On other ceremonial occasions, however, string bags are used merely as carriers. Once emptied, the *áti* are retrieved by their owners (Figure 24).

Other string bags are made and stored as future gifts. For example, mothers of adolescent boys set aside *áti* they will one day give to their sons' brides. These are important gifts as they convey several messages. A predominant association is that with adult womanhood and motherhood (see also MacKenzie 1991: 130). This gift, like other acts confirming the newcomer's welcome by the women with whom she will henceforth share most of her daily tasks, is expected. The act of giving is performed by the gesture of *áti jojegári*, in which the giver unfurls and opens up the string bag, ready for use. Both gift and gesture will be remembered, or reproachfully commented upon if not performed by the new wife.

So, string bags are versatile objects; they are made by women with different objectives and for diverse functions, which in some cases influence the choice of materials used. Nylon thread, being easily obtainable, durable, colourful and saving the woman many hours of work is preferred in most cases in the production of the utilitarian kind of string bags used to carry garden produce and to cradle infants. The importance of women's work in the production of garden food and the reproduction of children is reflected in the ceremonial giving of string bags in the context of life-cycle ceremonies, as well as the mother-in-law's gift to the new bride. A world of values is embodied in these objects throughout their technical, social and ritual lives. First of all, they represent women's patient work, as *tatáu* they affirm the values of maternity, as *jávo* they perform personal and clan identity, as *gámo áti* they embody the value of women as providers of abundance. When given, they express the value of the relations involved. Next, I will follow the life of another utilitarian item of women's wealth— the pandanus mat.

Making pandanus mats

Korafe women make two types of mats. *Gháito*, considered as the truly autochthonous mat, is made by sewing together a double layer of wide strips of *gháito* leaves from the *mónga* (Pandanus pistillaris) plant, which is a bush variety with wide leaves. *Savásava* mats are made by weaving together narrower strips of leaves of the *jégha* (Pandanus tectorius, Pandanus Sanderi) or *saságha* (Pandanus englerianus, Pandanus kruaelianus) varieties. The *savásava* mat is as common as the *gháito* in Korafe households, but it is regarded as a cultural import from Milne Bay. This resonates with the use of two similar types of mats among the Nalik of New Ireland: traditional stitched mats that are attributed with protective properties and used in ritual; and the more common plaited mats, which are used for sitting and sleeping, and believed to have been introduced by Polynesian missionaries (Were 2013: 594).

Mats are made by most adult women, but it is not an activity in which women engage every day. A mat may be made in a few days of concentrated work, particularly in the dry season. While women tend to stockpile string bags for future exchanges, mats are made as required. A woman wishing to make a mat begins by going to search for pandanus plants, which usually grow spontaneously in the bush. Tall plants may be cut down in order to harvest the leaves; however, it is preferable to take the leaves from shorter plants, taking care not to damage the growth tip, so that in time new leaves may be harvested.

Pandanus leaves are tough and lined along the edges and midrib by stiff and sharp thorns; women usually remove the thorns before tying the leaves into bundles and carrying them home. Finding, harvesting and carrying the leaves home is considered to be the most physically demanding part of the task of making mats. Women may enlist helpers from among their immediate family. Once a woman has gathered sufficient leaves, she begins treating them; turning the fresh, bright green, tough leaves with their longitudinal ribbing into flat, soft, smooth, pliable strips of material to be woven or sewn together. The work of transformation involves the whole woman's body adopting postures and making gestures that are mutually constitutive: defining the female body while giving shape and form to the object (cf. Hermkens 2013: 74 ff. on similar processes involved in Maisin women's production of barkcloth).

Independently of the type of mat, the same processes are required to prepare the leaves. Each leaf has to be laid out in the sun for a couple of hours to soften, then brought back into the shade of the verandah. Here the woman places two leaves at a time on top of each other, with the leaves' central fold upwards, she presses down with the heel of her hand along the length of the softened leaves to flatten them, obtaining two smooth strips. These she rolls tightly, if necessary she sits on them using her weight to flatten them further. Then she vigorously scrapes each leaf with the sandpaper-like *bíkororo* (ficus wassa) leaves to render its surface smooth and pleasing to the touch and facilitate the drying process (Figure 25).

If the woman wishes to make a plaited mat, the leaves are sliced into narrow strips. Women making *gháito* can decide to scratch patterns onto about half their strips, although frequently they are left undecorated. The design can be anything that pleases the woman, usually a simple geometric motif repeated along the length of each strip of pandanus, but different on each strip. Typically, the *gháito* will then be made of alternating plain and decorated strips. Next, the woman loosely rolls the leaves individually and places them in the sun to dry further, making the patterns stand out. When the leaves begin to dry, women unroll them and roll them up in the opposite direction, so that the strips lie flat without curling. Finally, the woman can sit down to sew or plait her mat. Some women embellish their *savásava* by dyeing some strips blue or purple by boiling them in a pot of water to which is added store-purchased dye (Figure 26).

Figure 25. Ethel flattening and scraping the pandanus leaf with a *bikororo* leaf

Source. Photographed by Elisabetta Gnecchi-Ruscone, 17 January 2014, and used with Ethel's permission

Figure 26. Elma making a *savasava*

Source. Photographed by Elisabetta Gnecchi-Ruscone, 16 January 2014, and used with Elma's permission

Although younger women told me that they favoured making *savásava* because plaiting was easier than stitching, *gháito* makers said that sewing was the easier part of the work. Given this different evaluation, I asked the women which part of the work they preferred. They explained that since they needed mats, they knew that they had to go to the bush to get pandanus leaves, remove thorns, scrape and dry the leaves in the sun and then sew or plait the mat: all parts of the work were necessary and they had no preference. Their work was not considered in terms of pleasure, but as the outcome of their intentions, an expression of agency. As Richard Eves in his article on dance objects argues, 'agency should be seen in terms of practice, as centrally concerned with the realisation of projects through bodily action and movement which connect people in their intersubjective world' (2009: 251). Women undertake the work of making mats with specific intentions in mind, whether it is to use it in their own home, give it to a friend, contribute it to a formal exchange or use it in ceremony. This motivates their work in all the stages of production.

In order to sew the pandanus strips to make a *gháito,* a woman must procure *songa* bark and transform it by cutting, stripping, peeling and rinsing it to obtain a hardwearing strand of binding material, the same as that used to tie together the flooring slats of local houses. She starts with four strips of pandanus leaf placed on top of each other: two strips are laid back to back so that the *gómo* (belly) sides of the leaves face outwards, these are sandwiched between two more strips, with their *gúka* (back) side outwards. She sews the layers together along one length, then folds back the two outer strips concealing the stitches inside the fold. She thus obtains two double-layered strips of pandanus with the belly side visible on both sides. She then takes two further leaves, uses them to sandwich the second strip, back side outwards, and tacks these together along the outer edge before folding back the outer strips, concealing the stitches and revealing the belly of the leaf. The process is repeated until the desired length (to accommodate a sleeping person) is obtained. The woman periodically smooths down the pandanus with her hands, applying the whole weight of her arms and upper body to the task (Figure 27). After paring down any longer strips to make straight edges, she folds the *gháito* in two longitudinally, pressing down strongly to make a permanent crease.

Figure 27. Jessette folds the mat

Source. Photographed by Elisabetta Gnecchi-Ruscone, 25 January 2014, and used with Jessette's permission

The last stage in manufacturing a stitched mat involves sewing three longitudinal rows of stitches; the only visible stitching on a *ghàito*, these are regarded as essential for its structural durability. First, a woman sews the two rows of stitches bordering the long sides of the mat (no sewing is required along the short sides). A couple of strands of *songa* fibre, the same length as the mat, are knotted together making small tassels at both ends. The strands are secured, about one centimetre in from the mat's edge, with small, tight-knit stitches crossing over them. The stitches (*diti*, lit. 'eyes') are visible on both sides of the mat, but the strands of *songa* are applied on one side only, visible when the mat is folded but on the underside when it is laid out. Finally, the woman stitches along the longitudinal crease created by folding the mat in half (Figure 28). This time she carefully sews only through the top layer, as these stitches (*gonia*, lit. 'buttocks') are to be visible only on the side of the mat on which people sit, and remain inside when the mat is folded.

Figure 28. Side-stitching the mat

Source. Photographed by Elisabetta Gnecchi-Ruscone, 21 January 2014

There is a very physical quality in the rapport between maker, materials and the mat in the making: on the one hand, there is a deep knowledge of the properties of the materials that 'grows out of a lifetime of intimate gestural and sensory engagement' with their craft; on the other, the 'intelligent gesture, at once technically effective and perceptually attentive' (Ingold 2013: 42, 132). The knowledge and skills needed to make mats are not acquired through formal instruction but through observing and copying older women. The actions involved are just some of the many tasks that fill a woman's daily life. She fits them into her daily routine, and may enlist the help of any willing girl—in the process, she creates the conditions for girls to experience the actions involved and passes on technical knowledge. Girls accompany their mothers into the bush, observe them harvesting leaves and help out in the casual manner arising from sharing daily life in the village. They may be asked to go and pick some leaves for scraping the pandanus, or to roll the strips and help by shifting them from sun to shade. Equally, they might choose to join in the fun when their grandmother is scratching patterns on the leaves, or their aunt is steeping narrow strips of pandanus in a pot filled with purple dye. Thus, informally, girls acquire skills that are considered part of every adult women's repertoire (Young Leslie 2007: 13) (Figure 29).

Figure 29. Jessette and granddaughters scratching patterns into pandanus leaves

Source. Photographed by Elisabetta Gnecchi-Ruscone, 19 January 2014

In short, it is through a woman's actions, through postures and gestures that are typical of women only, that bush material is transformed into household objects, used daily by her family for sleeping, eating and socialising. The intimate, physical actions of the woman's body upon bush pandanus leaves produce an artefact that may be described as creating domesticity. As expressed by two women from Goodenough village: 'Mats are important because they are part of life in a house, everyone in the family needs a mat to sleep on' (Elma, 18 January 2014); and 'If you have a house, you must have mats for your family to sleep on, and for guests to sit on' (Lila, 15 January 2014).

Using mats

Women thus domesticate bush pandanus leaves to make artefacts that create delimited spaces separate from the surrounding clutter of everyday activities, defining safe spaces where family members sleep and eat. Graeme Were comments on the protective properties attributed to pandanus mats, referring to the well-documented protective function of woven wrappings in Oceania in general (2013: 590–91). By observing the ways in which Korafe women use their mats, I wish to show that the protective function of *ghàito* is not limited to the rare circumstances in which they are used as covering.

Clever women, as well as knowing how to make mats, also know how to use and care for them to ensure they last a long time. While older mats are left lying on the veranda, new ones are preserved from soiling and wear by storing them in the beams of the roof when not in use. A *savàsava* mat is rolled up, while a *ghàito* is folded according to a specific sequence similar to folding a map (*gaghàri*). Women accompany the actions of unfurling and laying (*javuregàri* and *duràri*) a mat on the ground with a smoothing gesture of their open hands, to flatten it and brush away particles of dirt. A gesture with which we are familiar from having observed the women making the mat: one instance of the flowing of things between production and use (Ingold 2013), but also of the way in which the gestures that make a thing also define its maker (Hermkens 2013).

At the most mundane level, mats are used for sitting, eating and sleeping on. Mothers labour on mats, and babies are born on them. Married couples share the same mat, and the association between mats and conjugal life is remembered in mourning songs and laments (Gnecchi-Ruscone 2007). While Jessette was showing me how to fold a *ghàito*, she was telling me that different sizes may be made: smaller for children, larger for married couples, and so on. Her husband, who was listening from the rear verandah reminded her that in pre-Christian days a polygamous man and his two wives would share a wider mat, the husband sleeping in between the two women. Jessette then explained that in this case the mat would have four rows of vertical stitching, delimiting each sleeper's space on the mat, which was accordingly folded vertically in three parts, instead of two. She added that each woman would cook for her husband, and that he would make sure to eat from each of his wives' pots, if he did not want to hurt the women's feelings and cause arguments. The connection between mats, sleeping, eating and reciprocal conjugal duties is manifest.

In all cases, the mat defines a space separate from its surroundings where people may safely perform acts that potentially make them vulnerable: eating, sleeping and giving birth. This safe space is transportable, and mats may also be carried when travelling, to create a domestic space for the family away from home. They may also be used to build makeshift shelters on canoe platforms or on the ground.

When a visitor climbs the steps to the verandah, a great show is made of seeking out the best mat, unfolding and laying it down. These are the first gestures of hospitality and define the space reserved for guests, separate from other occupants, where they may feel comfortable and able to relax, eat and rest. At the same time, the mat limits the guest's movements; he or she will remain in the designated space without venturing inside the house. In households whose status implies that they often entertain visitors, the 'best' mat is kept in the rafters of the sitting platform ready to use. It is said that if a sorcerer should visit, the mat he sat on would be given to him to take away, as it would be too dangerous for others to use it after him. These attentions reserved for welcome guests respond to the vulnerability felt by Korafe when away from home, their fear of sorcery or contamination: a clean, freshly laid out mat provides a safe space within a potentially dangerous environment.

Gháito also figure in several ceremonial occasions, where they define a space separate from its surroundings. In the final stages of the initiation ceremony held for the eldest son or daughter of a couple, the initiand, after being decorated with the clan insignia by his or her maternal uncles, sits on a mat in the village clearing where the conclusive exchange of gifts between the parents and maternal uncles occurs. Similarly, the widow who is decorated by her deceased husband's sisters to mark the end of mourning sits on a mat while the all-night singing of *ghaséga* takes place (Gnecchi-Ruscone 2007). When a groom fetches his bride to take her to his village, the couple is made to sit on a mat in the centre of the village while they are addressed by the bride's brothers regarding the marriage agreement and the gifts to follow, and by the bride's mother and other senior women about the behaviour she should adopt in her new village.

On all these occasions, those sitting on the mat are in a state of transition. The *gháito* defines a safe space on which the transformation of the person through speech, actions and transactions occurs. In the central village clearing the most intimate of domestic objects—on which couples sleep, babies are born, family and friends partake of their meals—becomes a space where persons may safely be subjected to transformation.

Gháito are also used in burial. The body is wrapped in a sheet and placed at the bottom of a pit in the ground, a layer of sticks is laid perpendicularly over the body and covered with a new mat, protecting the body from the soil used to fill the grave. Another new *gháito* is placed over the mound of earth, and a small shelter is built above it. In another way, the mat seems to be defining and delimiting the space for the dead person's body, isolating it from dirt, even underground.

The material qualities of mats—their proportions, shape, texture, softness, visible and invisible stitching—perceptibly delimit a space apart from surrounding clutter and dirt. By the simple performative gestures of unfolding and laying a mat on the ground, women create the most intimate spaces of domestic family life, secure spaces for welcome guests to relax in, and provide safe spaces for protagonists of life-cycle ceremonies to publicly undergo social transformations. Mats also enter into formal and informal exchanges, creating and sustaining relations well beyond the domestic sphere.

Exchanging mats

A woman may produce mats to give informally to friends and relatives as part of the ongoing exchange relationships. She may decide to make a mat for a father, son or brother, especially if they are unmarried. Such gifts are sometimes solicited. Reciprocation is not immediate or equivalent, it is one of the ingredients of a continuous kinship or friendly relationship. Women also trade mats for clay pots with Ubir women from Wanigela, or sell them at the market, although this represents a slim and discontinuous source of earnings—the mats earn between 5 and 10 kina each.

Women's intentions are central to the production of such mats, which 'should be seen as embodiments of intentionality and agency made visible in the intersubjective social field' (Eves 2009: 251). For example, during January 2014, Elma was busy preparing three *savásava* mats to give to her teenage son when he embarked on the dinghy that would take him to Popondetta for the beginning of the school year. Elma made them to thank the family that took care of her son while he was boarding at school, and to reaffirm their mutual friendship.

Being the wet season, the process involved constant surveillance of the drying rolls. Elma enlisted the help of her husband for collecting the leaves, of her younger children for rolling and moving the strips of pandanus in and out of the sun, and of her older daughters and sister-in-law for dyeing and plaiting the mats. She thus mobilised her whole family, drawing on their work to produce mats that would reaffirm relations in a wider social field. Interestingly, Graeme Were observed among the Nalik a similar use of woven, as opposed to stitched, mats in an informal gift economy extending beyond New Ireland, which 'serve[d] to strengthen and consolidate social relations through the individualized productivity of female mat-makers' (2013: 595). He showed that the social and material properties of the pandanus used in woven mats allowed these to map 'an image of a wider network of individualized relations that require[d] renewal less often', while stitched mats map 'an image of localized, traditional social networks, sustained over a shorter, intense duration through its production and usage at life-cycle events' (2013: 596).[4]

Of a different order are the exchanges that occur for ceremonial occasions, such as marriage and initiation. Women produce a surplus of mats in anticipation of such events, as great numbers are required. Each woman will make at least 10 mats for such exchanges, and they compete among each other to demonstrate greater generosity. Great piles of gifts are built up by the women on each side of the exchange. Among these piles are mats, but also other women's artefacts like string bags, clay pots and tapa cloths. All these artefacts can be defined as valuables because they incorporate the work of women, and in virtue of their inclusion in such ceremonial gift exchanges.

Unlike the personal informal gifts described above, each woman's gifts enter into the cumulative gift made by one clan to another. Women may contribute to the gifts made by their husband's or brothers' group. From the performative point of view, there is a difference: a woman will publicly present her contribution to the gift made by her husband's clan by adding them to the pile of his clan. If she chooses to act as supporter to her brothers' clan, she will instead deliver them to its members, who will make the public gesture of adding them to their pile. Therefore, although acting as helpers to their brothers' clan is within the range of possibilities open to women, and is a frequently made choice, only their contribution to their husbands' clan appears to be prescribed.[5] The gifts will be shared among the group of recipients and their supporters. A woman who gives generously can expect social recognition and a greater share of the return gifts.

---

4   Korafe say that both kinds of pandanus mats may be given as formal and informal gifts; however, a difference does seem to be relevant in ritual situations, in which *gháito* are preferred over plaited mats.
5   This distinction does not occur when the brothers' and husband's clans are the direct protagonists of the exchange: once bride price has been paid, a woman helps her husband to make gifts to give to her brothers. Women's agency in this regard applies when more distant relations are the main players in the exchange, and a woman may choose to side with her brothers.

Figure 30. Pig laid on mat and covered with tapa
Source. Photographed by Elisabetta Gnecchi-Ruscone, 1988

Some of the most important exchanges are those following the satisfactory payment of bride price by the husband to his wife's brothers. The woman has effectively been separated from her brothers and cooperates with her husband in making gifts to give to her brothers for the sake of establishing and acknowledging the ties between them and her children. This series of exchanges used to culminate in the *vujári* ceremony in which the maternal uncles put their mark on their sister's eldest child by decorating him or her with their clan emblems, at the same time sanctioning his/her right to decoration, and consolidating their lifelong allegiance to their uncles' clan.[6] One such exchange involved the gift of a pig, raised by the initiate's mother and father, to the mother's brothers, who will reciprocate by giving the child an heirloom such as his or her maternal grandfather's pigs' tusks. The trussed pig is laid on a pandanus mat and covered with a piece of tapa (Figure 30). After the pig has been slaughtered and butchered for distribution among the uncles' clan, the grandmother washes any blood that may have spilt on the mats and tapa and uses them herself.

---

6   This ceremony, like many others, is harder to organise, and most people opt for a muted version of *vujári*, or birthday party, in which the maternal uncles give the initiate new clothes and a mirror; string bags are still exchanged in these occasions.

Both these items are associated with women. They are produced by the initiate's mother and given to the grandmother for having borne the weight of the baby's mother. At a subsequent stage, once the child has been decorated by his mother's brothers with their clan emblems, the child is accompanied out of the house. He or she steps over the maternal grandmother's back before walking on a row of mats to reach the *gháito* prepared at the centre of the village clearing, where the final and exuberant exchange of gifts between the maternal and paternal clans takes place. The initiate's mother gives mats and other gifts to her brothers and their helpers, and she receives gifts in return from the mother's brothers' wives and from her mother's sisters. The initiate's maternal grandmother is given string bags and taro; this time for bearing the initiate's own weight. While string bags, like the mat, are produced by women, the taro and pig are the product of the joint work of the child's mother and father.

Mats are also part of the exchanges occurring at marriage. When a wife goes to live in her husband's village, women from her own village, her mothers and sisters, will give her several mats to take with her to use in her married life. In turn, these women will receive part of the gift made some time later by the bridegroom to the bride's brothers. Although the groom's return gift is referred to as a gift for the bride's brothers, in fact part of it is shared out to the women of the bride's group of origin, in recognition of their contribution of items made by them. There is a distinction perhaps to be made between the performative moment of the gift giving—when a pile of goods is placed in the centre of the village (a gift from one group to another)—and the redistribution within the group—when individual women, who had given a mat to the bride to take with her, will claim and be given a share of this collective gift.

Conclusions

Both string bags and mats are first of all ordinary objects, used and valued by women in the course of everyday work. But they enter into social contexts when women choose to give them informally to friends and family, or more ceremonially as part of their brothers' or husband's clan gifts to another clan, thus forging or reinforcing social ties. They are also involved in ritual life, in different ways contributing to the work of transforming and publicly acknowledging the changed status of the protagonists of the ritual. Different domains of life are connected by the shared material qualities of these two objects that 'play a determinant role in the non-verbal expression of the principles and values that underlie social relations' (Lemmonier 2013: 136, my translation).

Considering the various life histories of these mundane objects, different kinds of observations can be made. From the point of view of everyday life, string bags and pandanus mats have been with Korafe for a long time. Their value at a prosaic level is the use they are made of by their makers' family members. My interest in these two items lies in the fact that they are used daily by all women and men throughout their lives, they are not just taken out of storage for ceremonial occasions. This does not imply a greater adherence to 'traditional' appearance or aesthetics. Indeed, there is a difference between the two objects in this respect: mats are more 'traditional' in appearance than string bags in which foreign materials designs and techniques are incorporated to a greater extent. However, this difference does not detract from notions of authenticity.

I have selected these two items because of their ordinariness; they are part of every Korafe woman's accoutrement of goods. The skills involved in their manufacture are within the normal repertoire pertaining to adult women. In their very ordinariness lies their relevance for the identity of the women who make, use and give them. It is nonetheless interesting that these same artefacts figure in ceremonial occasions as ritual devices, and also as items of exchange. The values expressed in each context varies; however, the question remains as to the appropriateness of defining them as women's wealth.

In summary, the material value of string bags and mats is embedded in everyday village life, as expressed by their omnipresence. Further, from their involvement in exchanges one may derive a tangible value that is inevitably linked to the immaterial, social significance inherent in the relationships negotiated by the transactions. Both string bags and mats are therefore good examples of artefacts that stimulate us 'to *think together* about domains that are usually *analysed apart*' (Coupaye 2013: 251, italics in original). The cultural values expressed by the material nature of these objects are inextricably linked to the women's world at different levels. In the case of mats, the first is the process of transformation of bush material into an artefact that defines domestic space. The second is the movement of the same artefact from the domestic realm into that of social and economic relations, through its introduction into the exchange system. The third is the use of, again the same artefact, to create a safe ritual space for the protagonists of ceremony. In all these contexts, these things may be seen to act on people (see also Gell 1998): on the women who make and use them by determining activities, postures and gestures that are typically and exclusively feminine; on those who receive them as gifts and thus become enmeshed in relations of reciprocity; but also on those who use them to restrict their freedom of movement, which, at the same time, allays their fears in situations of vulnerability.

Though these two items may act on people, it is only through the will, knowledge and actions of women who make and use them that they do so. In response to Lissant Bolton's (2001: 266) suggestion that the agency of things should be analysed in terms of the relationships in which they operate, Eves' argues that 'what things do is often not so inseparable from what things are or what is done to or with them' (2009: 260). Further, according to Coupaye, the properties of an object originate from the materials and actions constituting its productive process considered within its social context, the maker's status and the social value attached to her work, and 'simultaneously her/his network of reasons and intentionalities permeates, surrounds and informs the actual artefact s/he produced' (2013: 92).

It is therefore clear that string bags and mats are strongly associated with women's gender identity. They embody the values of women's work and express their intentionality and agency. The value attributed to these two ordinary artefacts is conveyed by two Korafe idiomatic terms for 'wealth': *guguá,* which literally translates as 'roll of pandanus mats' referring to possessions assembled to take on a trading voyage; and *áti ghayáfa*, or those string bags filled with other valuables and given in exchange feasts—the same term is now used to refer to a commercial bank, where one's wealth in money is deposited (Farr et al. 2008: 731). Obviously they are valuable items, part of the family's possessions, avowedly produced and managed by women both in daily life and in exchanges. Nonetheless, I am reluctant to draw the conclusion that this makes them women's wealth. Though women may gain in reputation for the quality or quantity of items given, and demonstrate considerable agency and autonomy in making and giving mats and string bags, this is not translatable into a separate realm in which women compete among themselves for power and prestige through gift exchange.

Bolton (2003: 123–24) shows that textiles embody women's commitment to the social relationships in which they are enmeshed, an investment in relationships that does not start and end with the exchange, but is born in the making of the objects. Similar observations were made by MacKenzie concerning string bags (1991: 142, 150–52). It is at this point, I contend, that women's relative autonomy and intentionality become relevant to our understanding of the significance of material objects in both informal and formal exchanges. When women give string bags or mats informally, they do so to affirm and strengthen personal ties, calling attention to their feelings and sentiment of caring for the recipient, be it a husband, son, brother, father or a sister.

When they give mats or string bags in ceremonial exchanges, women, it is true, do so as a contribution to a patrilineal clan's overall gift. By materially supporting the efforts of the clan, women actively and publicly affirm their affiliation to that patrilineal clan as sisters *or* wives, although not in all cases is this an either/or choice. Women can, independently of their husbands, decide to contribute to their brothers' clan gifts to a third clan. The different relationship of sisters and wives to the patrilineal clan is reflected by the more public and performative style of the wives' gifts, while sisters express caring for their clan of origin by bringing mats or string bags that their brothers' wives add to their piles of gifts. However, the point remains that women intentionally choose to contribute the things they have made to either patrilineal clan, that of their brothers and/or that of their husband. And that intentionality is fielded, as Bolton suggested, at the moment when they begin to collect the raw material for making the mats or string bags.

Annette Weiner's suggestion (1976: 126, 199) that we should consider brother–sister relations and sibling intimacy as critical and Maurice Godelier's (1999: 33–34) observation of the status of women in patrilineal clans relative to their husbands and brothers are both relevant when exploring questions of women's valuables and their roles in exchange.[7] In all cases, women see their contribution to clan exchanges as part of their work of caring for their kin and clan, this being one of the core values in the gendered identity of Korafe women. At the same time, the

---

7   Though this argument goes beyond the scope of this paper, it is my hunch that the different articulations of brother–sister relations in matrilineal and patrilineal societies may explain why women's wealth of the kind described in the Tobriands cannot be so easily found in patrilineal societies like that of the Korafe.

individual maker's contribution is recognised in the distribution of return gifts, and her work is not totally subsumed within the patrilineal clan, to whose prestige women choose to contribute with more or less work on each single occasion.

Acknowledgements

I wish to thank John Barker, Adine Gavazzi, Anna-Karina Hermkens, Kathy Lepani and Anna Paini for commenting on earlier versions of this text.

References

Appadurai, Arjun (ed.). 1986. *The Social Life of Things: Commodities in Cultural Perspective*. Cambridge: Cambridge University Press.

Barker, John. 2008. *Ancestral Lines: The Maisin of Papua New Guinea and the Fate of the Rainforest*. Toronto: University of Toronto Press.

Bolton, Lissant. 2001. 'Classifying the Material: Food Textiles and Status in North Vanuatu'. *Journal of Material Culture* 6(3): 251–268. DOI: 10.1177/135918350100600301.

——. 2003. *Unfolding the Moon: Enacting Women's* Kastom *in Vanuatu*. Honolulu: University of Hawai'i Press.

Coupaye, Ludovic. 2013. *Growing Artefacts, Displaying Relationships: Yams, Art and Artefacts amongst the Nyamicum Abelam of Papua New Guinea*. New York and Oxford: Berghahn Books.

Eves, Richard. 2009. 'Material Culture and the Magical Power of Dance Objects'. *Oceania* 79(3): 250–262. DOI: 10.1002/j.1834-4461.2009. tb00063.x.

Farr, James and Cynthia Farr, with Korafe and Yegha speakers. 2008. *Korafe-Yegha da Dikiseneri / The Korafe-Yegha Dictionary*. Online: www-01.sil.org/pacific/png/pubs/928474533810/Korafe_Dictionary_ Updated%20version.pdf (accessed 24 April 2017).

Gell, Alfred. 1998. *Art and Agency: An Anthropological Theory*. Oxford: Clarendon Press.

Gnecchi-Ruscone, Elisabetta. 1992. 'Power or Paradise? Korafe Christianity and Korafe Magic'. PhD thesis. Canberra: The Australian National University.

———. 2007. 'Parallel Journeys in Korafe Women's Laments (Oro Province, Papua New Guinea)'. *Journal de la Société des Océanistes* 124: 21–32.

Gnecchi-Ruscone, Elisabetta and Jan Hasselberg. 2012. 'Ad-dressing and De-vesting the Bodies: Changing Practices in Body Adornment, Coastal Oro Province, Papua New Guinea'. Paper presented at the 9th European Society for Oceanists Conference, Bergen.

Godelier, Maurice. 1999 [1996]. *The Enigma of the Gift.* Chicago: University of Chicago Press. Trans. from French by Nora Scott. 1996. *L'Enigme du don.* Paris: Libraire Arthéme Fayard.

Hermkens, Anna-Karina. 2013. *Engendering Objects: Dynamics of Barkcloth and Gender among the Maisin of Papua New Guinea.* Leiden: Sidestone Press.

Ingold, Tim. 2013. *Making: Anthropology, Archaeology, Art and Architecture.* Oxon and New York: Routledge.

Lemmonier, Pierre. 2012. *Mundane Objects. Materiality and Non-verbal Communication.* Walnut Creek, CA: Left Coast Press.

———. 2013. 'De l'immatériel dans le matériel… et réciproquement! Techniques et communication non verbale'. *Le Journal de la Société des Océanistes* 136–137: 15–26.

MacKenzie, Maureen. 1991. *Androgynous Objects: String Bags and Gender in Central New Guinea.* Chur and Melbourne: Harwood Academic Press.

Strathern, Marilyn. 1988. *The Gender of the Gift: Problems with Women and Problems with Society in Melanesia.* Berkeley: University of California Press.

Weiner, Annette. 1976. *Women of Value, Men of Renown: New Perspectives in Trobriand Exchange.* Austin, TX: University of Texas Press.

———. 1992. *Inalienable Possessions: The Paradox of Keeping-While-Giving.* Berkeley: University of California Press.

Were, Graeme. 2013. 'On the Materials of Mats: Thinking through Design in a Melanesian Society'. *Journal of the Royal Anthropological Institute* 19(3): 581–599. DOI: 10.1111/1467-9655.12051.

Young Leslie, Heather E. 2007. '…Like a Mat Being Woven'. In *Hybrid Textiles: Pragmatic Creativity and Authentic Innovations in Pacific Cloth*, ed. Heather Young Leslie, Ping-Ann Addo and Phyllis Herda. Special issue of *Journal of Pacific Arts* 3(5): 115–127.

Young Leslie, Heather, Ping-Ann Addo and Phyllis Herda (eds). 2007. *Hybrid Textiles: Pragmatic Creativity and Authentic Innovations in Pacific Cloth*. Special issue of *Journal of Pacific Arts* 3(5).

.

Poem: Making the Mark

Tessa Miller

Introduction

The following poem was written at a cultural art festival where I was to present a paper on tapa making. While at the festival, however, I felt that presenting a paper would be an act of redundancy. In comparison to the tapa making from many Pacific Island countries that was happening live, under tents just outside the building, the 'experts' presentations of papers and powerpoints on the subject felt unnecessary. The tapa makers from Fiji were Koto and Vetacini Matemosi, daughters of the late Makereta Matemosi. Makereta, the designer of the Fiji Airways logo, was at the centre of the tapa motif copyright application controversy brought by the airline. In providing Fiji Airways with the logo and 15 accompanying motifs, Makereta had drawn on the traditional designs of her husband's province. The divide between artist and corporation meant she had, unknowingly, handed over motifs to an airline looking to copyright cultural knowledge that, in truth, belong to the people.

Instead of presenting a paper on the technicalities of tapa making, her story inspired me to write this poem.

Part 1

Ode to Makereta Masi mark maker

An angel with a golden heart
Set down her guard to embark
Upon a quest to hail the mark
Of land and sea, bird and shark

And from the earth she gathered dust
By the father she laid her trust
To do great deeds her duties must
And of no glory did she lust

Drawing from far and wide
Sailing in on the ocean's tide
No identity was denied
As the strokes combined, side by side

A mighty flag to take hold
Of people united standing bold
To show the world, us treasures untold
Then suddenly, a knife sliced through her!

And a different story began to unfold …

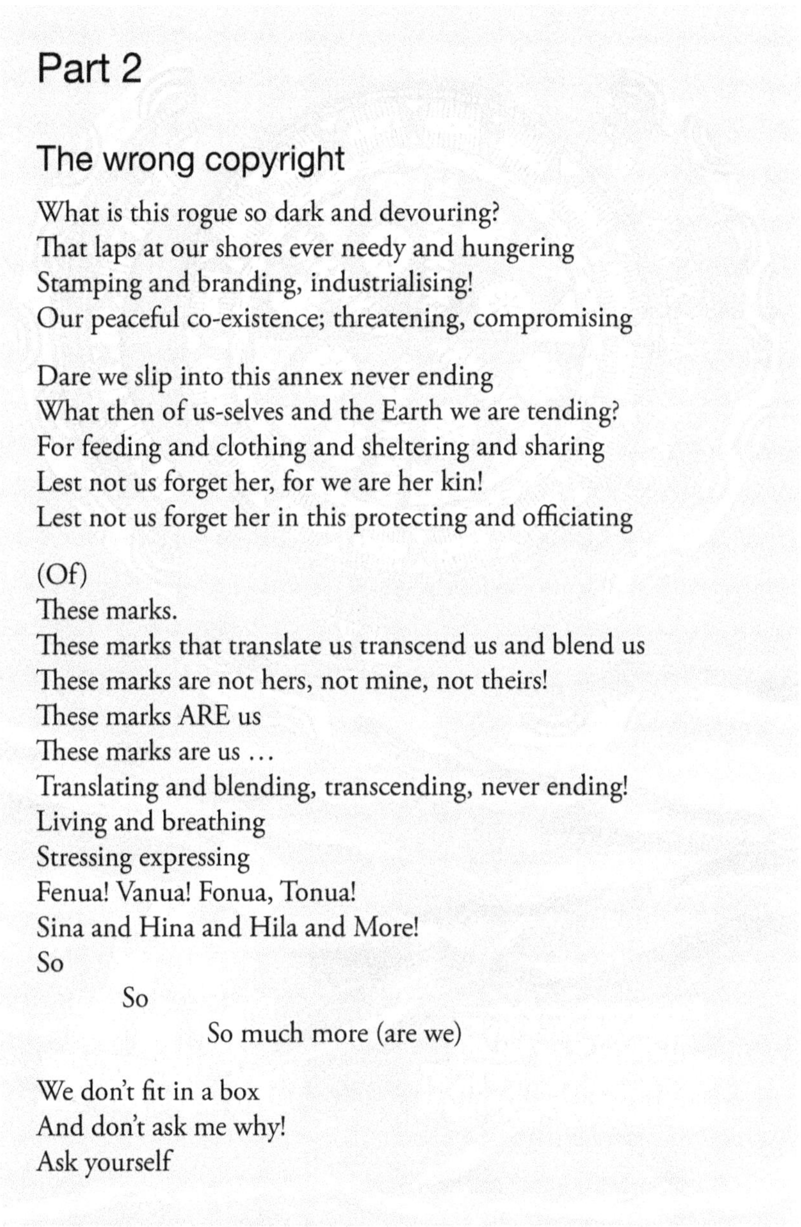

Part 2

The wrong copyright

What is this rogue so dark and devouring?
That laps at our shores ever needy and hungering
Stamping and branding, industrialising!
Our peaceful co-existence; threatening, compromising

Dare we slip into this annex never ending
What then of us-selves and the Earth we are tending?
For feeding and clothing and sheltering and sharing
Lest not us forget her, for we are her kin!
Lest not us forget her in this protecting and officiating

(Of)
These marks.
These marks that translate us transcend us and blend us
These marks are not hers, not mine, not theirs!
These marks ARE us
These marks are us …
Translating and blending, transcending, never ending!
Living and breathing
Stressing expressing
Fenua! Vanua! Fonua, Tonua!
Sina and Hina and Hila and More!
So
        So
                So much more (are we)

We don't fit in a box
And don't ask me why!
Ask yourself

Figure 31. Tessa Miller, *The Wrong Copyright*, earth pigments on barkcloth and laminated paper, 2015

6

Capturing the 'Female Essence'? Textile Wealth in Tonga[1]

Fanny Wonu Veys

Enveloped by *koloa*

On Tuesday 3 June 2003, at the beginning of the cooler season, Sela took me to a large house named *Sia ko Veiongo* in Kolomotu'a, the old part of the Kingdom of Tonga's capital, Nuku'alofa. Sela, who had always been involved with making and overseeing the production of *koloa*, including mats, barkcloth and coconut oil, was contributing textiles to the wedding bed (*mohenga mali*)[2] being prepared for 'Eiki Salote Lupepau'u Salamasina Purea Vahine Arii 'o e Hau Tuita and Matai'ulua-'i-Fonuamotu Fusitu'a.[3] The oldest daughter of Princess Pilolevu was to marry the son of a noble man, the Honorable Fusitu'a, whose estate is in Niuafo'ou.[4] As the composition of the wedding bed is the responsibility of the groom's mother, 'Eseta Fusitu'a accordingly had older female family members directing young men who were carrying heavy bales of mats and barkcloth

---

1   This chapter is published in a slightly altered form as Chapter 6 in my book *Unwrapping Tongan Barkcloth: Encounters, Creativity and Female Agency* (2017).

2   The couple is supposed to spend the first night of their married life on this wedding bed made up of textile wealth. Today, however, married couples often spend the wedding night on a European bed.

3   On 8 May 2008, Nuku'alofa Supreme Court granted Hon. Lupepau'u Tuita and Matai'ulua Fusitu'a a divorce (14 May 2008).

4   On 7 May 2014, a few days after the death of his father, the title of Fusitu'a was bestowed upon Matai'ulua-'i-Fonuamotu Fusitu'a, making him the estate holder of the villages of Faletanu, Ma'ofanga, parts of Angaha'a in Niuatoputapu and Sapa'ata in Niuafo'ou (Lavulo 2014).

in and out of the house, laying them down wherever they were asked to do so. The main and largest room of the house had several women sitting around a pile of mats that had been unfolded, and that covered almost the entire surface of the floor. The wedding bed was to consist of 40 mats (*fala*) and as many layers of *ngatu*. One woman functioned as a secretary, writing down the order of the mats that were used, a task complicated by the numerous times mats were pulled out while others were put on top of the pile. The actions of some of the younger women, helped by the young men, were prompted by the phrase '*Ko e hā falá?*' (Which mat?), which led to discussions among some of the older women. When the women had reached mat 23, they started pulling out more mats to keep them apart and make them ready to present to the bride's side. The 40th and last mat of the pile was carefully oiled with *lolo niu* (scented coconut oil). Once the female relatives of the groom Mataiʻulua (including his mother, ʻEseta Fusituʻa) had finished preparing the mats, they joined a small group of women who had started folding the *ngatu lau tefuhi*—a 100 *langanga* (section of about 40 cm) long barkcloth. Here again, young men carried the large barkcloths and spread them out under the vigilant eye of the women present. The barkcloths were folded to the same width as the mats by tucking in the borders (Figure 32) or by cutting small strips of excess *ngatu*. It was on this same neat pile of barkcloth and mats—the sequence of which visually and materially translated the ideas about the rank that elder, knowledgeable women hold—that the wedding couple seated themselves a week later on Wednesday 11 June 2003, to undergo the traditional royal wedding ceremony (*tuʻuvala*).[5] Sitting on this large pile of barkcloth, the couple not only elevated their status but also became the centre of everyone's attention—a process known as *fakalāngilangi* (bringing splendour) (Figure 33). Moreover, the couple and their attendants (*faʻe tangata*)[6] were dressed in *kie hingoa* (fine mats with genealogies) and the bride was dripping with coconut oil.

---

5   Churchward (1959: 522) describes *tuʻuvala* as the exchange of gifts and cloths between bride and groom in a Tongan way.

6   *Faʻe tangata* (also called *tuʻasine*) are the biological and classificatory brothers of the mothers of the bride and groom. During the wedding ceremony, the bride and groom will sit in their laps and other *faʻe tangata* may sit at their feet (Douaire-Marsaudon 1998: 304; Aoyagi 1966: 168).

Figure 32. Folding a dark barkcloth (*ngatu 'uli*) decorated with motifs inspired from historical museum barkcloths to incorporate in the wedding bed (*mohenga mali*). Sia ko Veiongo, Kolomotu'a, Tongatapu

Source. Photographed by Fanny Wonu Veys, 3 June 2003

Figure 33. 'Eiki Salote Lupepau'u Salamasina Purea Vahine Arii 'o e Hau Tuita and Matai'ulua-'i-Fonuamotu Fusitu'a sitting on the wedding bed (*mohenga mali*), which forms a throne showing their elevated status. Mala'e Pangai Lahi, Nuku'alofa, Tongatapu

Source. Photographed by Fanny Wonu Veys, 11 June 2003

Barkcloth, mats and coconut oil have long been crucial elements in wedding ceremonies. While the previous description concerned only a small part of the 10-day wedding celebrations, the Wesleyan missionary James Watkin witnessed, on 9 April 1833, a wedding ceremony that included similar materials that, through their materiality, allowed for the wrapping of people. As he wrote:

> Married a couple this morning in the presence of great numbers of people [;] they are two interesting young persons and both chiefs of considerable rank, they were beautifully attired in the native style in dresses that were a burden to carry, and their persons were anointed or rather drenched in perfumed oil, considerable preparation had been made for feasting, hogs and yams in abundance having been prepared for the parties concerned and for unconcerned spectators if such they might be called who had been attracted by the fine sight and the more tempting as well as substantial feast. The *gnatoo* [*ngatu*] drapery and mats of fine texture are tastefully adjusted to the person, and produce a pretty if not an imposing effect, it pleases me as much as the more flaring and more costly habiliments of the 'great ones' of more civilised parts of the earth. After the performance of the marriage ceremony they proceeded to the habitation of the bride groom and after a change of attire a few of the harmless ceremonies which obtained in former times on such occasion were gone through, one was walking in state from the house in which they were enrobed to another at a short distance and back again, in walking from the house the Lady preceded in returning the gentleman, after a repetition of this the bride was pretty well bedaubed with a superposition of oil and turmeric and conducted to a sort of throne or elevated seat formed with large quantities of *gnatoo* [*ngatu*] and mats of superior workmanship on which she was seated to continue in [mueaz?] state for a considerable time after which she is disencumbered of her load of a dress and privileged with use of the bath by which the matrimonial ceremony terminated. A marriage in high life is an affair of 'pomp and circumstance' here as well as elsewhere. I have held the usual service this day which was well attended and was pleased to see the bride and bridegroom present the former in a dress that required more strength than her own[,] the latter too was in matrimonial attire (Watkin 1833).

The presentation of large amounts of goods and food during ceremonial occasions in Tonga has been discussed extensively in anthropological literature. Based on nineteenth-century observations and twentieth-century scholarship, a broad distinction is generally asserted between objects made by men and those made by women. The latter, comprising a variety of textile valuables as well as coconut oil and sometimes baskets, are termed *koloa faka-Tonga*, or succinctly *koloa*, and are often categorised as the women's wealth of Tonga's island nation (Kaeppler 1999a). However, from both earlier vignettes, it appears that men as well as women manipulate *koloa* and are enveloped by it. In this chapter, I want to explore how *koloa* have been defined historically and in contemporary Tonga. I will then engage in the debate of how and why *koloa* are valued to finally question the notion of gendered objects in which *koloa* are viewed exclusively as women's wealth.

Defining *koloa*

William Mariner, a shipwrecked clerk who was adopted by Tongans after most of the crew of the *Port-au-Prince* had been killed in 1806,[7] explained in his account of his adventures, specifically in the introduction to a chapter entitled 'Arts and Manufactures', that in early nineteenth-century Tonga there was a difference between objects produced by skilled male professionals (*toofunga* [*tufunga*]) and those that do not require expert skills (Mariner 1827, vol. 2: 192). In the latter category, he moreover made a distinction between objects made by women and those produced by men. While Mariner did not name the different categories, he did make an attempt at defining groups of objects both in terms of gender and of the skill required to make them.

Tongans and scholars today refer to groups of objects that are considered precious, have special value and can be presented and given during ceremonies. The classification is made up of mats, barkcloth and coconut oil[8] in the first group; decorated baskets, combs and chiefs' ornaments in the second; and clubs, spears, canoes, carved whale's tooth, wooden head rests and kava bowls in the third (Douaire-Marsaudon 1998: 124; Kaeppler 1990: 59). The first category is generally coined *koloa* and will be at the centre of this discussion. It seems that the objects in the second group were made only by high-ranking women, but could be used by both men and women in the chiefly classes (Douaire-Marsaudon 1998: 124). The third group of objects was created by specialised male artisans (*tufunga*) who worked for chiefs, was used by men and was not distributed but kept and inherited (Douaire-Marsaudon 1998: 124). Still, historical

---

7   William Mariner was finally picked up by the brig *Favourite*, which took him to Macao from where he continued his voyage to London aboard an East India merchant vessel, arriving in June 1811. John Martin, a London doctor, who became fascinated with William Mariner's story when he met him a few years after his return to England, composed the narrative for him (Smith 2000: 193–94).

8   Kaeppler (1990: 59) claims scented coconut oil belongs to the second category named *teuteu*.

texts testify to the presentation to Europeans of items created by *tufunga*. George Forster remarked in October 1773 that 'arms' were presented to Cook's crew (Forster 1999, vol. 1: 244). Mariner told how all foreigners who came to Tonga received canoes (1827, vol. 1: 257). Also, the presence of hundreds of weapons in museum collections demonstrates that weapons created by male artisans were exchanged and gifted (Mills 2007). Wood incising has, however, with the disappearance of traditional warfare and the influence of Christianity, almost completely ceased (Kaeppler 1990: 59) and been relegated to the ceremonial sphere. Adrienne Kaeppler (1999a) states that some forms of *ngāue fakame'a'a* (material treasures), such as elaborately carved weapons, are no longer gifted because they are now not necessary for daily use. Tongan scholars including 'Okusitino Māhina (2004: 87–88) and Futa Helu (1995: 197) agree that many carved wooden objects are more likely to be appreciated as historical objects associated with and enhancing the status of specific male *tufunga*, or creators, builders and constructors of artistic or beautiful things. In 2008, during King George Tupou V's *taumafa kava*, the kava ceremony to mark the investiture of a Tongan royal, the attendants carried relatively newly carved clubs over their shoulders.

Different interpretations of *koloa* exist. They often depend on the varying degree of knowledge to which people have access, as well as the historical period, geographic area and rank of the person and his/her family. For example, Kaeppler's discussion on *koloa* is based on information given by aristocratic women in Tongatapu and the estate (*tofi'a*) on Tungua, an island in the Ha'apai Islands. Heather Young Leslie (2007), however, did fieldwork among commoner women from Kauvai Island in Ha'apai. In a booklet put out by the Free Wesleyan Church of Tonga, *Ko e kava mo e ngaahi Koloa Faka-Tonga* (Kava and Tongan prestigious objects) (2002),[9] it is explained that *koloa* comprise barkcloth, fine mats, coconut oil and baskets. Young Leslie (2007) asserts that *koloa* encompasses mainly textile wealth, as does Ping-Ann Addo (2013) who works among the diaspora communities in New Zealand. Her definition of *koloa* refers to 'things that women exchange' or 'a category of valuable objects made and presented ceremonially only by women, and associated with women's generative powers' (Addo 2013: 2, 34–35, 200). Actually, many definitions do not include baskets. Kaeppler (1990: 59) and Françoise Douaire-Marsaudon (1998: 124) classify baskets with objects that were made exclusively by

---

9   Author's translation.

high-ranking women. I suggest that as combs and chiefs' ornaments and headdresses are no longer made, the decorated baskets have joined the group of valuables termed *koloa*.

On numerous occasions during the 2006 funerary rites of King Tupou IV, fresh flower arrangements or cut pieces of plant materials constructed to represent new flowers were laid on flat woven coconut palm leaf baskets (*kato kakala*) and were presented. On Saturday 16 September 2006, during a presentation presided over by Princess Pilolevu, the only daughter of the then recently deceased king, and two of Pilolevu's daughters, Lupe'olo Halaevalu Mohe'ofo and Fane Tupou Vava'u, a large number of *kato kakala* were laid out in the east marquee by Queen Sālote school girls. No mention is made of *kato kakala* in historical sources, but this innovative way of processing Tongan material is in accordance with the Methodist missionary ideals of teaching Islanders 'a work of patience' (Eves 1996: 148). On Thursday 21 September 2006, under the east marquee, women holding crocheted bedspreads (*kafu niti*) and patchwork quilts (*monomono*) formed a circle around other goods gifted by female presenters. Both quilted and crocheted bedspreads were included in this particular presentation. Crocheted and quilted bedspreads, or *kafu*, have been made in Tonga for decades. The wives of missionaries and the French Marist nuns introduced these techniques. Therefore, in Tonga, crocheting and quilting are associated with Christianity (Veys 2009). Moreover, sewing, embroidery and lace-making were imparted to Tongan women by missionaries intent on colonisation in the hope that they would create an image more befitting Victorian femininity (Küchler and Were 2005: 183–84). Phyllis Herda (1999) argues that from the 1970s, crocheted and quilted bedspreads acquired a significance beyond mere bed linen. This was exemplified in the exhibition curated by Kolokesa Uafā Māhina-Tuai and Manuēsina 'Ofa-Ki-Hautolo Māhina (2011) in Auckland, showcasing exceptionally artistic items of Tongan crochet and embroidery. They have become a form of textile wealth, albeit an inferior one to barkcloth and mats.

The presentation to the royal family, on Thursday 21 September 2006, by the Catholic school children of 'Api Fo'ou School included at least 200 cakes. The school delegation entered via the southwest gates with the girls in front carrying *ngatu* and mats, followed by other girls with cakes, which were put down in the centre under the direction of a Catholic nun. Then came other goods such as kava roots and items of food that were carried by the Catholic schoolboys and their teachers. Cakes are usually bought in one of the many bakeries of Tonga's capital, Nuku'alofa, and then wrapped in cling film for public occasions; they are part of any contemporary celebration and ceremony such as birthdays, *misinale* (yearly church donations) and funerals. Women who can decoratively ice cakes share their skills through membership of cake-baking groups, or *langa fonua* groups, which are organised along the same lines as the *langa fonua* groups that make barkcloth (Jowitt and Lay 2002).

Tongan women have been making cakes, rich in sugar and fat, since the Langa Fonua established by Queen Sālote encouraged the use of western kitchens with stoves to cook and ovens to bake (Addo 2013: 69; Wood-Ellem 1999: 265). Later that day (21 September 2006), a presentation took place under the west marquee and involved goods such as mats and bedspreads and large numbers of sweets presented in *kato lole* and on screens (*tapu lole*). The *kato lole* are either plastic containers or Chinese rattan baskets filled with oranges, apples, crisps, chocolates, chewing gum and sweets. The containers are wrapped in cellophane. *Tapu lole* are rectangular screens, have two legs and are covered with shiny wrapping paper (Figure 34). Cadbury and Nestlé chocolate and packets of crisps are neatly arranged in rows. These screens are traditionally made of *ngatu* and mats or flowers and are meant to serve as grave decoration (Churchward 1959: 457). The cling film–wrapped cakes, the *kato lole* enveloped in cellophane and the *tapu lole* with their glistening paper possess a similar shininess to oil-rubbed *ngatu*, mats and baskets. The superimposition of layers and colours found in all these objects may be considered a central theme in Tongan objects of presentation. The fat and the sugar present in cakes, *kato lole* and *tapu lole* are in addition highly appreciated in Tongan culture (Cottino 2015; Veys 2009).

In the twentieth century, these objects have acquired the status of *koloa si'i*, so-called lesser or minor *koloa*, through their association with Christianity in the case of crocheted or knitted covers (*kafu niti*), patchwork quilts (*monomono*), fleece blankets (*kafu sipi*) and flower baskets (*kato kakala*), and through their affiliation with the involvement of women in the Tongan economy—thus increasing their access to cash capital and transnational connections in the case of cakes (*keke*), sweets panels (*tapu lole*) and baskets with sweets (*kato lole*) (Addo 2013: 35; Veys 2009: 138–40). The emergence of *koloa si'i* is also closely connected to the decrease of women who are capable or willing—often because of the time constraints that today's white-collar jobs entail—to produce *koloa* (Besnier 2011: 105). These lesser valuables that complement the traditional textile wealth have become an appropriate material for use in ceremonial presentations and exchanges.

Figure 34. *Koloa si'i* including crocheted bedspreads (*kafu niti*), sweets panels (*tapu lole*) and baskets with sweets (*kato lole*) presented at the marquee on the palace grounds. Nuku'alofa, Tongatapu

Source. Photographed by Fanny Wonu Veys, 20 September 2006

How can we translate a word expressing a notion as complex as *koloa*? The dictionary compiled by the Marist missionaries describes it as 'riches, every precious object, what one possesses' (Colomb and Missionnaires Maristes 1890: 165).[10] The linguist Maxwell C. Churchward (1959: 270) proposes 'goods, wealth, riches, possessions'. Kaeppler (1990) often uses 'treasures', while Douaire-Marsaudon (1998) talks about 'riches'. Addo (2013) uses different wordings, including 'thing of value', 'wealth' and 'women's valuables'. In analogy with the New Zealand Māori, *taonga*, usually coined as 'treasure' (Veys 2010), Addo (2013) also uses the term 'treasure' to translate *koloa*. I prefer the designation 'prestigious objects' because this encapsulates the role played by *koloa* in certain contexts and the skill and particular materials needed to make these objects. Whatever definition of *koloa* is used, everyone agrees that these objects are valuable to Tongans, as they materialise the skill and effort of women who ensure that *koloa* can participate in ceremonial exchanges, and thus potentially form the physical manifestation of past events.

---

10 Original quote in French: 'richesses, tout objet précieux, ce qu'on possède' (Colomb and Missionnaires Maristes 1890: 165).

The value of *koloa*

Koloa materialises 'what one values' through its close linkage with women. Manufactured and presented by women, it reflects the high status sisters occupy vis-à-vis their brothers whose labours and crafts are deemed *ngāue* (work) (Herda 1999: 149). Hence Kaeppler (1999b: 219) asserts that *koloa* captures the 'female essence'. Consequently, the value of *koloa* corresponds to the value of women. In doing so, the valuing of *koloa* foregrounds 'a predisposition to equate the value of objects with the value of people' (Crăciun 2015: 2).

Tongan women are characterised by and held in esteem because of their female *mana* (potency), which Maxwell Churchward (1959: 330) translated as 'miracle, supernatural act or event; supernatural power or influence or attendant circumstances'. Actually, in the past, *mana* was inseparable from rank in its practical efficacy (Shore 1989: 138). An obvious consequence was that solely high-ranking women could influence objects by their *mana* so as to create *koloa*. Therefore, the eighteenth- and nineteenth-century manufacture of *ngatu*, for example, happened under the supervision of chiefly women. Valuable barkcloth was created only by women in the presence of a high-ranking female. *Koloa* as such were valuable not because they were made by women, but because they were imbued with the *mana* of a high-ranking woman. This is exactly what Herda (1999: 160) points out when she argues that, in the past, a piece of barkcloth did not become *koloa* until the chiefly woman acted upon it in a chiefly manner. Thus commoners' labour did not make the piece of barkcloth automatically *koloa*. Following the Tongan notion of chiefliness, it was the *mana* of the chiefly woman, her presence and skill that was imbued within the cloth. As anthropologists theorising value have emphasised, value depends on the context, and therefore changes in context will impact on value (Graeber 2001; Munn 1986; Thomas 1991). It can therefore be argued that the word *koloa* does not simply refer to the type of object—barkcloth, mats, etc.—but also to the context, more specifically a Tongan context, that allowed for the *mana* of a chiefly person to be incorporated into a particular object.

Kaeppler (2007) argues that what happened in the past is essentially still the case in contemporary Tonga, but it has become restricted to objects used in an aristocratic context. Once ordinary objects, specifically textiles, play a role in ceremonies they become prestigious. Their status of *koloa* resides in the context they are used in and the specific materials—ranked hierarchically—of which they are made (Kaeppler 2007: 145–46). However, Addo (2013) demonstrates that, in a diasporic context, the simple fact of a Tongan woman manipulating the cloth suffices to make it *koloa*. Actually Meredith Filihia (2001: 384) believes that all women, including commoner women, have always enjoyed an elevated status, even though, in pre-Christian times, commoners' souls might not have entered the Tongan afterworld *Pulotu*.[11] Now, objects are considered *koloa* because they are made by women. This transformation in conception in what constitutes *koloa* is also a consequence of an important shift occurring in the social organisation of barkcloth production spurred on by the 1875 Declaration of Rights,[12] which guaranteed the personal freedom of chiefs (*hou'eiki* [s. *'eiki*]) and commoners (*tu'a*) alike (Campbell 2001: 98). According to Maxine Tamahori (1963: 134–37), the Declaration of Rights changed the residence of the commoners and the interests of chiefly women. In this void, the *kautaha*[13] (textile wealth-making group) emerged in the twentieth century. Catherine Small (1987: 145) agrees with this 'vacuum theory' as she puts it, but adds that while chiefly women removed themselves from village leadership, commoner women were empowered with new incentives of their own, allowing them to create *koloa* without the intervention of a chiefly woman.

Tongan women themselves emphasise the need for having and producing barkcloth. The women of several Tongan families in Tongatapu and Vava'u proudly showed me the pile of barkcloth and mats they had accumulated in order to be ready for any funeral or wedding occurring within the extended family. Women take great pride in doing *koka'anga* work, and are respected for it by both male and female members of the village community. Getting together to perform the work strengthens the bonds among them. Addo (2013: 45) acknowledges that Tongan women perform the highest value of Tongan society, *'ofa* (love), because they work with love in creating something that is beautiful (*faka'ofa'ofa*).

---

11 *Pulotu* is the Tongan afterworld. In Tongan mythology, it is perceived as being an island located somewhere to the west of Tonga (Filihia 2001: 377–78).

12 The Declaration of Rights was part of the 1875 Constitution, which was modelled on English law and which dealt with three important matters: the declaration of rights, describing a form of government, and the issue of land (Campbell 2001: 98).

13 Churchward (1959: 257) defines *kautaha* as 'union, association, company, firm, club, society, league, alliance, organisation'. Tamahori (1963: 129) claims that many organisations in Tonga might be called *kautaha*, but the term has evolved to refer to associations organising the production of *ngatu*. Now, the words *toulanganga* and *toulālanga* for barkcloth-making and mat-weaving groups respectively are more often used (Addo 2013).

The necessity of producing barkcloth is a theme that occurs in other places in the Pacific. Steven Hooper (1995: 151) states that, in the great majority, female members of a Lauan (Eastern Fiji) household, even those based at Suva, consider it necessary and desirable to have a supply of barkcloth and mats in order to be able to participate in regular rituals. Eastern Fijian women stress that they require a *gatu* (barkcloth) for a wedding in order to demonstrate skill, industriousness and respect. This fact can be connected to the idea of barkcloth being considered valuable as it appears the more energy that is put into its production the more it is worth, hence the particular high repute of the *ngatu'uli* (black barkcloth), for example. Anna-Karina Hermkens (2013: 99) explains that also for the Maisin people, living along the shores of Collingwood Bay in Papua New Guinea, women are expected to make tapa. Women told her it was not only a custom Maisin people had grown up with, but that now it also constituted their living, giving them money with which they can buy other goods.

Jehanne Teilhet (1983: 53) states, with respect to women's birth-giving capacities and hence control over life and death, that women are believed to have greater innate powers than men. In this context, *mana* is a 'generative potency' that can act upon 'organic creations' (Shore 1989: 140). There is a clear link between fecundity and *mana*. This means that without children the family lineage dies, as do all the ancestors who live in the supernatural world because there is no one left to honour them. Thus, women establish the continuity between the past and the present. Since they were given the natural power to create and control, their products have the same effect. In a broader Polynesian context, the notions of *noa* and *tapu* are often used. According to Shore (1989: 138–50), Polynesian women are perceived as being *noa*, meaning 'free', 'nothing', 'unmarked', 'unconstrained'. Therefore they have the capacity of neutralising things, places or people who are in a *tapu* state. *Tapu*, as opposed to *noa*, signifies 'contained', 'bound', but has a distinctive passive and active usage. As an active quality, *tapu* suggests a contained potency of some thing, place or person. In its passive usage, it refers to what is forbidden or dangerous.[14]

---

14 I have not encountered the word *noa* being associated with women in a Tongan context. This also equally does not agree with the rather negative definition given in the dictionary compiled by Churchward (1959: 379), where he states that *noa* means 'any kind of, any old, of no particular kind, common, ordinary, of no value or importance, worthless, unimportant, causeless, meaningless, aimless, futile, without payment or without result, unreal, purely imaginary'.

Figure 35. Pathway of *ngatu tāhina* (rusty-brown barkcloth) extending from the palace to the royal tombs. Mala'e Kula, Nuku'alofa, Tongatapu
Source. Photographed by Fanny Wonu Veys, 19 September 2006

In its social manipulation or management, textile wealth plays a role in protecting people in liminal and therefore potentially dangerous situations during life rituals. Wrapping and binding, thus enclosing and separating, are conceptually linked in the notion of 'protection'. Not only are people being wrapped and bound, ritual spaces undergo the same protective measures. This happened in nineteenth-century Tonga, but also in present-day Tonga, which was exemplified by pathways of barkcloth laid out in front of the Wesleyan centennial church during the 2003 royal wedding, the coronation of King George Tupou V and from the palace to the royal tombs (*mala'e kula*) for the funerals of both Tupou IV and V (Figure 35). The power of the protection is exponentially increased through the presence of women lining the female product—*ngatu*—which thus extends the protection to a cosmological level. *Koloa*, or prestigious objects, enshrine the *mana* of the maker and/or donor. *Koloa* is thus a metaphor for female potency, which is particularly important when dealing with bodies: women give birth, nurture and raise children. Similarly, women create and arrange the distribution, wrapping and cutting up of textile wealth. Garth Rogers summarises that 'words, titles, land, houses, and political authority, including jural control over the children, are transmitted through males; ritual honours and mystical powers are transmitted through females' (1977: 171). Through women and the nurturing qualities of their products, the social fabric of Tonga is supported, explaining why its production and use persist to this day.

Women and their products thus bring human life into the world, nurture it, protect it and accompany it out of the world (Hooper 1995: 165). This nurturing has no physical connotation. It has more to do with mental feeding, embedding a person in a culture and by doing so incorporating him or her in the society, thus generating social and cultural life. Moreover, by participating in the rituals and interceding with their products, the women ensure that the transitions in a person's life are facilitated. *Koloa*, are, like the women themselves, valuable, while *ngāue* are like men, powerful (Kaeppler 1990).

Understanding the value of *koloa* also requires taking into account its material qualities that contribute to the quest for *fiemālie* (feelings of being comfortable and contented) when making and giving them. *Koloa* including *koloa si'i*, are large, have contrasting colours and glisten; they have nice perfumes and their production and presentation go hand in hand with melodious beating sounds, with the agreeable rustling of plant fibres and the assured voices of the women presenting their work (Veys 2013). In short, they display a sense of abundance (Cottino 2015). These are all qualities that correspond to Tongan sensibilities. The importance of *koloa* lies in the combination of the reproductive *mana* inherent in women and the sense of abundance that women's specialist skills produce (Veys 2009).

Are *koloa* gendered?

Complementary object categories were central to Marcel Mauss's important 1950 essay *Essai sur le don* (Mauss 1990). In Samoa specifically, the sociologist Mauss juxtaposes masculine goods versus feminine goods, termed respectively *'oloa*, objects that belong to the husband, and *tonga*,[15] permanent paraphernalia, particularly mats given at marriage (Mauss 1990: 98–100). The anthropologist Serge Tcherkézoff (1997: 193–223) remarks that the man–woman dualism is actually more complex. According to

---

15   *Oloa* and *tonga* is the spelling used by Marcel Mauss (1990: 98–100). Contemporary Samoan spelling is *'oloa* and *'ie tōga*.

Tcherkézoff (1997: 212), Mauss naïvely based his analysis of gifts in Samoa on just one missionary ethnography made by the Reverend George Turner that only treated matrimonial exchange. Based on Turner's limited observations, Mauss concluded that all exchanges of goods in Samoa were gendered. According to Tcherkézoff (1997: 212), Mauss naïvely based his analysis of gifts in Samoa on just one missionary ethnography made by the Reverend George Turner that only treated matrimonial exchange. Based on Turner's limited observations, Mauss concluded that all exchanges of goods in Samoa were gendered. However, Tcherkézoff (1997: 193–223) argues that '*oloa* is cognate to the Tongan term *koloa*, which in the Samoan context encompasses all kinds of valued objects. Turner actually never suggested that '*oloa* and *tōga* were gendered, but rather referred to them as 'foreign property' and 'native property' respectively. Nevertheless, the notion of gendered objects has influenced many anthropologists, including Annette Weiner (1992), who, based on extensive fieldwork in the Trobriand Islands and shorter fieldwork in Western Samoa, theorises on fibre-based objects in societies of Polynesia, Papua New Guinea and Australia. She convincingly argues that these fibre-based objects, which she glosses 'cloth', give women who are generally the producers, exchangers and conservators, power in the political process (Weiner 1992).

Even though men and women are enveloped by and handle *koloa*, it is mostly women who beat, paste, weave, boil, dry, dye and decorate *koloa*. Evidenced in the 2003 royal wedding and 2006 royal funeral, women not only play a prominent role in making it, but also in sequencing, presenting and exchanging it at significant life stages, including births, weddings, funerals and investiture, and also events such as graduations and 21st birthdays (Addo 2013; Hooper 1995; Kaeppler 1995: 119). However, the involvement with *koloa* is not an exclusive female activity. On 26 April 2003, I witnessed a husband beating bark (*tutu*) together with his wife in their home in 'Ohonua, the capital of 'Eua, the island southeast of Tongatapu. He was helping out his wife, who had to prepare strips of beaten barkcloth for the *toulanganga* (the barkcloth-making club) she was attending later that day. The husband felt it was inappropriate for him to engage in this kind of activity and absolutely did not want me to photograph him doing this, claiming he was not good at *tutu*. Men and boys also help with growing the paper mulberry tree, carrying large bales of *ngatu* and *lālanga* (woven textiles) onto the presentation grounds and putting them into storage containers. This was strikingly obvious during the 2006 funerary rituals of King Taufa'ahau Tupou IV. Men also bring food to cater for the women's weekly get-togethers for the *koka'anga* process, young boys climb the *koka* tree (Bischofia javanica) to collect its scrapings in order to make dye and help with swinging the *fautaukoka* (hibiscus fibre dye wringer) over a pole, which wrings the *koka* dye out of it. Addo (2013: 48) asked an older woman how she felt about a younger man demonstrating the workings of the *misini tutu* (barkcloth-beating machine), which had been introduced in the early 1980s by Geoffrey Houghland, a former Peace Corps Volunteer. She feared, however, the woman would feel uncomfortable with a man being so closely involved with the barkcloth-making process. The woman replied that as a younger man he was performing his duty helping an older female family member. Addo (2013: 48) concludes that 'the importance of accomplishing work related to textile production—with varied materials—seems to be more important than expressly delineating textile work along gender lines in all situations'. As long as women are able to control and feel the responsibility of the different aspects involved in making and manipulating barkcloth, the help of men is welcome.

When driving around the main island of Tongatapu in 2012, I noticed the growing number of *kautaha nō pa'anga* (financial establishments). In these businesses, women and also men trade in *koloa faka-Tonga* only. This differentiates them from the western pawnshop on which they are modelled (Besnier 2011: 104). The pawnshop emerged in the 1980s and really developed from 2006 onwards, when a whole group of civil servants wanted to do something with the redundancy packages they had received in an attempt to downsize the Tongan civil service. Moreover, the decrease in the number of women who had the time and willingness to make *koloa*, even though they were faced with the ever-increasing demand of *koloa* for ceremonial use, played a part in the creation of the pawnshop. The business of the pawnbroker is notoriously lucrative, but because they are making money on the backs of people who are already cash poor, they also operate on the social fringe (Addo and Besnier 2008: 40–41; Besnier 2011: 104–06). Dotted with these 'money-borrowing companies', the Tongan landscape had considerably changed since my initial stay in 2003 and subsequent research visits. An unwanted consequence of these money-making 'banks' were the raids on the premises by young boys, who stole all the *koloa* stored in order to resell them (Lucy Moala Mafi, personal communication, March 2012). As such, the emergence of the pawnshop has contributed to a growing involvement of men with *koloa*.

Many anthropologists theorising women's wealth in Tonga understand *koloa* to be the complementary domain to *ngāue*,[16] products derived from agricultural work and animal husbandry (Addo 2013; Douaire-Marsaudon 1998: 207; Herda 1999; Kaeppler 1995: 103; Kaeppler 2007: 146; Young Leslie 1999). They form complementary oppositions, which exist between men and women (Chave-Dartoen 2012: 96), and by extension between goods produced through female or male intervention. The notions of *koloa* and *ngāue* constitute an organising principle for values, status, responsibility, temporality and space (Chave-Dartoen 2012: 96–97). They both play a role at key moments of every *kātoanga* (ceremony). While the distinction between *koloa* and *ngāue* is not explicitly discussed in historical texts, the two groups are represented separately in the description of most important ceremonial occasions (Amos 1853; Mariner 1827, vol. 1: 122–23; Watkin 1833; Williams 1841: 276). *Koloa* can be redistributed, but the most precious ones will be conserved by the chiefs and can be inherited, while *ngāue* have to be consumed, eaten in order to fulfil their function. Kaeppler explains that the contrast between *ngāue* and *koloa* reflects the high status of women in Tongan society: *ngāue* can be ritually offered to equals, while *koloa*, like the prestige they embody, should move upward to someone of higher rank, or to someone whose status should be recognised because of illustrious ancestral connections (Kaeppler 1999b: 170). Kaeppler's vision is nuanced by Addo (2013: 4), who stresses that the gifting of especially long yams, kava and pigs was the prerogative of commoner men to their chiefs. Under Taufaʻahau Tupou I, the first king in the contemporary royal dynasty, commoners could acquire their own wealth in the form of *koloa* and *ngāue*. The latter could even contribute to paying taxes to the church (Addo 2013: 7–8). However, some elites continued to make gifts of *koloa* and *ngāue* (Addo 2013: 37). The association of *koloa* and *ngāue*, with men's and women's labour respectively, has prompted many scholars to assert that these categories are 'strongly gendered' (Douaire-Marsaudon 2004: 207).

---

16   Depending on the scholar, the male goods cultivated, baked, cooked or presented by men receive various names. Douaire-Marsaudon (2008) uses the word *kai* for the male goods that are presented during *kātoanga*. Strictly speaking, *kai* refers to food and could in theory also be food that is produced by women. Therefore not all *kai* is suitable to represent group identity. Sometimes the word *ngoue* is used (Addo 2013: 94; 2004). Again, this only includes agricultural produce, and therefore excludes all men's wealth, which results from animal husbandry. *Ngāue*, on the other hand, is a wide concept that can encompass different types of goods and is closely connected to the 'work' men do for a ceremonial presentation.

To a certain extent, all objects are gendered. As Niko Besnier infers, when objects and people meet, one encounters gender: 'Objects are gendered through their production, consumption, and circulation, and bodies are gendered by default' (2011: 26). He does offer a note of caution by saying that the gendering often operates in subtle ways, which perhaps is a reflection of the complex hierarchies of Tongan society where women rank higher than their brothers but lower than their husbands (Besnier 2011: 26; Kaeppler 1971: 175). Thus, the father's side (*kāinga 'i tamai*) is higher than the mother's side (*kāinga 'i fa'ē*).[17] Kaeppler (1971: 177) and Elizabeth Bott (1981: 19) add a third principle within the *kāinga*, which includes everyone to whom one can bilaterally trace a relationship. Older is ranked higher than younger. The gendering is also found on a societal level in the distinction between *kāinga*[18] (kinsmen) and *ha'a* (a form of societal ranking by which titles and their holders are organised): the rank acquired through women—within the *kāinga*—is personal, while the rank acquired through men—within the *ha'a*—is the impersonal public rank of title and office (Biersack 1982: 196; 2006: 241). So cultural value is derived from women, while political 'power' is received through men.

While most scholars agree that goods in Tonga *are* gendered, some accentuate the fluctuating nature of this dualistic view of *koloa* and *ngāue* as respectively female and male. Jehanne Teilhet-Fisk (1991: 47, 62) and Kerry James (1988: 33–36), for example, explain that a very old kava bowl can be considered *koloa* because it has transcended its pure utilitarian value to acquire a transactional or exchange value. Conversely, *ngāue* is often used to refer to any kind of work. Teilhet-Fisk (1991: 47, 62) has even recorded women referring to making *ngatu* as *ngāue*. Both *ngāue* and *koloa* are concepts that can take on different meanings depending on the context in which they are circulating. Moreover, items incorporating barkcloth and sold as souvenirs or handicrafts[19] to tourists are not *koloa* (Addo 2013: 36), because they are objects that have been adapted in size, style and function to what people can and want to take with them. Besnier

---

17　Bott (1981: 19) explains that the *kāinga 'i fa'ā* includes the set of brothers and brothers' children to whom the mother and her children are superior.

18　Shulamit R. Decktor Korn (1974: 9) sees *kāinga* as a form of domestic kin group next to and sometimes overlapping with *'api* (the household group) and *fāmili* (family, village based action group).

19　The most common handicraft objects are placemats, baskets, fans and jewellery, decorated with or in the shape of turtles, dolphins and the map of Tonga. These handicrafts are available at the main Talamahu market, on temporary stalls set up for cruise ship tourists coming on land and at the Langa Fonua 'ae Fefine Tonga, the women's cooperative that Queen Sālote Tupou III founded in 1953 (von Gizycki 1997).

(2011: 108) warns that because Tongans, when speaking English, use the word 'handicraft' both for tourist items and for *koloa*, it devalues *koloa*. This is particularly the case when this conflation occurs in interactions with people who are unfamiliar with the local context of both *koloa* and handicrafts.

There are objections to viewing objects as gendered, because female objects or objects made by women do not 'automatically represent "femaleness"' (Hermkens 2013: 108). I believe Hermkens makes an important point here. Tongan textile wealth does not simply represent the division of labour or ideological concepts relating to what it means to be a woman. *Koloa* indexes the *mana* of Tongan women by virtue of the work and love (*'ofa*) they have put into it. Taking into account historical and contemporary developments, I believe that most textile wealth, through its connection with mainly chiefly women in the past and all Tongan women today, has the potential to be considered *koloa*, especially when performing its role of protecting people in liminal situations, masking vulnerabilities, revealing abundance and linking society. It is also in this context that I refrain from calling *koloa* women's wealth or even women's property—as Weiner (1992) perhaps too readily does—but argue for using 'prestigious objects' to translate the word *koloa*.

References

Addo, Ping-Ann. 2004. 'We Pieced Together Cloth, We Pieced Together Culture: Reflections on Tongan Women's Textile-making in Oakland'. *Textile Society of America Symposium Proceedings Paper* 469: 352–359. Online: digitalcommons.unl.edu/tsaconf/469 (accessed 3 July 2015).

———. 2013. *Creating a Nation with Cloth: Women, Wealth, and Tradition in the Tongan Diaspora*. Volume 4. ASAO Studies in Pacific Anthropology. New York and Oxford: Berghahn.

Addo, Ping-Ann and Niko Besnier. 2008. 'When Gifts Become Commodities: Pawnshops, Valuables, and Shame in Tonga and the Tongan Diaspora'. *Journal of the Royal Anthropological Institute* 14(1): 39–59. DOI: 10.1111/j.1467-9655.2007.00477.x.

Amos, Richard. 1853. 'Extracts from the journal of Richard Amos'. In *Wesleyan Methodist Missionary Society, Australasia Correspondence, Tonga 1852–1853*. Microfiche 14, Box 533, no. 633. London: School of Oriental and African Studies.

Anderson, Atholl, Kaye Green and Foss Leach (eds). 2007. *Vastly Ingenious: The Archaeology of Pacific Material Culture, in Honour of Janet M. Davidson*. Dunedin: Otago University Press.

Aoyagi, Machiko. 1966. 'Kinship Organisation and Behaviour in a Contemporary Tongan Village'. *Journal of the Polynesian Society* 75(2): 141–176.

Baba, Tupini, Okusitino Māhina, Nuhisifa Williams and Unaisi Nabobo-Baba (eds). 2004. *Researching the Pacific and Indigenous Peoples: Issues and Perspectives*. Auckland: Centre for Pacific Studies, University of Auckland.

Barberani, Silvia, Gaia Cottino, Fredrica Riva and Michela Badii (eds). 2015. *Sguardi etnografici sul cibo*. Milano: Fondazione Giangiacomo Feltrinelli.

Besnier, Niko. 2011. *On the Edge of the Global: Modern Anxieties in a Pacific Island Nation*. Contemporary Issues in Asian and the Pacific. Stanford, CA: Stanford University Press.

Biersack, Aletta. 1982. 'Tongan Exchange Structures: Beyond Descent and Alliance'. *Journal of the Polynesian Society* 91(2): 181–212.

——. 2006. 'Rivals and Wives: Affinal Politics and the Tongan Ramage'. In *Origin, Ancestry and Alliance. Explorations in Austronesian Ethnography*, ed. James J. Fox and Clifford Sather, pp. 237–279. Canberra: ANU E Press. Online: press.anu.edu.au/publications/series/comparative-austronesian-series/origins-ancestry-and-alliance/download (accessed 23 February 2017).

Bott, Elizabeth. 1981. 'Power and Rank in the Kingdom of Tonga'. *Journal of the Polynesian Society* 90(1): 7–81.

Campbell, Ian Christopher. 2001. *Island Kingdom: Tonga Ancient and Modern*. Christchurch, NZ: Canterbury University Press.

Chave-Dartoen, Sophie. 2012. 'Opposition masculin/féminin à Wallis (Polynésie occidentale). Espaces, circulations et responsabilités rituelles'. *L'Information géographique* 76(2): 95–107. DOI: 10.3917/lig.762.0095.

Churchward, C. Maxwell. 1959. *Tongan Dictionary (Tongan–English and English–Tongan)*. Tonga: Government Printing Press.

Colomb, Antoine and Missionnaires Maristes. 1890. *Dictionnaire Toga-Français-Anglais et Français-Toga-Anglais, précédé d'une grammaire et de quelques notes sur l'archipel par les missionnaires maristes*. Paris: C. Chadenat.

Cottino, Gaia. 2015. 'Il paese dalle "grandi cosce": l'abbondanza nelle isole del regno di Tonga'. In *Sguardi etnografici sul cibo*, ed. Silvia Barberani, Gaia Cottino, Fredrica Riva and Michela Badii, pp. 12–29. Milano: Fondazione Giangiacomo Feltrinelli.

Crăciun, Magdalena. 2015. 'Bobbles and Values: An Ethnography of De-bobbling Garments in Postsocialist Urban Romania'. *Journal of Material Culture* 20(1): 3–20. DOI: 10.1177/1359183514564132.

Douaire-Marsaudon, Françoise. 1998. *Les premiers fruits. Parenté, identité sexuelle et pouvoirs en Polynésie occidentale (Tonga, Wallis et Futuna)*. Paris: Centre National de la Recherche Scientifique Editions, Editions de la Maison des Sciences de l'Homme.

——. 2008. 'Food and Wealth: Ceremonial Objects as Signs of Identity in Tonga and in Wallis'. In *The Changing South Pacific. Identities and Transformations*, ed. Serge Tcherkézoff and Françoise Douaire-Marsaudon, pp. 207–229. Canberra: ANU E Press. Online: press-files.anu.edu.au/downloads/press/p90711/pdf/ch10.pdf (accessed 18 February 2017).

Durell. 1853. 'A Tongan Royal Wedding'. Unpublished, privately held.

Eves, Richard. 1996. 'Colonialism, Corporeality, and Character: Methodist Missions and the Refashioning of Bodies in the Pacific.' *History and Anthropology* 10(1): 85–138. DOI: 10.1080/02757206.1996.9960893.

Filihia, Meredith. 2001. 'Men are from *Maama*, Women are from *Pulotu*: Female Status in Tongan Society'. *Journal of Polynesian Society* 110(4): 377–390.

Forster, George. 1999. *George Forster 1754–1794: A Voyage Round the World*, ed. Nicholas Thomas and Oliver Berghof. 2 vols. Honolulu: University of Hawai'i Press.

Fox, James J. and Clifford Sather (eds). 2006. *Origin, Ancestry and Alliance: Explorations in Austronesian Ethnography*. Canberra: The Australian National University.

Free Wesleyan Church of Tonga. 2002. *Ko e Kava mo e ngaahi Koloa faka-Tonga. Nuku'alofa, Tonga: 'Ofisi Ako 'o e Siasi Uesiliana Tau'atāina 'o Tonga*, Free Wesleyan Church of Tonga (Education Department).

Graeber, David. 2001. *Toward an Anthropological Theory of Value: The False Coin of Our Own Dreams*. New York: Palgrave.

Helu, Futa. 1995. 'Brother/Sister and Gender Relations in Ancient and Modern Tonga'. *Journal de la Société des Océanistes* 100–101(1–2): 191–200.

Herda, Phyllis S. 1999. 'The Changing Texture of Textiles in Tonga'. *Journal of the Polynesian Society* 108(2): 149–167.

Hermkens, Anna-Karina. 2013. *Engendering Objects: Dynamics of Barkcloth and Gender among the Maisin of Papua New Guinea*. Leiden: Sidestone Press.

'Hon. Lupepau'u Divorces Matai'ulua'. *Matangi Tonga Online*. 14 May 2008. Online: matangitonga.to/2008/05/14/hon-lupepauu-divorces-mataiulua (accessed 5 July 2015).

Hooper, Steven. 1995. 'Gatu Vakaviti: The Great Bark Cloths of Southern Lau, Fiji'. In *Pacific Material Culture. Mededelingen van het Rijksmuseum voor Volkenkunde, Leiden*, ed. Dirk A.M. Smidt, Pieter ter Keurs and Albert Trouwborst, pp. 149–166. Leiden 28: Rijksmuseum voor Volkenkunde.

James, Kerry. 1988. 'O, Lead Us Not into "Commoditisation" … Christine Ward Gailey's Changing Gender Values in the Tongan Islands'. *Journal of the Polynesian Society* 97(1): 31–48.

Jowitt, Glen and Graeme Lay. 2002. *Feasts and Festivals: A Celebration of Pacific Island Culture in New Zealand*. Auckland: New Holland Publishers.

Kaeppler, Adrienne L. 1971. 'Rank in Tonga'. *Ethnology* 10(2): 174–193. DOI: 10.2307/3773008.

——. 1990. 'Art, Aesthetics, and Social Structure'. In *Tongan Culture and History. Papers from the 1st Tongan History Conference held in Canberra 14–17 January 1987*, ed. Phyllis Herda, Jennifer Terrell and Niel Gunson, pp. 59–71. Canberra: Dept. of Pacific and Southeast Asian History, The Australian National University.

——. 1995. 'Poetics and Politics of Tongan Bark Cloth'. In *Pacific Material Culture. Mededelingen van het Rijksmuseum voor Volkenkunde, Leiden*, ed. Dirk A.M. Smidt, Pieter ter Keurs and Albert Trouwborst, pp. 101–121. Leiden 28: Rijksmuseum voor Volkenkunde.

——. 1999a. *From the Stone Age to the Space Age in 2000 Years: Tongan Art and Society on the Eve of the Millennium*. Tofoa, Kingdom of Tonga: The Tongan National Museum.

——. 1999b. '*Kie hingoa*: Mats of Power, Rank, Prestige and History'. *Journal of the Polynesian Society* 108(2): 168–231.

——. 2007. 'Me'a Lalanga and the Category Koloa: Intertwining Value and History in Tonga'. In *Vastly Ingenious. The Archaeology of Pacific Material Culture, in honour of Janet M. Davidson*, ed. Atholl Anderson, Kaye Green and Foss Leach, pp. 145–154. Dunedin: Otago University Press.

Korn, Shulamit R. Decktor. 1974. 'Tongan Kin Groups: The Noble and the Common View'. *Journal of the Polynesian Society* 83(1): 5–13.

Küchler, Susanne and Graeme Were. 2005. *Pacific Pattern*. London: Thames & Hudson.

Lavulo, Elizabeth. 2014. 'The Installation of Lord Fusitu'a in the Kingdom of Tonga'. *Whatitdo.com: The Urban Island Review*. 10 June 2014. Online: www.thewhatitdo.com/2014/06/10/the-installation-of-lord-fusitua-in-the-kingdom-of-tonga-2/ (accessed 25 July 2017).

Māhina, 'Okusitino. 2004. 'Art as Tā-vā, "Time-Space" Transformation'. In *Researching the Pacific and Indigenous Peoples: Issues and Perspectives*, ed. Tupini Baba, Okusitino Māhina, Nuhisifa Williams and Unaisi Nabobo-Baba, pp. 86–93. Auckland, New Zealand: Centre for Pacific Studies, University of Auckland.

Māhina-Tuai, Kolokesa Uafā and Manuēsina 'Ofa-Ki-Hautolo Māhina. 2011. *Nimamea'a: The Fine Arts of Tongan Embroidery and Crochet.* Auckland: Objectspace.

Mariner, William. 1827. *An Account of the Natives of the Tonga Islands, in the South Pacific Ocean: With an Original Grammar and Vocabulary of Their Language. Compiled and Arranged from the Extensive Communications of William Mariner, Several Years Resident of those Islands by John Martin.* 2 vols. Edinburgh and London: Constable (3rd edition).

Mauss, Marcel. 1990. *The Gift: The Form and Reason for Exchange in Archaic Societies.* London and New York: Routledge Classics. Original edition, *Essai sur le don*, first published 1950 by Presses Universitaires de France en Sociologie et Anthropologie.

Mead, Sidney M. and Bernie Kernot (eds). 1983. *Art and Artists of Oceania.* Palmerston North: Dunmore Press.

Mesenhöller, Peter and Oliver Lueb. 2013. *Tapa – Kunst und Lebenswelten / Art and Social Landscapes. Made in Oceania.* Köln: Rautenstrauch-Joest-Museum Kulturen der Welt.

Mills, Andy N. 2007. 'Tufunga Tongi 'Akau. Tongan Club Carvers & Their Arts'. 2 vols. PhD thesis. Sainsbury Research Unit, University of East Anglia, Norwich.

Munn, Nancy. 1986. *The Fame of Gawa: A Symbolic Study of Value Transformation in a Massim (Papua New Guinea) Society.* Cambridge: Cambridge University Press.

Rogers, Garth. 1977. '"The Father's Sister is Black": A Consideration of Female Rank and Powers in Tonga'. *Journal of the Polynesian Society* 86(2): 157–182.

Schindlbeck, Markus (ed.). 1997. *Gestern und heute - Traditionen in der Südsee. Festschrift zum 75. Geburtstag von Gerd Koch.* Berlin: Baessler-archiv. Beträge zur Völkerkunde. Neue Folge Band XLV.

Shore, Bradd. 1989. 'Mana and Tapu'. In *Developments in Polynesian Ethnology*, ed. Alan Howard and Robert Borofsky, pp. 137–173. Honolulu: University of Hawaii Press.

Small, Catherine Ann. 1987. 'Women's Organisations and their Pursuit of Wealth in Tonga: A Study in Social Change'. PhD thesis. Philadelphia, PA: Temple University.

Smidt, Dirk A.M., Pieter ter Keurs and Albert Trouwborst (eds). 1995. *Pacific Material Culture: Mededelingen van het Rijksmuseum voor Volkenkunde*, Leiden 28. Leiden: Rijksmuseum voor Volkenkunde.

Smith, Vanessa. 2000. 'William Mariner: Missiles and Missives'. In *Exploration & Exchange. A South Seas Anthology 1680–1900*, ed. Jonathan Lamb, Vanessa Smith and Nicholas Thomas, pp. 191–204. Chicago, London: University of Chicago Press.

Tamahori, Maxine J. 1963. 'Cultural Change in Tonga Bark-cloth Manufacture'. MA thesis. Department of Anthropology, University of Auckland.

Tcherkézoff, Serge. 1997. 'Le mana, le fait «total» et l' «esprit» dans la chose donnée. Marcel Mauss, les «cadeaux à Samoa» et la méthode comparative en Polynésie'. *Anthropologie et Sociétés* 21(2–3): 193–223. DOI: 10.7202/015491ar.

Tcherkézoff, Serge and Françoise Douaire-Marsaudon (eds). 2008. *The Changing South Pacific: Identities and Transformations*. Canberra: ANU E Press. Online: press.anu.edu.au?p=90711 (accessed 3 July 2015).

Teilhet, Jehanne. 1983. 'The Role of Women Artists in Polynesia and Melanesia'. In *Art and Artists of Oceania*, ed. Sidney M. Mead and Bernie Kernot, pp. 45–56. Palmerston North: Dunmore Press.

Teilhet-Fisk, Jehanne H. 1991. 'To Beat or Not to Beat, That is the Question: A Study on Acculturation and Change in Art-making Process and its Relation to Gender Structures'. *Pacific Studies* 14(3): 41–68.

Thomas, Nicholas. 1991. *Entangled Objects: Exchange, Material Culture, and Colonialism in the Pacific*. Cambridge, MA and London: Harvard University Press.

Veys, Fanny Wonu. 2009. 'Materialising the King: The Royal Funeral of King Taufa'ahau Tupou IV of Tonga'. *The Australian Journal of Anthropology* 20: 131–149. DOI: 10.1111/j.1757-6547.2009.00007.x.

———. 2010. *Mana Maori: The Power of New Zealand's First Inhabitants.* Leiden: Leiden University Press.

———. 2013. 'Duty and Multi-sensorial Qualities of Barkcloth During Royal Ceremonies in Tonga'. In *Tapa – Kunst und Lebenswelten / Art and Social Landscapes. Made in Oceania*, ed. Peter Mesenhöller and Oliver Lueb, pp. 38–51. Köln: Rautenstrauch-Joest-Museum Kulturen der Welt.

———. 2017. *Unwrapping Tongan Barkcloth: Encounters, Creativity and Female Agency.* London: Bloomsbury.

von Gizycki, Renate. 1997. 'Tapa in Tonga – Gestern und heute. Aufzeichnungen zur begegnung mit den Frauen von Langa fonua 'ae fefine Tonga'. In *Gestern und heute – Traditionen in der Südsee. Festschrift zum 75. Geburtstag von Gerd Koch*, ed. Markus Schindlbeck, pp. 63–84. Berlin: Baessler-archiv. Beträge zur Völkerkunde. Neue Folge Band XLV.

Watkin, James. 1833. 'Extracts Journal of James Watkin'. In Wesleyan Methodist Missionary Society, Australasia Correspondence, Tonga 1822–1835, 1833, Microfiche 12, Box 541, No 560. London: School of Oriental and African Studies.

Weiner, Annette B. 1992. *Inalienable Possessions: The Paradox of Keeping-While-Giving.* Berkeley: University of California Press.

Williams, John. 1841. *A Narrative of Missionary Enterprises in the South Sea Islands.* London: John Snow.

Wood-Ellem, Elizabeth. 1999. *Queen Sālote of Tonga: The Story of an Era 1900–1965.* Auckland: Auckland University Press.

Young Leslie, Heather. 1999. *Inventing Health: Tradition, Textiles and Maternal Obligationin the Kingdom of Tonga.* Toronto: York University.

———. 2007. 'Tonga' [Political Reviews]. *The Contemporary Pacific* 19(1): 262–276. DOI: 10.1353/cp.2007.0021.

7

Passing on, and Passing on Wealth: Compelling Values in Tongan Exchange

Ping-Ann Addo

Introduction: A life adorned with *koloa*

Throughout her life, Kalo has always been intimately involved with *koloa*—the textiles that comprise the most important category of traditional wealth for people from the Kingdom of Tonga. One of five sisters and one brother, Kalo grew up in Vava'u, Tonga, learning everything about *koloa* that her mother could teach her. After all of her sisters married and moved away from the family home—two of them moving as far away as Auckland, New Zealand—Kalo remained her mother's ardent supporter in the making, caring for, gifting, receiving and sorting of *koloa*. In this chapter, I examine the ways in which *koloa* is integrated into Kalo's end of life experience as she transitions into becoming an ancestor. Taking a retrospective and introspective outlook, as Kalo herself did in conversations I had with her in early 2012, I examine the meanings of women's wealth across generations and changing social contexts for Tongans in diaspora.

Tongans have long honoured people of status in their communities with gifts of *koloa*, accompanied by food and, more recently, by cash. The wife of a Methodist church pastor, Kalo's mother had, over the course of her married life, received and reciprocated innumerable pieces of *koloa* from people in their community. Having never married, Kalo lived at home and helped her mother with these tasks until the older woman died in the early 1970s. Then Kalo succeeded in caring for her mother's *koloa* herself, contributing it to collective gifts and life crisis celebrations in her *kāinga*, or extended family. In 1978, when she moved to Auckland to join her younger sister who had lived there for several years, Kalo took several of her mother's much-loved *koloa* as part of the wealth she would use to continue the cultural tradition of ceremonial gifting, or *fai fatongia*. When I met Kalo in 2000, she lived alone in a small apartment near her Tongan Methodist church in an Auckland suburb. Kalo's dedication to *koloa* was expressed throughout her living space. The apartment had three bedrooms, one of which was entirely devoted to the storage of *koloa*, which included fine mats plaited from pandanus leaves and barkcloth made from both natural and synthetic materials. In the other two bedrooms, beneath the mattresses, lay carefully folded pieces of *koloa*. Kalo rarely slept on these beds, preferring to sleep on several layers of fine mats on her living room floor. In bags and boxes around her apartment were skeins of coloured yarn and packets of wide-eyed needles for embellishing or fixing the decorative edges on some varieties of fine mats. Sometimes there were containers of leftover dye from a barkcloth-making session stored under her kitchen sink.

Thus, even in diaspora, Kalo continued to adorn her life with *koloa*, and she ensured that *koloa* of all types remain intimately connected to the spiritual life of her family. As is the case for many Tongan women, Kalo's involvement with *koloa* seemed to be inseparable from her devotion to God and her church (Figure 36). Whenever there was a family ritual—a wedding, first birthday, 21st birthday, or christening—it would be celebrated, at least in part, in the Methodist church next door. Kalo's sisters, their children and grandchildren, would first assemble at Kalo's house to prepare for the celebration. They would unfold, sweep, sun and layer appropriate combinations of *koloa*—usually a fine mat, barkcloth, and a quilt—for presentation to key members of the celebrants' lineages. They would don *ta'ovala* (waist mat worn wrapped around the hips in formal Tongan dress styles) that Kalo had chosen for each of them over the long-sleeved or long-skirted church outfits, taking Kalo's correction on how to wrap and tie it around their waists with belts made of plaited coconut fibre or braided synthetic hair decorated with coloured beads.

Figure 36. Kalo delivers a sermon at her church. The altar and tables in front and behind her are draped in fine mats

Source. Photographed by Ping-Ann Addo, Auckland, December 2007 and used with Kalo's permission

After the event, the entire family typically returned to Kalo's small house for a cup of tea and some biscuits, or for a more elaborate meal catered by the younger women in the family. Before eating, Kalo would carefully store the *koloa* that her relatives had worn for future occasions (see Figure 37). Hymnal practices for the family's presentations at special church services were also held in Kalo's small living room. Indeed, her home provided an important venue for the transmission of cultural knowledge and practices regarding *koloa*.

In 2012, at the age of 78, Kalo moved to live her with 'daughter' 'Ana—a niece whom she had raised. Kalo transitioned from participating in weekly Tongan cultural activities to staying home and reading her Bible, or watching television, but primarily catching up with relatives or friends on the phone. After the move, she ceased many activities that tied her to the broader Tongan community. For example, she no longer held or even attended weekly meetings of her all-women's rotating credit group that had, for years, met every Tuesday in her apartment. In a rotating credit group, members each contribute weekly a set amount of cash, and one member takes home the pool. This rotates until every member has received a payout, and the cycle can stop at that point or continue for further cycles. She no longer participated in the textile-making work that had been the most culturally important, shared activity of the women in the rotating credit group. For many years, these women had gathered to embroider pillow cases and decorate fine mats, and when they had money—which they received sometimes from outside funding agencies (see Addo 2013)—they would engage in textile making with materials sourced primarily in New Zealand.

Figure 37. Kalo (centre), her daughter, 'Ana, and great-nephew dressed for the New Year's Day service at their church

Source. Photographed by Ping-Ann Addo, Auckland, December 2007

Thus these women were crucial in the ceremonial lives of their families, but many of them acknowledged that they sought Kalo's advice about choosing *koloa*. In this sense, Kalo was a special node of connection in the maintenance and transfer of knowledge about and social relations embodied in *koloa* among diasporic Tongans in New Zealand. Indeed, one day, as Kalo and I sat in her living room, a car pulled up outside and a young man delivered a folded fine mat that his aunt—one of Kalo's counterparts in the textile-making group—charged him with delivering as her thanks to Kalo for her help with arranging *koloa* for her daughter's recent wedding.

When I visited Kalo in early 2013, I was shocked to find out that she no longer had any *koloa* in her possession, save for a few *ta'ovala* (waist mats) that she wore for church or ritual occasions and a barkcloth and a fine mat she had saved from her own mother. I asked to whom she had given these things and what she received in return:

> I gave a few to [friends from the textile-making group] Seilose, Olga and Talita. You remember Talita is my cousin, yes? The *koloa* that my mother left to me ... I gave some to my sisters. I told Mele, the one after me, which ones I wanted to be buried in when my time comes ... the *ta'ovala* I am to wear and the one I want my coffin wrapped in. But I took a lot of the *koloa* to Mele's daughters and to my nieces and gave it to them. I told them how to keep the [mats and barkcloth] folded under their mattresses so they do not wrinkle the faces [of the cloth] ... What did they give me back? Nothing ... But I don't need anything. It's [from] my love.

'Why did you do this?' I wondered out loud, knowing that she had always been the one to have some *koloa* around. 'I have to leave them *something*', came her earnest reply. I duly noted that this purposeful detaching of wealth items from herself was an exercise in preparing some sort of bequest for members of younger generations in her *kāinga*. At its root it was about passing on something prestige-laden, tangible and personal to her descendants.

In this chapter, I explore how the notion of *koloa* as wealth can be borne out in old age for (diasporic) Tongan women as they negotiate their relationships of authority and obligation with younger generations of their kin groups. Objects, like relationships, are not static, and objects embedded in relations *between* people help us understand what is of value to actors whose modernity—whether deliberately or by proxy—includes traditional wealth items. I analyse how Kalo has used wealth to respond to, but also to redirect, the life course of others in her kin group based on their shared cultural values. She deploys *koloa* during life crises ceremonies and other moments of transition in order to effect agency in their successful and happy futures—futures that she hopes will be anchored in Tongan culture and tied to Tonga as an ethnic homeland. The meanings of wealth objects are never guaranteed, and are subject to multiple interpretations (Keane 2005). These meanings may change along with the contexts in which individuals, and those most closely related to them, experience the often disruptive effects of life's transition moments.

I use the lens of *koloa* in Kalo's life transitions to explore how the specificities of the hopes that Kalo holds for her *koloa* translate into a range of meanings for the wealth items. I follow Jennifer Johnson-Hanks, who suggests that 'we move away from thinking about transition events as the things that organize socially made lives' and 'instead ... focus on institutions and aspirations, recognizing that these aspirations are multiple, changeable, and apply over a variety of temporal frames' (Johnson-Hanks 2002: 867). Kalo's outlook is one that is at once retrospective and forward looking, which is common in ageing subjects (Albert and Cattell 1994; Counts and Counts 1985). It is a perspective that is worth examining for how we understand objects to embody value and convey meaning, even as value and meaning change over the course of a life. Kalo is an elderly migrant woman who is considering her impending death, but also reflecting on her kin group as one that has a deep and long history, as well as a future as a *kāinga* that identifies, and can be identified, as *Tongan*. Her aspiration now is to actively infuse her kin-group members' lives with Tongan tradition in the form of sensibilities, practices and icons such as wealth objects.

Through my analysis of *koloa* as Kalo deploys them in her family relationships, I suggest that the wealth-related aspects of women's valuables can be better understood by examining the life course of women associated with them. The life course 'refers to a sequence of age-graded events and social roles that are embedded in social structure and historical change' (Elder 2001: 8818). A life course perspective thus allows us to consider how different people in a group experience a particular kind of identity project—in this case, how to be demonstrably Tongan—based on their particular age-grade vantage points. Life stories of non-chiefly Tongan women have been published (for example, Fanua 1996), but a life-course perspective is missing from the academic study of Tongan women's wealth. Looking at how commoner women at different points in the course of their lives and in different generations relate through *koloa* allows us to consider the diverse ways women make wealth meaningful. I go so far as to suggest that the life course includes the experiences and responsibilities a woman expects to have even *after* she has died. Tongans—the vast majority of whom are Christian faith-keepers—believe in an afterlife as well as in the efficacy of those who have passed on.[1]

---

1   Ancestors are ever-present members of Tongan families, as exemplified in their visiting those left behind in dreams, their graves being cared for regularly by kin, and the frequent naming of newborn babies after (recently) deceased relatives. Babies and children who are thus named may even be spoken to as if they are the specific ancestor.

A native Pacific Islander is almost never more authoritative than when she is an ancestor, or close to becoming one. As Dorothy Ayers Counts and David R. Counts (1985) have documented, women in Pacific societies often enjoy increased authority in the public domain on entering 'old age'. This was certainly true of Kalo in the years when I first knew her, and she certainly still retains a strong sense of her own authority vis-à-vis the younger people in her kin group, as well as strong hopes that they will continue to live by Tongan values after she has passed on. However, since she moved in with 'Ana, Kalo seems to have a different relationship with public life, working more behind the scenes to impart knowledge about wealth to her descendants, but also maintaining the authority to compel others to act in particular ways. This authority rests on the status of *koloa* as wealth—that Kalo's womanhood is framed by a life spent knowing, making and gifting *koloa* makes her an appropriate agent to declare her hopes to her descendants *through* such wealth.

Transitions, paths, influences

Koloa link individuals together into communities. Like so many forms of Oceanic wealth, they are usually exchanged at rituals of transition that matter to lineages and community for their collective history and their self-realisation in the present. Heather Young Leslie states '*koloa* is redolent with several sets of meanings, including … locating an individual within a social network that spans generations' (1999: 259). As I show below, *koloa* have often been important anchors to places and people during transitions in Kalo's life. Indeed, Kalo's life course may be categorised as a bundle of transitions—transitions that were made more manageable by having and deploying *koloa*.

During the late 1970s, when she was in her mid-40s, Kalo underwent a major transition: she moved from her native Tonga to the city of Auckland, New Zealand. As a member of one of the earliest migrations of commoner Tongans to white-majority nations in the Pacific, Kalo did so-called unskilled work (in a fish canning factory), lived with relatives (two of her sisters who had emigrated before her) and helped raise these relatives' children. At first she merely cared for one particular sister's daughters while living with them in their biological mother's house. However, wishing to live closer to the church that she regularly attended three times a week—as is normal in devout Methodist Tongan families—she applied to her church administrators for permission to rent a small apartment near the church. She moved into the small three-bedroom apartment in the late 1980s.

This move, effectively, to live in the church's 'backyard', was another key moment of transition for Kalo. She has always been autonomous but, as Tongan women do, she uses that autonomy to benefit her sisters and their kin.[2]

> In this little apartment I could take care of my own things. But I couldn't live alone. I asked my sister Mele to let me take [raise] her two eldest ones: Sela and 'Ana. Mela married again, too, and she had just had the baby girl. She was happy to let me take her girls. They lived here with me, they took the bus to school. For a while Amelia [her late sister Tivinia's daughter] lived with us, too (Discussion with Kalo, Auckland, 2001).

Here Kalo raised 'Ana and Sela into adulthood, taking them to church each week, and giving and receiving *koloa* as their *mother* at their 16th birthdays and weddings. Today, as women with children of their own, 'Ana and Sela still honour Kalo by referring to her as their 'Mum'. Their own children refer to Kalo as their grandmother, while still remaining close to their biological grandmother, Mele.[3]

During the 25 years that she lived in her apartment, Kalo, being devoutly Christian, attended church three times a week and regularly donated to the church a large portion of her small pension and the money her daughters gave her from their jobs. She also played the role of a 'focalwoman', a term I borrow from Tressa Berman (2003: 83), who refers to 'focalpeople' as those (usually elders) who attain a position of leadership and respect based on consensus by members of their community. In particular, a focalwoman is admired for her exemplary participation in relations of reciprocity, relations that are so often crucial to the economy of indigenous communities. Ever since she moved to Auckland to join her younger sister and to raise children, Kalo had been the focalwoman in her *kāinga* when it came to ceremonial exchange. It has been largely through her efforts to source, store, select and provision others in her kin group with *koloa* that they have been able to participate in ritual presentations of wealth that many consider especially traditional. She not only advised people about

---

2   As her brother's older sister, she generally would gain things from, rather than give wealth to, his children. Kalo's brother and his family live in Tonga, so she does not ask for much materially from them. Wealth transfers typically flow from those in the diaspora to their kinspeople in the Kingdom of Tonga.

3   The *pusiaki* (adoptive) system for raising children guarantees that children know, respect and acknowledge both their biological parents and their social parents. If materially possible, a child will support both sets of parents, but it is not usually considered necessary, as biological parents will probably have other children to support them—they are not likely to have 'given up' the child in the first place if the transaction would leave them childless.

and arranged *koloa*, she often donated the cloths they presented, adding her time, advice, leadership and prayers to the collective gift. She did this not only for kin but also for women in her congregation, especially if they were part of her rotating credit association group. Kalo could not remember just how many gifts of combinations of *koloa* (barkcloth and fine mats, quilts and bedspreads), food and cash she had been part of since she moved to New Zealand, but she had recounted several of these moments over the decade that I had known her.

When both of her daughters, Sela and 'Ana, got married in the late 1980s and 1990s respectively, Kalo presented *koloa* to the grooms' mothers, their fathers' sisters, and to the pastors who officiated or even just attended the ceremonies. When all of Sela's four children and 'Ana's three were christened and then celebrated their first birthdays, Kalo provided her daughters with *koloa* to present to the pastors who officiated or otherwise prayed over and blessed the children. Her daughters were usually the ones to provide the cash part of these gifts. When her own younger sister, Tivinia, died of cancer in 2007, Kalo presented *koloa* to the pastors who prayed for and with her, and *kāinga* for the safe passage of Tivinia's soul the Heaven. In 2010, when Sela's eldest daughter—and the oldest of Kalo's grandchildren—turned 21, the family threw her a large birthday celebration, and Kalo provided *koloa* for gifting to the relatives of the child's father and to pastors and other special guests who attended that occasion as well. When I saw her in early 2013, the most recent life ritual she had been involved in was the christening celebration organised by her great-niece, Anita, who had borne a baby boy several months before.

Exchanges like this take place regularly in both homeland and diasporic Tongan communities, and are crucial to the social status, expression of Tonganness and economic stability of Tongan families everywhere. At any given point in time, one or another member of a given *kāinga* is in debt to someone in another *kāinga*, and it is everyone's responsibility in the first *kāinga* to contribute what they can—materially, spiritually and symbolically—to repay these debts. In receiving a reciprocal gift, kin groups incur further debt but also reaffirm the relationships between them. Focalwomen like Kalo tend to be experts in modelling to their relations how best to continue the cycles of reciprocity that have sustained them all materially and spiritually since they arrived in New Zealand. That said, wealth exchange can be contested and emotionally charged for these women, as well as for others in their community who benefit from the 'to- and fro-ing of [backcloth] and mats and things, [which] strengthens the relationships between family members' (Fanua 1996: 2).

Tongans themselves often debate the utility of symbolic wealth exchange, when labour might 'best' be put towards earning money in the cash economy. Yet, histories of wealth exchange have continued to direct what Tongan exchange looks like globally today. Contemporary diaspora-based relations are rooted in the homeland, for different kin groups were certainly interacting there before emigrating out. Thus, the *who*, rather than the *where* or even the *when*, of a history of exchange is what matters, even when individuals prefer to express cultural values by exchanging other valuables such as cash. It is from repeated acts of declaring one's identity *as a Tongan* through exchange that a sense of collective history, community and nation-building, both in Tonga and abroad, continue to be embedded in cultural wealth. *Koloa*, which historically have been made by groups of women, or at least by an individual woman working communally, are icons of this history. To women like Kalo, *koloa*, as a system of objects embedded in relations that span time and space, is thus inalienable—essential to Tongan identity (Addo 2013).

Koloa and their wealth-like characteristics

Anthropologists generally agree that it is through their associations with powerful people, deities and other efficacious entities that particular objects come to be considered wealth (Graeber 1996). Theorists of women's wealth in Tonga (Herda 1999; James 1997; Kaeppler 1999; Young Leslie 1999 and 2004) suggest that *koloa* are valued because of their origin in the hands of women and their association with the sacred status of women vis-à-vis their brothers. Women involved in *koloa* production imbue the cloths with womanly *mana* (sacred potency) when, working in groups, they hammer, paste, dye and pattern barkcloth from paper mulberry tree bark (Filihia 2001). Other important women's wealth items include large fine mats for gifting and waist mats called *ta'ovala*. These constitute smaller fine mats such as *kie tonga*, single-layered mats (1 metre by 1.5 metres [about 3 feet by 5 feet]) that are off-white in colour and decorated with brightly coloured, store-bought feathers and yarn. A special category of *koloa*, *fala paongo*, constitutes undecorated, two-layered mats of a medium-brown colour that women make from a special species of pandanus and that can be big enough to cover the floor of a large room (see Veys this volume). Also important in the *koloa* system are a variety of store-bought and machine-made quilts, bedspreads with matching pillow cases and decorated baskets filled with bottles of coconut oil, perfume and other toiletries (Herda 1999).

Phyllis Herda begins her 1999 essay, 'The Changing Texture of Textiles in Tonga', with this note: 'certain types of barkcloth and mats are categorized by Tongans as *koloa,* a term translated as *(1) "wealth", (2) "possessions", (3) "what one values"'* (149), or prestigious objects (see Veys's designation, this volume). It is useful for analysts to think about the value of wealth items as a process of reinforcing, for oneself and others, just what it is that 'one values'. For Kalo, such a process is one in which women produce meaning from making, exchanging and influencing the lives of others with *koloa.* Through her bequests of wealth, Kalo intends to impart not just material value, but her entire outlook on and approach to contemporary Tongan life.

Kalo hopes her *koloa* will prove to be meaningful to the kin-group members to whom she has bequeathed them. Specifically, she hopes that her relatives will perform the meanings of *koloa* as cultural objects in the ways *she* has made them meaningful in her life and precisely *because* she has performed such value for them in her very acts of bequest. Some of these ways include using *koloa* as adornment for bodies, homes and ritual spaces; negating the relative fragility of textiles by purposefully keeping them as signs of the endurance of the kin group; employing *koloa* as a medium for compelling particular behaviours and sensibilities in others; using them to transmit efficacy from herself to others and from one generation to another; and trusting textiles to leave specific traces of herself through memories, associations, textures and smells evoked by or embedded in the *koloa.* Kalo characterises *koloa* as wealth because they afford her agency in ensuring that what she hopes for her kin-group members will indeed come true.

Wealth adorns

Koloa play a number of crucial roles in Tongan families' ritual life-stage events. Kin from both mothers' and fathers' sides gather to recognise each other's role in the celebrant's achievement of particular status. Individuals who attend are considered to be in a ritual state. They wear *koloa,* usually in the form of *ta'ovala,* over their stitched clothing to contain their *mana* and as signs of respect for those with greater *mana* than themselves (Figure 38). Women like Kalo often embellish *ta'ovala* in New Zealand (Figure 39).

Figure 38. A family dressed for a special service at church. The father and three young sons are all adorned in *ta'ovala* (waist mats)

Source. Photographed by Ping-Ann Addo, Auckland, December 2007

Figure 39. Kalo (seated at rear) and her textile group fellow work together on decorating a fine mat in her living room

Source. Photographed by Ping-Ann Addo, Auckland, August 2001

Women from a given kin group proceed into the gathering bearing fine mats and barkcloth, blankets and store-bought bedding. Sometimes they unfurl them for all to admire before they gift them, sometimes literally, at the feet of key members of a recipient's family. Finally, women will often have decorated the hall or space where the event is being held with *koloa*: barkcloth line the walls; fine mats line the floors under tables laden with Tongan food; durable pieces of *koloa* (like single-layer fine mats with brightly coloured yarn decorations) are draped over chairs where high-ranking guests like chiefly people and religious ministers will sit; and small gifts like cakes resting atop folded pieces of *koloa* are presented to certain guests (Figure 40).

David Graeber remarks on the commonality of wealth items being crucial to societal notions of value and performances of identity:

> Insofar as wealth is an object of display, it is always in some sense an adornment to the person. In countless societies the most treasured forms of wealth consist of objects of adornment in the literal sense (Graeber 1996: 5).

Figure 40. *Koloa* presented at Kalo's relative's 60th birthday celebration; note the barkcloth-covered tables at centre, fine mat-draped floor and chair at left, and cakes presented to honour guests at right

Source. Photographed by Ping-Ann Addo, Auckland, January 2001

Tongan women's textile wealth has been used to embellish people's homes, celebrations, lives and personhood, especially those of women, and they have done so for as long as Tongans can remember. *Koloa* have played a role as adornment in Tongan culture because they are things that Tongans have always used to visually announce their identity, values and sense of uniqueness and worth—ideal kinship relations, women's *mana* and women's work, mutual help and (the Kingdom of Tonga's) history. *Koloa* are thus, at a number of symbolic levels, 'privileged emblems of a group's identity' (Douaire-Marsaudon 2008: 213), embodying ideas about both cultural wealth and personal wealth. This idea that wealth can be visibly enacted as a sign of identity is no less true among Tongans in the diaspora.

Wealth endures

When I first interviewed Kalo in 2001, when she was 68 years old, she emphasised that she thought about what she could leave her daughters and grandchildren. Just as she raised her daughters, she has taught her grandchildren about their cultural responsibilities—to mind family and attend church. She said, at that time, that when she died she would want to leave them a sense of devotion to the (Methodist) church to which most of her family belongs, and 'whatever money' she had then. However, as long as I have known Kalo, cash is the resource that she is least likely to have on hand, for what little money she does have tends to be spent on buying textiles for use in religious and family functions, in addition to making donations to the church (Addo 2013: 108).

Often in Kalo's relationship to wealth, she would have very little money, but she could always fall back on traditional textile wealth if she needed to contribute to a collective family gift. Indeed, she had told me years ago that she preferred managing her relationships with *koloa*, traditional wealth, because 'cash just fell through her fingers'. Ten years after telling me she wanted to leave her children some cash, she was basically suggesting that money was neither the most important form of wealth nor the kind that had sufficient symbolic density to convey the efficacy she wanted to impart through her bequest.[4]

As long as Kalo has had *koloa* she could always keep track of her wealth and has never 'felt poor'. She chose, in this later stage of her life, to adhere to and pass down a form of wealth that could potentially endure over time: *koloa*. The endurance of *koloa* is entirely purposeful, for, like most textiles, if they are not assiduously maintained they may fade, rot, tear, be eaten (by pests) or pilfered away. As Annette Weiner states, 'Because cloth is subject to physical disintegration, keeping an old cloth despite all the ravages of time and the pressure to give it to others adds immeasurably to its value' (1989: 52). Furthermore, in families such as Kalo's, cloths are valued because they 'carry the histories of past relationships' (52), such as the relationship between Kalo and her mother.

Endurance of the physical form is a main characteristic of wealth everywhere (Sykes 2005), and there is deep meaning in the fact that wealth can potentially outlast those exchanging it at a given moment. Tongans value, source prestige from and basically have no social identity if they do not actively engage and maintain their kin ties by exchanging wealth. Thus, wealth endures so that *kāinga* may materially and symbolically endure. That is, through the particular and directed deployment of wealth, a woman further enables her kin group to endure.

---

4   With the concept of symbolic density, Weiner (1994) suggests that some objects in a system of wealth items are relatively strongly associated with their owner's or custodian's 'fame, ancestral histories, secrecy, sacredness, and aesthetic and economic values' (394); they become weighty with cultural meaning and value and, thus, tend to be kept rather than given (away) in exchange.

Wealth compels

A real turning point for the entire *kāinga* occurred when Kalo's great-niece Anita announced she was going to give birth to her first child. The announcement came just a few months before Kalo moved into 'Ana's house. To the surprise of many people in the family, Kalo gave Anita two beautiful pieces of *koloa*—a fine mat and a barkcloth—before the baby's birth, with instructions that she, in turn, gift these to the baby's father's sisters. No one in Anita's generation had received *koloa* from Kalo directly; commonly in Tongan ceremonial exchange, *koloa* is gifted to someone of significance in the celebrant's lineage—in such a case it would be to the baby's father's sister, for example—and rarely to the celebrant herself. Yet, when I asked her why she had made such a gift to her great-niece, Kalo replied, 'Because she is going to be a mother soon'. The young woman would need wealth to exchange in order to legitimate her status as a Tongan woman and, moreover, as an appropriate mother.

Later, as her time to move to 'Ana's house drew near, Kalo began giving some of her other great-nieces and her granddaughters *koloa* as well. Yet, these *koloa* were meant to constitute more than an individual bequest of wealth. These cloths were valuables that—in Kalo's aspirations—were meant to maintain the status of the family. Kalo intended for the younger women to use them in ritual presentations that they would eventually participate in, and she instructed them on appropriate occasions and ways to gift them. The great-niece who had already born her first child had done so out of wedlock. Even though she was not married to the baby boy's father, the *kāinga* was already engaged in reciprocal relations with his kin group. That they are Samoan-New Zealanders made this as appropriate as it would have been had they been Tongans; Samoan families similarly express their cultural values through exchanges of food, cash and textile. Known collectively as *fa'alavelave*, these ceremonies are similar to Tongan life-crisis ceremonies in marking ritual occasions with kin-based, public exchanges of ceremonial wealth (Gershon 2012).

When I asked Kalo why she gave *koloa* to the girls who were not yet mothers—why hadn't she waited until they had had their first children like Anita had—she replied: 'I don't want them to rush to have babies … and I might not be here when they become mothers'. With these gifts of *koloa*, Kalo meant to compel these younger women to be mothers in the same way that she had been a mother to their (biological) mothers. For the girls who were still without children, there was a deeper message:

stay on the 'straight and narrow', don't get pregnant and finish school (four of the five girls in that generation were enrolled in or have graduated from the University of Auckland).

She said what she most hoped the younger women would do with the *koloa* was '*fai fatongia*'; that is, present it ritually as gifts (literally: 'do duty'). She wished they could *make koloa*, but recognised that was an unrealistic expectation, as textile making was older women's work if it was done in diaspora at all (see Addo 2013). Thus, by passing textiles to them, Kalo was provisioning these young women to be generators of wealth in their own right. With these bequeathed wealth objects, she is compelling them to 'do duty'. In the past, I have seen Kalo work at imparting these younger women with knowledge about *koloa*—telling them how to fold and carry the things, as well as the order in which they should be laid out for presentation. They have always obeyed, encouraged by their aunts or their own mothers, and have usually done a satisfactory job. However, Kalo believes that they still require more knowledge and skill around choosing *koloa*, preparing them for gifting and gifting them in appropriate combinations at particular ceremonial occasions. Kalo intends to supply them with these skills with what remains of her life.

Wealth transmits knowledge and efficacy

Symbolically speaking, *koloa* is intimately tied to transmission of value, of knowledge and *mana* (Addo 2013; Herda 1999; Kaeppler 1999; Veys 2009; Young Leslie 2004). Meredith Filihia defines *koloa* as ancestral wealth and notes that the act of making *koloa* is itself a process of transmitting *mana* to people through things when the '*mana* of ancient women is hammered into barkcloth' (2001: 387). Kalo constitutes, therefore, a crucial link in 'an unbroken line' between generations of Tongan women: their own ancestresses and the women their daughters, granddaughters and great-nieces would grow to be (381).

In this vein, Kalo had used a bequest of *koloa* to honour her ancestors—including her own mother from whom she initially acquired her notable knowledge of *koloa*—and to foreground her own impending status as an ancestor. Kalo has provisioned her younger women relatives with the wealth they need to do her proud now and after her death. To even the most devout Christian Tongans, ancestors are ever-present family members—people to be honoured and sometimes feared. It is my contention that what Kalo was trying to do was to compel and prepare these descendants of hers so that they could fulfill *her* desired destiny *for them* as cultural actors. The wealth objects bind them in ritual obligation to her, even after her death. Yet, if these younger women are to appropriately touch others with her *mana* through these cloths, then her opportunity to train them with the knowledge and skills to channel her efficacy is *now*.

Bequeathed wealth, when passed on, conveys a sense of stability both *within* the lineage and *of* the lineage (Brenner 2006), and thus it carries with it a sense that it has always existed. I use stability in both an abstract and a literal way. In the abstract sense, valuables must contribute to a notion of identity, culture and kin group as abiding and prompting people to think or respond 'we have always done it this way'. And in the literal sense: if a valuable does not feel like it will outlast the persons exchanging it, it is unlikely to be made to retain its status as the supreme form of wealth or to be given heirloom status. These are the roles that *koloa* had always played for Kalo. Indeed, the two pieces she had retained the longest were a fine mat and a barkcloth that her mother handmade many years ago in their village in Vava'u. Kalo had taken them to Auckland in 1978 when she first moved there, and she had kept these *koloa* for many decades, folded between sheets and other *koloa* under her mattress. A few other pieces that had belonged to her mother were among the *koloa* that she passed on to her younger kinswomen. The *mana* of Kalo's mother, the maker of these particular *koloa*, was part of her legacy to give to these younger women.

Thus, bequeathed objects also index death (the giver's) and are laden with many senses of obligation. By bestowing the wealth on them *before* her death Kalo can both compel her descendants to be givers of cloth and exemplify such giving to them. The cloths themselves are direct links to Kalo. They serve as reminders of her impending death, and are embedded with her mandate for the kin group to do right by her once she has passed away. Through simply passing on the cloth, Kalo *hopefully* leaves traces of herself and her desires that have effects across many generations.

Gifted wealth leaves traces of the self

When a woman launches knowledge and *mana* into the universe through her *koloa*, she also leaves traces of herself in the very physicality of cloth, as well as in associated memory and stories. As Suzanne Brenner states in relation to the gold that Sumbanese women pass on to their descendants, such a bequest constitutes an 'object of condensed value that literally and figuratively attaches to women' (Brenner 2006: 179). Some of the important works in the anthropology of the gift focus on the inalienabilty of objects/valuables in order to think about how (cultural) identities are established and augmented through the exchange of things *as gifts* (Kuehling 2005; Mauss 1990; Munn 1992; Strathern 1990; Weiner 1992; see also Hermkens and Lepani this volume). Yet Webb Keane (2001: 73) reminds us that wealth items (whether money or exchange goods) have multiple uses and possess features of mobility and durability, allowing them to extend the agency of actors, but also making them easily detachable therefrom. This quality of detachability is essential to wealth—otherwise one could not actually exchange it for anything with anyone else—but it is not synonymous with alienability. As Weiner (1992) has argued, to give is not to alienate, but to reinforce connections through *both* giving and keeping. Even as women detach things from themselves in acts of giving, they create attachments to, or between, others. That which is kept purposefully is retained on behalf of lineages, communities and nations, for the longevity of their intertwined histories. Remember that Kalo kept *koloa* that her own mother had made *in Tonga*, specifically to be used as a wrapping for her corpse or coffin at her own death. Thus, intergenerational attachment and connection across space remain sources of value in women's lives.

Since these objects are acquired as gifts, they are also accompanied by obligations. While Kalo's provision of *koloa*, and her modelling of the actions around ceremonial gifting are only suggestions as to what she would hope for, they are bound up with the honour of the family. So rather than doing the work of arranging practically all aspects of the ceremonial gifting of *koloa*, Kalo has set up a situation in which younger members of her family would have to do right by her (even after her death) by showing their Tonganness with these *koloa*. Not only would they have to get involved in the intricacies of *koloa*—how to store and differentiate different pieces of the textiles, how to care for them, and how to match the quality of a piece appropriately to a specific celebratory event—they would have to actually gift the cloths. This is what she claims she explained to her great-niece when instructing the younger woman on how to prepare *koloa* for gifting at her baby boy's christening.

When a woman specifically leaves cloths with younger women—hand-picking each cloth for a specific person to receive, with the intent that the recipient uses these wealth items for further exchange—she is actually projecting her own desires and intents vis-à-vis a wider community.

My contention is that Kalo is clearly making claims on the resources, emotions and intentions of future generations of her family by locating *herself* as a key individual 'within [the] social networks' that will 'span generations' of their *kāinga* (Young Leslie 1999: 259). She further indexes that although the specific *koloa* are no longer in her immediate possession and thus detached from her (see Keane 2001: 73), they remain identified with her. As such, these *koloa* are inalienable—at least in the younger women's mental, emotional and cultural associations. Thus Kalo will have agency after her death. As an ancestor, she will act *through others*, and her hope is that these young women in her kin group will become the primary enactors of her lifelong womanly compulsion to gift *koloa*.

Conclusion

In this chapter, I have looked at a life of gift prestation as well as at how the specific hopes of one elderly woman relate to the provisioning of her female kin-group members with women's wealth. Kalo's new role of provisioning and instructing younger women in her family to be able to maintain the family identity through gifting is a crucial part of who she has become towards the end of her life. I began with Kalo's life story in order to analyse the life course as a series of transitions between phases or stages in the ontogeny of a kin group. In so doing, I have been able to examine how and why a person may, over the course of her life, express the values embodied in textile wealth in highly contextualised yet enduring ways. There is no irony in this statement: *koloa* have divergent forms and meanings and, like all objects that serve as valuables, they have efficacy through humans' evolving relations with one another.

Writing at the intersection of *kāinga* relations, gender and life course, I have argued that how women who gift wealth objects imbue them with efficacy and meaning can change over the givers' life course, based on their specific hopes for the recipient's future life course. People entrust that wealth items will do many things, such as materialise the idea that a kin group will endure, transmit efficacy, compel action and ultimately leave traces of the self. Thus, wealth can indeed have powerful effects on *kāinga* members' identities and the relationships between them. However, we must understand the specific ways in which moments in the life course of people who give and receive wealth intersect in order to ascertain specific meanings and influential effects of wealth in moulding persons. Using the case study of a family I know well, I have focused on how an ageing woman uses *koloa* to guide her descendants, rather than on how she uses them to augment the reputation of her wider *kāinga*, as she would do when she exchanges textiles with members of another kin group. Thus, I have also been able to examine exchange as a phenomenon that is as formative of how individuals relate *within a kāinga* as it is of the family's status and reputation, which is normally based on exchange between *kāinga*.

Descendants and textiles are among a woman's *koloa*, or 'what one values'. Since Kalo will one day die and leave behind both her descendants and her *koloa*, I have considered the ways that she connects these categories of valued entities together *in her own mind* based on the kinds of cultural lives she hopes her descendants will embrace. Looking at how Kalo prepares her kinswomen for a future she hopes will be filled with *koloa* exchange shifts the focus on socialisation away from life stages and rights-of-passage rituals to less temporally bounded, everyday relationships that women like Kalo have been cultivating with others. Over the typical Tongan life course, a person becomes connected cosmologically, politically, socially, religiously and culturally to others *through* the exchange of wealth, such that one commoner woman's life story has much to teach us about why and how people matter to each other, rather than why objects matter in themselves.

References

Addo, Ping-Ann. 2013. *Creating a Nation with Cloth: Women, Wealth, and Tradition in the Tongan Diaspora*. Volume. 4. ASAO Studies in Pacific Anthropology. New York, Oxford: Berghahn.

Albert, Steven M. and Maria G. Cattell. 1994. *Old Age in Global Perspective: Cross Cultural and Cross National Perspectives*. New York: G.K. Hall & Co.

Berman, Tressa. 2003. *Circle of Goods: Women, Work, and Welfare in a Reservation Community*. Albany: State University of New York Press.

Brenner, Suzanne April. 2006. *The Domestication of Desire: Women, Wealth, and Modernity in Java*. Princeton: Princeton University Press.

Counts, Dorothy Ayers and David R. Counts. 1985. 'Introduction: Linking Concepts, Aging and Gender, Aging and Death'. In *Aging and Its Transformations: Moving Toward Death in Pacific Societies*, ed. Dorothy Ayres Counts and David R. Counts, pp. 1–24. Pittsburgh: University of Pittsburgh.

Douaire-Marsaudon, Françoise. 2008. 'Food and Wealth: Ceremonial Objects as Signs of Identity in Tonga and in Wallis'. In *The Changing South Pacific. Identities and Transformations*, ed. Serge Tcherkézoff and Françoise Douaire-Marsaudon, pp. 207–229. Canberra: ANU E Press. Online: press-files.anu.edu.au/downloads/press/p90711/pdf/ch10.pdf (accessed 18 February 2017).

Elder, G.H. Jr. 2001. 'Life Course: Sociological Perspectives'. In *International Encyclopedia of the Social and Behavioral Sciences*, pp. 8817–8821. Oxford: Pergamon.

Fanua, Tupo Posesi. 1996. *Mālō Tupou: An Oral History* (as told to Lois Wimberg Webster). Auckland: Pasifika Press.

Filihia, Meredith. 2001. 'Men are from Maama, Women are from *Pulotu*: Female Status in Tongan Society'. *Journal of Polynesian Society* 110(4): 377–390.

Gershon, Ilana. 2012. *No Family is an Island: Cultural Expertise among Samoans in Diaspora*. Ithaca, NY: Cornell University Press.

Graeber, David. 1996. 'Beads and Money: Notes towards a Theory of Wealth and Power'. *American Ethnologist* 23(1): 4–24. DOI: 10.1525/ae.1996.23.1.02a00010.

———. 2001. *Toward an Anthropological Theory of Value: The False Coin of Our Own Dreams*. New York: Palgrave.

Herda, Phyllis S. 1999. 'The Changing Texture of Textiles in Tonga'. *Journal of the Polynesian Society* 108(2): 149–167.

James, Kerry. 1997. 'Reading the Leaves: The Role of Tongan Women's Traditional Wealth and Other "Contraflows" in the Processes of Modern Migration and Remittance'. *Pacific Studies* 20(1): 1–27.

Johnson-Hanks, Jennifer. 2002. 'The Limits of Life Stages in Ethnography: Toward a Theory of Vital Conjunctures'. *American Anthropologist* 104(3): 865–880. DOI: 10.1525/aa.2002.104.3.865.

Kaeppler, Adrienne L. 1999. 'Kie Hingoa: Mats of Power, Rank, Prestige and History'. *Journal of the Polynesian Society* 108(2): 168–231.

Keane, Webb. 2001. 'Money is No Object: Materiality, Desire, and Modernity in an Indonesian Society'. In *The Empire of Things: Regimes of Value and Material Culture*, ed. Fred R. Myers, pp. 65–90. Santa Fe, NM: School of American Research Press.

Kuehling, Suzanne. 2005. *Dobu: The Ethics of Exchange on a Massim Island, Papua New Guinea*. Honolulu: University of Hawai'i Press.

Mauss, Marcel. 1990. *The Gift: The Form and Reason for Exchange in Archaic Societies*. London and New York: Routledge Classics. Original edition, *Essai sur le don*, first published 1950 by Presses Universitaires de France en *Sociologie et Anthropologie*.

Munn, Nancy. 1992 [1986]. *The Fame of Gawa: A Symbolic Study of Value Transformation in a Massim Society*. Durham, NC: Duke University Press.

Strathern, Marilyn. 1990 [1988]. *The Gender of the Gift: Problems with Women and Problems with Society in Melanesia*. Berkeley: University of California Press.

Sykes, Karen Margaret. 2005. *Arguing with Anthropology: An Introduction to Critical Theories of the Gift*. London: Routledge.

Veys, Fanny Wonu. 2009. 'Materialising the King: The Royal Funeral of King Taufa'ahau Tupou IV of Tonga'. *The Australian Journal of Anthropology* 20: 131–149. DOI: 10.1111/j.1757-6547.2009. 00007.x.

Weiner, Annette B. 1989. 'Why Cloth? Wealth, Gender and Power in Oceania'. In *Cloth and Human Experience*, ed. Annette B. Weiner and J. Schneider, pp. 33–72. Washington DC: Smithsonian Institution Press.

——. 1992. *Inalienable Possessions: The Paradox of Keeping-While-Giving*. Berkeley, CA: University of California Press.

——. 1994. 'Cultural Difference and the Density of Objects'. *American Ethnologist* 21(2): 391–403. DOI: 10.1525/ae.1994.21.2.02a00090.

Young Leslie, Heather. 1999. 'Tradition, Textiles and Maternal Obligation in the Kingdom of Tonga'. PhD thesis. Toronto: York University.

———. 2004. 'Pushing Children Up: Maternal Obligation, Modernity, and Medicine in the Tongan Ethnoscape'. In *Globalization and Culture Change in the Pacific Islands*, ed. Victoria Lockwood, pp. 390–413. Upper Saddle River, NJ: Prentice Hall.

8

Cook Islands *Tivaivai* and the Haircutting Ceremony in Auckland: Ritual Action, Money and the Parameters of Value

Jane Horan

Introduction

The large cavernous Ātiu hall in Mangere—the community focus of the Cook Islands Ātiuan community in Auckland where most Cook Islanders live[1]—was already packed with 500 people or more when I arrived late for the haircutting (*pākoti'anga 'o'ora*) of Māmā Lucy's nephew. I was shown to a seat at the front of the hall and felt the weight of the large crowd behind me. Everyone was seated at trestle tables facing towards the stage where the boy, who was no more than seven or eight,[2] sat on a wide, deep

---

1   The island of Ātiu is one of 15 islands in the Cook Islands archipelago, but some 61,839 Cook Islanders live in New Zealand (Statistics New Zealand 2013), and less than 18,000 (Ministry of Finance and Economic Management 2017) reside in the island homelands. Of these, at least half live in Auckland. Cook Islanders in New Zealand 'make place' by the establishment of halls like the Ātiu Hall, and there is also a Pukapuka Hall, Manihiki Hall, as well as a Cook Islands Hall in South Auckland. These are all used extensively by the various island communities to stage ceremonial economy events.

2   The age of the boy having his hair ritually cut varies. Of the haircuttings I attended, three were for younger boys aged around seven or eight, which seems to be the average age, although I attended another haircutting that was for an older youth of 18. I heard about at least one other haircutting that was for a 21-year-old, which was combined with his 21st birthday celebrations and was staged

armchair with rolled arms, which had been covered by a finely stitched *tivaivai taorei*, an 'unquilted quilt' in the piecework style.[3] Such textiles, made for the most part by women, are considered the most elite valuables in the Cook Islands ceremonial economy (Horan 2011, 2012, 2013). The haircutting is the Cook Islands male rite-of-passage ceremony that transitions a 'boy to man',[4] and like other ceremonial economy events, such as weddings, funerals, public presentations to ministers and other dignitaries, *tivaivai* feature significantly and ostentatiously as the gift and/ or as decoration and adornment of people and ritual contexts.

The boy looked small and bewildered. His hair was braided into about 150 single locks each tied with a royal blue or a white ribbon, and it was these that were about to be ritually cut from his head as part of his haircutting. What these locks of hair were to be exchanged for, what constituted the other aspect of the rite of passage aside from the physical cutting of his hair, and defined the very specific form of adulthood that the boy was entering, were envelopes that boldly, explicitly bore the name of the giver—and contained a sum of money. The boy was about to be gifted money 'wrapped' in envelopes, but what he and his kin group were maintaining or acquiring were a set of obligations to reciprocate in kind as a form of connection. The focus on connection is countenanced,

---

as a large, prestigious event in the National Auditorium in Avarua in Rarotonga. Loomis (1983: 227) notes that for those who subscribe to the precontact origins of the rite, most assert that the 'traditional' age of the boy was generally older, over 20.

3   There are three main types of *tivaivai*: *tivaivai taorei*, which is made in the patchwork style; *tivaivai tātaura*, which feature several colours of appliquéd fabric with embroidery embellishment; and *tivaivai manu*, the simplest form, which consists of a pattern cut from one piece of fabric that is then appliquéd to a base fabric.

4   There is some debate about how traditional the haircutting ceremony actually is, but most agree that it is more common now than it used to be, especially in New Zealand (Ama 2003). Some of the people I spoke to about haircuttings said that it was a tradition that dated from the time before the missionaries came. However, others have scoffed at this and declared that it was a convention introduced by the missionaries. One woman told me 'it's a new thing'. Some think that the haircutting ceremony is just for title holders, others for the oldest son only of a nuclear family. Antony Hooper indicated that he neither saw nor was told about haircutting ceremonies amongst the Auckland Cook Islander population at the time of his research (late 1950s), and that it was his opinion that the current haircutting ceremony was essentially a copy of the Niuean event (personal correspondence cited in Loomis 1983: 230). In his own writing, Hooper asserts that it was the 21st celebration that was the key *kōpū tangata* (extended kin) event of an individual's life (1961: 172) for both males and females. Now, because young women have never had a rite-of-passage celebration like the haircutting, 21st birthday celebrations are used to mark a more contemporary female transition, as are the presentation of *tivaivai* during an *'o'ora* at the conclusion of a wedding ceremony. A wedding *'o'ora* used to done by the bride and her mother to present *tivaivai* and other household textiles to the new husband/son-in-law, but this is changing. Because fewer women make *tivaivai* now, the wedding *'o'ora* has evolved into a medium to pass on *tivaivai* to 'worthy' daughters, and to demonstrate the quality of the mother–daughter relationship (Horan 2012).

for the most part, by nonagonistic gifting. But the staging of the ritual arena—including the strategic use of specific *tivaivai* made by his female relatives, and other textiles in what constitutes a hierarchy of textiles—was especially efficacious and, I argue, integral to both the rite-of-passage process *and* the exchange of valuables because *tivaivai* effectively dignify the gifting of money in the service of Cook Islands kinship obligations and values.

The small boy sat wide-eyed on the chair, looking out over the assembled crowd of his extended family and invited guests, like me. From where I sat, the boy appeared at the centre of a profusion of textiles: propped either side of him, nestling him into the depths of the chair were cushions with blowsheet covers.[5] Another *tivaivai*, in the *manu* style was draped around his legs. The stage area surrounds and the set of tables in front of the stage (for the honoured child, his friends and close family during the feasting part of the haircutting) were all festooned with blowsheets. The front face of the stage was also covered with blowsheets and propped along the edge of the stage, placed side by side, was a row of cushions with blowsheet covers edged with lace. On the floor, where the blowsheet-covered tables were placed, were plastic fibre mats, and in front of the children's main table was a chair draped with a *tivaivai* that was ready for the *'o'ora*, a subsequent gifting event that was to come, where the boy was to be gifted *tivaivai*, as well as other textiles and household items. The overall effect of the ritual scene was of wrapped containment via a profusion of ranked textiles with the neophyte at the centre. It seemed to me that the small boy was effectively wrapped in concentric layers of cloth made by his female relatives. The layers of textiles radiated out from him: *tivaivai*, as the most elite textile, wrapped him at the centre; lesser textiles efficaciously wrapped the ritual arena and the honoured guests who sat in the front part of the hall.

---

5   Blowsheets are made by laying out plain cotton sheeting on the ground. Stencils of various motifs like flowers, leaves, birds, bunches of grapes, etc. are arrayed on the sheet in a decorative pattern. Then women take pots of paint, suck paint up into straws, and then literally blow it over the stencils. Several colours of paint are used, and the process done enough times so that once the stencils are removed, the pattern is revealed by the negative spaces. To make the most of the paint used, women also lay another cotton sheet over the paint covered stencils to imprint the stencil patterns to create a positive image on the other sheet. Blowsheets have the advantage of being quick and cheap to produce. On one particular day, I watched Māmā Lucy and other women from the Enuamanu Va'ine tini (*tivaivai*-making group) produce upwards of 100 blowsheets, some of these featured in the haircutting detailed in this chapter.

This textile-adorned ritual context was to facilitate the transition the boy was making into a Cook Islanders' version of manhood. This public haircutting ritual was about conjoinment and the setting up for the boy of 'a particular future through exchange relationships' (Gershon 2007: 484) because a Cook Islands adult is one who is enmeshed in such a matrix of obligations. But as David Graeber (2001: 167) notes:

> One cannot hope to understand circulation of valuables in a 'gift economy' ... without first taking into account more fundamental processes by which the human person is created and dissolved. And then when such general principles as action and reflection, or the movement between abstract potential and concrete form do appear—which they generally do—these too are always aspects of persons before they are aspects of things.

The making and use of a *tivaivai* as 'women's wealth' is really about 'how forms of value emerge to regulate a process which is ultimately about the creation of people' (Graeber 2001: 142). According to Terence Turner (2012: 501), values are what drive 'and constitute the most general purpose of social action and the most important qualities of personal identity'. For Cook Islanders, such values are about kinship and the performance of *aro'a* (glossed as love, see below). These values dramatically inform the social activities and goals of most Cook Islanders in New Zealand, as well as elsewhere, to one degree or another, including the ritual action inherent in the haircutting ceremony, where, as with other ceremonial economy events, those values are materialised—literally and figuratively— by *tivaivai*.

This chapter is about the relationship between *tivaivai* made as a form of 'women's valuable' to be given as the gift and used as adornment of people and ceremonial venues, *and* the movement of money in the haircutting. I cast this relationship in the broader context of value (Turner 2006a, 2006b, 2008) as a structural component of the way Cook Islanders 'create their universe', to paraphrase Graeber (2013), and the way values are a refraction of value, while valuables are the materialisation of values. I argue that how and why *tivaivai* are in the very specific category of 'things that matter' (Miller 1998) is because they operate in ritual contexts as semiotic media of value (Turner 2008). The haircutting ceremony comprises an array of exchanges of material valuables that underscore the circulation of social values (Fajans 1993). In particular, the ritual complex 'fronted' by *tivaivai* is about highlighting, maintaining and creating new relationships for the neophyte as an emerging man and eventual husband and father, as well as signifying that the child is becoming a fully fledged adult member of his kin group. But it is also about the display of femaleness in the Cook Islands, and *aro'a* and the performance of *tivaivai* in particular as valuables, as well as the public gifting of money wrapped in envelopes. However, the fact that the haircutting is being elaborated and ritual decoration with *tivaivai* in particular is intensifying, as the gifting of money is becoming more judicious is, I argue, in response to the broader capitalist context that Cook Islanders live in. The relationship among value, values and valuables is being ameliorated and elaborated for contemporary Cook Islanders such as Māmā Lucy, her nephew and their wider extended family. These layers are what this chapter is about.

The ritual action at Māmā Lucy's nephew's haircutting

As I took my designated seat towards the front of the hall for the haircutting, Māmā Vero, the most genealogically senior woman in the Auckland Ātiu community, had already begun to recite the boy's genealogy for all to hear. She stood in front of the crowd with a microphone in hand addressing the large audience. As the holder of the genealogies, Māmā Vero spoke as one who was used to commanding a room. An imposing woman, she was resplendent in a green-and-white *pāreu* fabric *mu'umu'u*, her long white-grey hair was plaited in a single braid, and she wore a finely worked pandanus hat. Her attire adorned her as a woman of substance and *mana* (power, prestige). As she spoke, her skill as an orator was apparent. Her rapid Ātiuan was lost upon me but she used changes in tone, pauses and gestures to tell the story and command the attention of the crowd in a way that emanated *mana*. She had a direct, authoritative way about her that made everybody listen as she systematically linked virtually all of the people in the audience to the boy sitting on the stage: by birth, marriage and adoption, back through time to the islands and then to New Zealand. The timbre of her voice rose and fell as she told the history of the movement of kin backwards and forwards between the islands in the Cooks and beyond. The boy's place of birth, his *'enua'ānau*, was New Zealand, but his *ipukarea*, his homeland and ancestral home, was Ātiu and the other islands to which he and his family were connected. Everyone in the room was drawn together, all heard, the older ones remembered and the younger ones learned. Māmā Vero was mesmerising and it seemed to me that as she spoke, she literally talked the ritual into being (Keane 2001: 74). As she related the knowledge of where the little boy and the greater part of the audience belonged, this too was wrapped in the worked-upon array of textiles that adorned the hall and the boy. That wrapping with textiles and Māmā Vero's reciting of the genealogy set the ritual context for the exchanges that were about to happen, but also effectively 'circulated' values to do with the importance of kinship.

After the recitation of the genealogy, it was time to cut the locks of hair from the child's head. The Master of Ceremonies (MC) instructed the most senior people to file up onto the stage first. All the guests had been allocated a ranking number, which designated their order (Loomis 1983: 228; Ama 2003: 121). The most elite guests, followed by close family members, filed up first. Several of these initial people, who were probably closer family members, adorned the boy with neck garlands ('ei) made from artificial flowers, lollies, shells, ribbons and cash money notes. They would then cut their lock of hair from the child's head. There was at least one NZ$100 note, multiple NZ$20 and a number of NZ$10 and NZ$5 notes, totalling around NZ$250. The boy was literally adorned and wrapped with various valuables—money and *tivaivai*.

After elite guests and close family, the remainder of the audience was sequentially invited to queue up in ranked order to take their turn on the stage and cut a lock of hair. Ushers worked from the front of the hall to the back, table by table, instructing the representatives of groups to line up. As these people filed up and took their turn on the stage to cut a lock of hair, I watched as each group handed an envelope that contained money to one or other of the parents who were attending their son. The envelope was tucked down beside the boy, and then the giver was handed a beribboned pair of scissors by one of the boy's parents and instructed by the other to cut a given lock of hair. Eventually, people at the section of tables where I was seated were ushered into the queue. As I filed up onto the stage and looked out over the large crowd, I was confronted by the noise and the expanse of people, and I wondered at the child's strained composure in the face of such public display. The three women in front of me were from a family of large Cook Islands women; they were wearing beautiful fragrant 'ei katu (head garlands) and their thick long black hair flowed down their backs. Two of these women were holding store-bought duvets in plastic packaging, which they intended to gift—in full view of the crowd—before cutting their lock of hair, thereby gaining maximum prestige (Loomis 1983: 220). They handed the textiles to Māmā Lucy, who was helping out on stage. The third woman had an envelope in her hand, which I noticed had her family's name on it; she handed this to the boy's mother and then cut her lock of hair. According to one of my informants, the giving of envelope-wrapped money and a gift, often a textile like a duvet, if not a *tivaivai*, is up to the individual. She said kin closest to the child usually give both, commensurate with their greater love for the boy and to signal their willingness to be a continuing part of his life in the future. She noted that 'sometimes you give money and sometimes you give money and a gift, it depends on your connection' (personal communication, Eva William, Auckland, 2011). But the money is always given in an envelope, so the name of the giver can be emblazoned on the front.

As I took my turn to cut the child's hair, I handed my envelope to the boy's mother; she placed the envelope in beside her son amid the growing pile of named envelopes. The boy's father handed me the scissors and instructed me where to cut a lock of hair between the ribbon and the boy's scalp. The child was still as my scissors bit into his hair, severing another lock from his head. I looked down at him, swaddled as he was in the profusion of textiles, and I was struck by the very public and drawn-out nature of the process; the drama of the ritual as each piece of hair was seemingly exchanged for envelope-wrapped money. I took my lock of hair and walked to the other side of the stage. I passed Māmā Lucy, who smiled at me as she ordered the growing pile of duvets and other textiles and gifts that were amassing at the side of the stage. I returned to my seat and watched the rest of the crowd file up, give their envelopes and cut off their lock of hair. As the ritual cutting of the hair proceeded, the music troupe behind the boy on the stage played popular Cook Islands songs. There was lots of noise as people chatted and laughed and the atmosphere was festive. Some of the older women danced to the music as they stood in line, waiting to cut their lock of hair. The process took about 45 minutes because of the large number of people.

When all the braided locks had been cut from the little boy's head, a relative who was adept at actually trimming hair gave the boy his first haircut and styled the unevenly cut hair in front of the crowd. Māmā Lucy and his parents then took the young boy to the back area behind the stage, out of view of the crowd. The boy and his parents effectively transitioned through an 'off stage' (Goffman 1959) moment, to emerge transformed. His brief disappearance was important because the transition he was making was punctuated with a full change for him and his parents into clothing of the same fabric. When all three emerged from the back stage area, the boy and his father now wore green-and-yellow hibiscus *pāreu* fabric shirts and dark trousers, and his mother had changed into a dress in the same fabric. The boy wore the money *'ei* around his neck and he wore a plaited pandanus hat with a garland of flowers on it over his newly cut hair. The change of clothing, of new textile wrappings in other words, heralded and underlined the transformation the boy had just made, as his hair was cut and he was gifted with what amounted to a sum in the vicinity of NZ$6,000–$8,000 as an education fund for his future.

The boy's parents lead him out into the hall area to loud and enthusiastic cheers from the crowd. As he came to stand in front of all the people, flanked by his parents, the young boy hung his head. He was trembling a little; he must have been finally overwhelmed by the crowd, the noise and the attention because he had started to cry. His mother coaxed and comforted him as he was paraded around the hall. Eventually, he was seated on the *tivaivai*-adorned chair that was placed in front of the head table at the front of the stage ready for the subsequent *'o'ora*, and eventually the feast. He was rapidly becoming a very specific type of man.

Tivaivai, value and values

The ritual action of a haircutting ceremony, like that of Māmā Lucy's nephew's, is effectively a performance of Cook Islands values, via the use of valuables in exchange and adornment, prescribed by the structural parameters of value as perceived by Cook Islanders. Such core values for Cook Islanders are orientated to varying degrees by two multifaceted concepts: kinship and *aro'a*. Contained in the very definitions of these concepts are the means and methods for *how* people as Cook Islanders are connected to one another, as well as *how* to actually act appropriately and exist in the world. These concepts also define what is considered right generally and, more specifically, how Cook Islanders honour one another publicly. To use Turner's (2006b: 1) terminology, kinship is 'the main locus of the value relation and serve[s] as the source of the principal forms of social value', whereby the main modus operandi is *aro'a*. Herein lies the mode of belonging, of acting appropriately, of accessing prestige as mana, and garnering power and gain, which all require traffic in value, the adherence to values and the wielding of valuables.

The Cook Islands kinship system links people to the land and to one another through membership via belonging, configured through cognatically reckoned extended family groups (Rasmussen 1995; Crocombe 1964). For Cook Islanders in New Zealand in particular, kinship links 'do not exist a priori' (Loomis 1983: 223). They need to be actualised via social interactions—for the most part via the public realm of the Cook Islands ceremonial economy—whereby all kin relationships are effectively a social construct that is either reproduced or neglected on a daily basis and 'dramatized in ritual' (1983: 223) in contexts like Māmā Lucy's nephew's haircutting ceremony. Connections forged via the gifting and use of *tivaivai* and other valuables 'define the person as a composite of relationships and features shared with others' (Gudeman 2008: 29). During kinship events, ceremonial processes turn the 'vast array of potential social relationships encoded in a person's or persons' kinship relationships into actual linkages traced and traceable ... by the flow of material wealth' (Evans 2001: 134). Those kinship linkages are maintained, underlined or manifested by the act *of* exchange because people 'do' kinship by the performance of *aro'a*. However, ultimately, they are actualised by the circulation of value and the performance of values that are created by the ritual, and materialised by the use of *tivaivai* in particular.

The word *aro'a* is an extremely complex term. The word is glossed as love but, linguistically, the notion of loving and showing love is contiguous with gifting as well as modes of decorum. From the dictionary, the word *aro'a* means:

1. greet, welcome, salute, offer good wishes to (especially to guests on arrival or departure)
2. to welcome with a gift, to present somebody with something (including publicly)
3. to forgive, have pity on
4. kindness, sympathy, sorrow, love as in divine love or loving kindness (Buse and Taringa 1995: 76).

Expressing *aro'a* is about actions rather than just words. To gift is to show *aro'a*, to be loving towards a child is to show *aro'a*, to extend hospitality to kin or others is to show *aro'a*. To wrap a child at his haircutting ceremony in *tivaivai* demonstrates the quality of *aro'a* in which he is held by his mother and/or his female relatives and wider kin group: it shows *how much* he is loved and *to whom* he belongs, and *how* he is cherished. To gift money to the neophyte is to acknowledge, support and express the desire to be connected to the individual and their kin group on display—but this is signalled as much by the amount of money in the envelope as by the name of the person/family group on the outside. These processes are all dignified by *tivaivai* as valuables, because the textiles in turn are ultimately the materialisation of values and the refraction of the structural parameters of value.

Aro'a is expressed and shown by gifting, but the obligation created by such action is what conjoins people in the Maussian sense (Mauss 1990: 5; Alexeyeff 2004: 70). In Kalissa Alexeyeff's (2004) analysis of the gifting of food done by the woman with whom she lived in the Cook Islands, she noted that the woman gifted to her relatives to:

> demonstrate her attachment to them and to incur obligation. This system of exchange was a central element of her understanding of relationships; goods and services are obtained primarily through gift exchange with relations and friends not by direct monetary payment. In this system, money could be given as a present, but it could not be given as a direct payment (2004: 74).

Alexeyeff was really writing about how Cook Islanders are conjoined. Her paper on food exchanges (2004) describes the food-giving part of a much bigger system of exchanges that interfaces with all aspects of Cook Islanders' lives; namely, the ceremonial economy that operates according to Cook Islands values via the exchange of valuables in an expanded notion of economy. Here, food is one of a number of valuables exchanged in this system; cash money and envelope-wrapped money are others, as are lesser textiles, the performance of dancing and locks of hair. However, overall, the most elite valuable is *tivaivai*. These effectively dignify the whole system because *tivaivai* are the valuables that express the most profound and closest of bonds in the domestic sphere. This mode is writ large in the public sphere (Graeber 2001: 73; 2013; Turner 2006b: 20) by the performance of the use and/or gifting of *tivaivai* in an ostentatiously public way, along with the public gifting of envelope-wrapped money.

Tivaivai and money—in specific ways—are objects that are turned into signs of invisible values. As a semiotic media of value, *tivaivai* are indexical symbols of the material activity that they mediate (Turner 2008); in doing so, *tivaivai* become seemingly able to dignify the gifting of money as an expression of *aro'a*. But, in effect, *tivaivai* are fetishised as the source of value because they materialise values as per the broader structural parameters of value. The combination of the textile decorations, the rhetoric of the genealogy, and the whole orchestrated ritual process that created a 'high formality of exchange', helped to:

> separate signification and utility, emphasising the semiotic character of objects that also bear use and market value … [whereby] such formality is part of the ongoing work effort it takes to keep gift and commodity distinct (Keane 2001: 73–74).

This formality was able to bring about the distinction between mere money and envelope-wrapped money because it referenced the specific parameters of value. The oratory, and the assiduous attention to the selection of specific textiles in wrapping and decoration, did 'work' in Webb Keane's sense. However, more fundamentally, they were about the circulation of value, the signalling of values, the materialisation of these as valuables and the evoking of the hierarchy of valuables.

Alfred Gell (1998) generally and Susanne Küchler (Küchler and Eimke 2009) specifically attribute agency to indexical qualities of the object and *tivaivai* respectively, in effect fetishising the source of value and agency. Whereas Turner (2006b, 2008) construes agency as emanating from the dynamic among value, values and valuables, which are the structural parameters of value within a given cultural group. Value is expressed as values, which are materialised in specific ways as valuables. Here, ideas of agency, the performance of actions and social consciousness are integrated with social organisation (Turner 2008: 43). This is what is happening when a child is wrapped in *tivaivai* at his haircutting ceremony.

Tivaivai as valuables and the materialisation of values

Tivaivai are a legacy of sorts of the colonisation of the Cook Islands, which began in 1821 with the arrival of the missionaries. Before *tivaivai* became the cloth of ceremony and prestige in the Cook Islands, woven mats and tapa cloth were used for ritual. These, made for the most part by women, had the power to sanctify by the process of physically wrapping (Kaeppler 2007; Sissons 2007). The arrival of the missionaries was the beginning of a process that changed the social nexus and, by the late 1800s, *tivaivai* were being valued, and were more than likely beginning to eclipse indigenous textiles, as the cloth of ceremony and ritual (Herda 2010, 2011). Effectively, the process of the missionary conversion of Cook Islanders was mirrored in the conversion of their textile system from that made from locally grown fibres into the cloth fabric of *tivaivai* (Thomas 2000: 211). But how this happened, I argue, was derived from changes taking place in the parameters of value and values, which, in turn, changed what were considered 'valuables'.

The changing social nexus, including the emergence of *tivaivai*, was powered by dual processes: a local response to the regional changes that were sweeping eastern Polynesia through the 1800s and early 1900s (Sissons 2007, 2008), and internal power machinations coupled with the manifestation of missionary agendas in the Cook Islands. These included a particular version of the accompanying cult of domesticity where the teaching of sewing was an important missionary-led process, because sewing was seen as a way to control hands and bodies (Eves 1996; Weber 2009). Hence, missionary zeal and evangelism were not confined to the saving of souls (Colchester 2003; Comaroff and Comaroff 1992; Douglas 1999; Eves 1996; Jolly and Macintyre 1989). Rather, the conversion process was concerned with 'bringing the wider pattern of social life into some sort of conformity with English Christian ideas of marriage and familial life' (Thomas 2000: 211). The social habits that ordered work, how people lived and with whom, gender roles along with clothing, cloth and the interiors of houses were converted as well (203). What was ultimately changing was the social nexus (Küchler and Eimke 2009; Sissons 2007), but what those changes were amounted to changes in the general parameters of value, and specifically to changes in the way kinship and *aro'a* as values were enacted and materialised as valuables. The subsequent inclusion of money in ceremonial gifting in a way that is subsumed below this performance of values in contemporary ceremonial contexts like Māmā Lucy's nephew's haircutting is a continuation and elaboration of this changing social nexus.

Tivaivai and matching pillowcases were initially made as decorations for the bed, which was the main piece of furniture in the home. As *tivaivai* have come to be fetishised as the paramount form of wealth in the Cook Islands ceremonial economy, they are concomitantly models of and models for femaleness, progeniture and kinship. Throughout the course of my research, time and time again, Cook Islands women told me 'you are not a woman without *tivaivai*'. What 'woman' means here has three facets to it: women as females, women as mothers (and/or grandmothers, and/or aunties) and women as Cook Islanders. The making and/or gifting of *tivaivai* is considered the ultimate expression of femaleness, of being a woman as an individual but also as part of how to publicly (for the most part) do relationships (Weiner 1976: 8). Women gift *tivaivai* to maintain, underline or create, as well as display, key relationships in their lives—of a son or nephew at his haircutting ceremony for example. But, in doing so, the making and/or use as decoration as well as the gifting of *tivaivai* effectively delineates a Cook Islands woman's essential muliebrity. At the same time, the use of *tivaivai* affects the wider assembled kin network at an event like a haircutting, whilst publicly defining who the emerging man is as an individual and as a member of a kin group. *Tivaivai*, as semiotic media of value, work on multiple levels, but always as refractions and materialisations of values and the broader structural parameters of value.

For older Cook Islands women, femaleness and womanliness have to do with mothering in particular ways: giving birth to and/or adopting children and raising them; dressing, behaving, carrying themselves in ways that show decorum and poise; being home makers and keeping house in a way that involves having *tivaivai*, in particular, with which to adorn their homes; and having the ability to sew *tivaivai* and being seen to do so. All of this has a public aspect to it which is very important. This muliebrity is performed when a woman gifts and/or uses her *tivaivai* as decoration and to adorn specific individuals at public ceremonial events. Most older women embody this ideology, and younger women, particularly those born and bred in the diaspora, have a different, ameliorated or abridged version. But regardless of the age of a woman or where she lives, *who* a woman is as a Cook Islander and mother, grandmother, auntie, extended kin, wife, is publicly displayed and broadcast when she gifts and/or uses *tivaivai*. In the process, for women as individuals or as groups of Cook Islands women, culturally sanctioned parameters of prestige as mana are created, because the making and/or use of *tivaivai* is the axis of and access to prestige. What is also circulated when *tivaivai* are used to adorn and wrap people and venues is a sense of what is symbolically essential about being a Cook Islander. The way *tivaivai* manifests, performs and signifies womanliness and mothering as the most important valuable interfaces with and underlines core values of the importance of kinship and the notion of *aro'a* as a mode of action for Cook Islanders.

Rites of passage like the haircutting event are 'inevitably moments of teaching, when the society seeks to make the individual most fully its own, weaving group values and understandings into the private psyche so that internally provided individual motivations replaces external controls' (Myerhoff 1982: 112). This was the case for the initiate as Māmā Vero rousingly recited his genealogy, but a comparable process was happening for the audience too. They were reminded to whom, how and where they belonged, whereby part of the 'ideological and dramaturgical "work" of the haircutting' (Loomis 1983: 230) is to galvanise and rouse kin to actively belong to the *kōpū tangata* (extended family). This, in turn, provides the appropriate ritual context to facilitate the gifting of money, which has become the most pragmatic way of being actively family, and showing and doing *aro'a*. Both these have added impetus in the diasporic context.

To have the boy sitting on a *tivaivai taorei* with a *tivaivai manu* draped over his knees was to publicly signal how cherished he was in his family. He was allotted other *tivaivai* in the *'o'ora* that followed the haircutting process, but such specific use of *tivaivai* in the haircutting ritual to wrap the boy evoked specific values and made him appear mothered—smothered even in the materialisation of Cook Islands femaleness and mothering. As he sat on the stage flanked by his parents and other relatives, including his auntie, Māmā Lucy, the *tivaivai* were a sign of the purported integrity and strength of the family. In the display on the stage, the values of the domestic sphere and the *aro'a* that ideologically operates there were being writ large, so to speak, in the public domain of the haircutting event (Turner 2006b: 12 and 20; Graeber 2001: 73) because of the use of *tivaivai* and other lower ranked textiles. The performance of the quality of kinship displayed in effect countenanced the motivation to gift envelope-wrapped money by the assembled group of extended kin. The wrapping and enthroning of the boy in elite textiles and the ritual stage area in lesser textiles accentuated the hierarchy of textiles that has such salience for Cook Islanders.

The symbolic change of clothing of both the boy and his parents was part of this dramaturgy, and showed that the boy was now connected to his parents and the kin networks they represented in a different way, and vice versa, as facilitated by the gifting of envelope-wrapped cash by the assembled extended kin. But the provision of good food, entertainment (generally Cook Islands dancing), the elaborately wrapped ceremonial venue and the judicious use of *tivaivai* in particular were essential parts of this because of the circulation of value (Fajans 1993) that they created and the exchange of valuables they ultimately contextualised. The ritual process facilitated the transition of the boy into a Cook Islands man *and* situated the gifts of money in what Stephen Gudeman (2008) calls the realm of mutuality vis-à-vis the realm of market.

Tivaivai and money

When people choose to attend an event like Māmā Lucy's nephew's haircutting ceremony, and gift money in exchange for a lock of hair, they do so for a number of reasons: from being a way to help kin and actually do and show *aroʻa*, or as a reciprocal gesture that answers a prior contribution from the family of the boy, or a desire to establish a link with a family or exert influence (Loomis 1983: 229). Regardless of the prime motivation, the gifts of textiles, money, food and services 'constitute *kaioʻu* "indebtedness"' (229). The recording of who gives what is done assiduously. After a haircutting, such a record constitutes a reference for the boy's interactions with his community of kindred in later life when he has become a man and is making his own way (229). One of my informants told me that there is always a book where who gives what and how much is noted in exacting detail at each event. She said, 'I always know what everyone gives' (personal communication, Eva William, Auckland, 2011), and it is important to know, because therein lies the relationship. Therein lies the ability to receive *and* eventually reciprocate. Therein lies the adherence to Cook Islands values and value via the movement of valuables. Terrence Loomis asserts that metaphorically, 'The strands of hair from the boy signify the reciprocal exchanges which bind participants together economically, symbolically and by kinship *piriʻanga* [custom]' (1983: 229). But this only works because the locks of hair and money are ranked as valuables in a broader structure of value.

Cook Islanders in New Zealand have been and remain marginalised (Loomis 1985, 1990), featuring too regularly in the worst statistics from unemployment rates to levels of education (Statistics New Zealand 2013). But I argue that the Cook Islands ceremonial economy, in particular the haircutting ceremony, has evolved to give a more or less explicit acknowledgement of the economic realities in which Cook Islanders live. Cook Islanders have a specific understanding of money as it moves in the ceremonial economy, which is inevitably articulated with and is a function of the value of money in the market economy in which they live in New Zealand, but the two are not synonymous. They are related and managed, but are ritually managed to be explicitly different. Cook Islanders have articulated the capitalist economy with a fully fledged active ceremonial economy, which accommodates money in its midst as an important but nonsterile valuable that services social relationships in the way a good gift should, creating the requisite obligations and binding people together.

People get by and do economy in a wider, more encompassing way that involves the realm of mutuality as well as market (Gudeman 2001, 2008). Nobody gets rich from participating in the Cook Islands ceremonial economy, but the system nonetheless operates to deliver sums of cash and quantities of food and support at key events in people's lives, and delivers cogent, powerful displays of values and modes of connection to all the participants in the ceremonies that mark those events.

Māmā Lucy's nephew was born in New Zealand, he is being raised and educated there, most of his extended family live there, and while he has the option of going back to the islands to live partly because he will have claims on land, he will more than likely end up living in New Zealand like two-thirds of the population of the Cook Islands. He has to function in a capitalist western economy. But the process of becoming a man to do this, from his Cook Islands family's point of view, was to be wrapped physically and metaphorically in textiles that trumpeted certain specific values about being a Cook Islander in New Zealand and about being a human being, and about ongoing relationships of belonging to his wider kin group. His hair was cut in exchange for sums of money, he was adorned with neck garlands that were embellished with cash money notes, and his passage to manhood was completed by a change of clothes, a feast and an 'o'ora where he was literally wrapped and adorned in more textiles, including tivaivai. What Māmā Lucy's nephew gained as his hair was cut was at least a nod to economic power, a network of kin to whom he is now obligated and conjoined, and he is now a Cook Islands man. The making and use of tivaivai as valuables is about 'how forms of value emerge to regulate a process which is ultimately about the creation of people' (Graeber 2001: 142).

Acknowledgements

I would like to thank Māmā Eva William and Māmā Lucy Papa for their help with this chapter. I am also grateful for the postdoctoral scholarship awarded to me by the Kate Edgar Educational Trust, which provided financial support while I researched and wrote about this topic.

References

Alexeyeff, Kalissa. 2004. 'Love Food: Exchange and Sustenance in the Cook Islands Diaspora'. *The Australian Journal of Anthropology* 15(1): 68–79. DOI: 10.1111/j.1835-9310.2004.tb00366.x.

Ama, 'Aka'iti. 2003. 'Maeva: Rites of Passage: Highlights of Family Life'. In *Akon'anga Maori: Cook Islands Culture*, ed. Ron Crocombe and Majorie Tua'inekore Crocombe, pp. 119–125. Suva: Institute of Pacific Studies and Cook Islands Extension Centre, University of the South Pacific in association with the Cook Islands Cultural and Historic Places Trust and the Ministry of Cultural Development.

Buse, Jasper with Raututi Taringa. 1995. *Cook Islands Maori Dictionary*, ed. Bruce Biggs and Rangi Moeka'a. The Ministry of Education, Government of the Cook Islands; The School of Oriental and African Studies, the University of London; The Institute of Pacific Studies, The University of Auckland; Pacific Linguistics, The Research School of Pacific and Asian Studies, The Australian National University.

Carrier, James (ed.). 2005. *The Handbook of Economic Anthropology*. Cheltenham: Edward Elgar.

Colchester, Chloë (ed.). 2003. *Clothing the Pacific*. Oxford and New York: Berg Publishers.

Comaroff, Jean and John Comaroff. 1992. *Of Revelation and Revolution: Christianity, Colonialism and Consciousness in South Africa*. Chicago: Chicago University Press.

Crocombe, Ron. 1964. *Land Tenure in the Cook Islands*. Melbourne: Oxford University Press.

Crocombe, Ron and Majorie Tua'inekore Crocombe (eds). 2003. *Akon'anga Maori: Cook Islands Culture*. Suva: Institute of Pacific Studies and Cook Islands Extension Centre, University of the South Pacific in association with the Cook Islands Cultural and Historic Places Trust and the Ministry of Cultural Development.

Douglas, Bronwen. 1999. 'Provocative Readings in Intransigent Archives: Finding Aneityumese Women'. *Oceania* 70(2): 111–129. DOI: 10.1002/j.1834-4461.1999.tb02996.x.

Evans, Mike. 2001. *Persistence of the Gift: Tongan Tradition in Transnational Context.* Waterloo: Wilfrid Laurier University Press.

Eves, Richard. 1996. 'Colonialism, Corporeality, and Character: Methodist Missions and the Refashioning of Bodies in the Pacific'. *History and Anthropology* 10(1): 85–138. DOI: 10.1080/02757206.1996.9960893.

Fajans, Jane (ed.). 1993. *Exchanging Products: Producing Exchange.* Oceania Monographs. Sydney: University of Sydney.

Gell, Alfred. 1998. *Art and Agency: An Anthropological Theory.* Oxford: Clarendon Press.

Gershon, Ilana. 2007. 'Viewing Diasporas from the Pacific: What Pacific Ethnographies Offer Pacific Diaspora Studies'. *The Contemporary Pacific* 19(2): 474–502.

Goffman, Erving. 1959. *The Presentation of Self in Everyday Life.* New York: Anchor Books.

Graeber, David. 2001. *Toward an Anthropological Theory of Value: The False Coin of Our Own Dreams.* New York: Palgrave.

———. 2005. 'Value: Anthropological Theories of Value'. In *The Handbook of Economic Anthropology*, ed. James Carrier, pp. 439–454. Cheltenham: Edward Elgar.

———. 2013. 'It is Value that Brings Universes into Being'. *Hau: Journal of Ethnographic Theory* 3(2): 219–243. DOI: 10.14318/hau3.2.012.

Gudeman, Stephen. 2001. *The Anthropology of Economy: Community, Market and Culture.* Malden: Blackwell Publishing.

———. 2008. *Economy's Tension: The Dialectics of Community and Market.* New York: Berghahn Books.

Hann, Chris and Keith Hart (eds). 2009. *Market and Society: The Great Transformation Today.* Cambridge: Cambridge University Press.

Herda, Phyllis. 2010. 'The Creation of a New Tradition: Women's Quilting in the Cook Islands'. Conference paper given at the Pacific Arts Association 10th International Symposium, Rarotonga, 9–11 August.

———. 2011. 'Tivaevae: Women's Quilting in the Cook Islands'. *Uncoverings* 32: 55–78.

Hooper, Antony. 1961. 'Cook Islanders in Auckland'. *Journal of the Polynesian Society* 70(2): 147–193.

Horan, Jane. 2011. 'Tivaivai and Value in the Cook Islands Ritual Economy: The Creation of Value, Values, and Valuables in a Diasporic Community'. In *Textile Economies: Power and Value from the Local to the Transnational*, ed. Walter E. Little and Patricia A. McAnany, pp. 57–76. New York: Altamira Press.

——. 2012. 'Tivaivai in the Cook Islands Ceremonial Economy: An Analysis of Value'. PhD thesis. University of Auckland.

——. 2013. 'Tivaivai and the Managing of "Community" Funding in Auckland, New Zealand.' In *Engaging with Capitalism: Cases from Oceania, Research in Economic Anthropology*, Research in Economic Anthropology Volume 33, ed. Fiona McCormack and Kate Barclay, pp. 83–106. Bingley: Emerald Group Publishing Ltd.

Jolly, Margaret and Martha Macintyre (eds). 1989. *Family and Gender in the Pacific*. Cambridge: Cambridge University Press.

Kaeppler, Adrienne. 2007. 'Containers of Divinity'. *Journal of the Polynesian Society* 116(2): 97–130.

Keane, Webb. 2001. 'Money is No Object: Materiality, Desire, and Modernity in an Indonesian Society'. In *The Empire of Things: Regimes of Value and Material Culture*, ed. Fred R. Myers, pp. 65–90. Santa Fe, NM: School of American Research Press.

Küchler, Susanne and Andrea Eimke. 2009. *Tivaivai: The Social Fabric of the Cook Islands*. London: British Museum Press.

Little, Walter E. and Patricia A. McAnany (eds). 2011. *Textile Economies: Power and Value from the Local to the Transnational*. New York: Altamira Press.

Loomis, Terrence. 1983. 'The Cook Islands Haircutting Ritual as Practised in New Zealand'. *Journal of the Polynesian Society* 92(2): 215–232.

——. 1985. *Samson in the South Pacific: Changes in the Symbolism of Hair in Polynesian-European Relations*. Occasional Paper No. 5. Auckland: The Social Research and Development Trust.

——. 1990. *Pacific Migrant Labour, Class and Racism in New Zealand: Fresh off the Boat.* Aldershot: Avebury.

Mauss, Marcel. 1990. *The Gift: The Form and Reason for Exchange in Archaic Societies.* New York: W.W. Norton. Original edition, *Essai sur le don*, first published 1950 by Presses Universitaires de France en *Sociologie et Anthropologie.*

Miller, David (ed.). 1998. *Material Cultures: Why Some Things Matter.* Chicago: University of Chicago Press.

Ministry of Finance and Economic Management. 2017. Census 2011. Government of the Cook Islands. Online: www.mfem.gov.ck/statistics/census-and-surveys/census/143-census-2011 (accessed 31 July 2017).

Myerhoff, Barbara. 1982. 'Rites of Passage: Process and Paradox'. In *Celebration: Studies in Festivity and Ritual*, ed. Victor Witter Turner, pp. 109–135. Washington: Smithsonian Institution Press.

Rasmussen, Wilkie Olaf Patua. 1995. 'The Sociopolitical Implications of Teina/Tuakana (Junior/Senior) Kinship Relationships among Tongareva People in South Auckland'. MA thesis. University of Auckland.

Sissons, Jeff. 2007. 'From Post to Pillar: God-houses and Social Fields in Nineteenth-century Rarotonga'. *Journal of Material Culture* 12(1): 47–63. DOI: 10.1177/1359183507074561.

——. 2008. 'Three Iconoclastic Episodes: Rematerializing Eastern Polynesia'. Conference paper given at the Joint Conference of the ASA, ASAANZ and AAS, Ownership and Appropriation, Auckland, 8–12 December.

Statistics New Zealand. 2008. *Cook Island Maori People in New Zealand.* Online: www.stats.govt.nz/Census/about-2006-census/pacific-profiles-2006/cook-island-maori-people-in-new-zealand.aspx/Cook-Island-Maori-profile-updated-May2008-1.pdf (accessed 21 January 2011).

——. 2013. *Census QuickStats about Culture and Identity/Pacific Peoples Ethnic Group.* Online: www.stats.govt.nz/Census/2013-census/profile-and-summary-reports/quickstats-culture-identity/pacific-peoples.aspx (accessed 17 May 2014).

Thomas, Nicholas. 2000. 'Technologies of Conversion: Cloth and Christianity in Polynesia'. In *Hybridity and Its Discontents: Politics, Science, Culture*, ed. Avtar Brah and Annie E. Coombes, pp. 198–215. Florence, KY: Routledge.

Turner, Terence. 2006a. 'The "Transformation Problem" in Relation to the General Applicability of Maxian Value Theory'. Unpublished manuscript.

———. 2006b. 'Kayapo Values: An Application of Marxian Value Theory to a Non-commodity Based System of Production'. Unpublished manuscript.

———. 2008. 'Marxian Value Theory: An Anthropological Perspective'. *Anthropological Theory* 8(1): 43–56. DOI: 10.1177/ 1463499607087494.

———. 2012. 'The Social Skin'. *Hau: Journal of Ethnographic Theory* 3(2): 219–243. Online: www.haujournal.org/index.php/hau/article/ view/236 (accessed 18 January 2014).

Turner, Victor Witter (ed.). 1982. *Celebration: Studies in Festivity and Ritual*. Washington: Smithsonian Institution Press.

Weber, Max. 2009. *The Protestant Ethic and the Spirit of Capitalism*, ed. Richard Swedberg. New York: W.W. Norton and Company Inc.

Weiner, Annette. 1976. *Women of Value, Men of Renown: New Perspectives in Trobriand Exchange*. Austin: University of Texas Press.

Poem: *urohs* language

Emelihter Kihleng

Figure 41. Evenglynn Andon with some of the *urohs* she sews and her sister's drawings. This poem, '*urohs* language', was written about Evenglynn

Source. Photographed by Emelihter Kihleng, 18 November 2012

urohs speak to her[1]
late at night as
she sews on her Janome

---

1   Machine-embroidered and appliquéd skirts made by Pohnpeian women from Pohnpei Island, Federated States of Micronesia.

the quiet doesn't faze her
she listens
her world is visual, physical
textile spiritual
fingers red from kool-aid
pwuh in her mouth
she is in the zone
colours and patterns zip past
the *misihn hummzz*

kisakis ieu
they call it
her self-taught gift
for sewing
she watched her mother
continued learning at NMHS
even taught her elder sister
who draws their *mwahi*
they communicate in their
sisterly speak
signing, enunciating with lips
and mouth
she grunts then points
her likes and dislikes
combining and creating
her own unique patterns
she has an eye
for what pops

sisters sit together
at the dining room table
wearing *urohs* and bra
too hot for t-shirts
always at the head
her sister beside her
hands pushing fabric
faces concentrating
flower designs forming in bright green
pieces of red, black and patterned fabric
scattered across the table
mermaids and *serehd* sketches

on the tile floor
next to babies fast asleep

when she finishes a new one she likes
she'll put it on
ih likauih seli[2]

Figure 42. Karly Tom with the *urohs* she sells at her store in Pehleng, Kitti, Pohnpei

Source. Photographed by Emelihter Kihleng, 14 December 2012

Reference

Kihleng, Emelihter. 2015. '*Menginpehn Lien Pohnpei*: A Poetic Ethnography of *Urohs* (Pohnpeian Skirts).' PhD thesis. Victoria University of Wellington.

---

2   'She'll wear it around.'

Epilogue: Sinuous Objects, Sensuous Bodies: Revaluing 'Women's Wealth' Across Time and Place

Margaret Jolly

Sinuous – 'having many twists and turns, moving and
bending in a smooth and attractive way'.

(Merriam Webster Dictionary)

This volume, like the objects of its study, might be read as sinuous. The authors evoke the sensuous processes of Pacific women's creative labour: pandanus being stripped, bleached and softened, plaited into mats or baskets; spun fibres from barks or forest vines, and ochres from the bush or string in vibrant, variegated hues from the store, looped into pliable bags to carry food, babies and other precious things; the bark of the paper mulberry or breadfruit tree made supple with beating and pounding, felted, patterned, dyed or painted; coils of clay twisted in spirals and fired to create fine, hard vessels; banana leaves, cut, scraped on incised boards, bleached in the sun and bundled; banana fibres tied and dyed to form colourful, multi-layered skirts; bolts of cloth fashioned into skirts reinscribing the moving arc of swaying 'grass skirts'; quilts crocheted or sewn with patchworks of cloth, sometimes layered with stuffing, appliqué and embroidery. Cloth artfully draping, protecting and transforming moving bodies; enormous bundles of leaves, baskets, tapa or textiles being exchanged in the complex twists and turns of gifting across time and place; cloth—pandanus, tapa, calico—wrapped around the dead lying still on their last winding journey to the other side.

As well as evoking the sinuous materiality of these different objects and their intimate relation to sensuous, gendered bodies, the editors and authors of this volume trace a more abstract sinuosity in the movement of these things through time and place; they coil through different regimes of value, between what has been dubbed 'mutuality and the market' (Horan this volume), often but not always in a 'smooth and attractive way'. The eight chapters in this volume trace winding paths across the contemporary Pacific, from the Trobriands in Milne Bay to Maisin, Wanigela and Korafe in Oro Province, Papua New Guinea, through the islands of Tonga to diasporic Tongan and Cook Islander communities in New Zealand. They cross over the borders of what has been called Melanesia and Polynesia, between the western and eastern Pacific, a demarcation with colonial origins that has too often segregated both Pacific peoples and scholarly studies of the Pacific (Spriggs 2009). There are also historical twists in time travel as the editors and authors reflect on the changing values and significance of these objects, in the context of colonialism, Christian conversion, collecting and the heightened globalisation of contemporary capitalist economy. Scholarly debates have also taken some radical twists and turns since such objects were dubbed 'women's wealth' by Annette Weiner (1976) 40 years ago. So, before I reflect on this volume's timely and innovative contributions, let me return to that moment when Annette Weiner and Marilyn Strathern debated 'women's wealth', a debate that continues to haunt contemporary feminist anthropology and this volume of essays, grounded in fine, twenty-first-century ethnography (Weiner 1976, 1980, 1988, 1989, 1992; Strathern 1981).

The fertility of fibres: *Doba* and 'women's wealth' in the Trobriands

From her first monograph (1976), *doba* were central to Weiner's revisioning of the Trobriands from 'a woman's point of view'. She challenged Bronisław Malinowski's androcentrism, suggesting that he failed to witness the source of the distinctive power of women, that he was so fixated on men and the exchange of shell valuables in the *kula* that he ignored women's prominent exchanges of banana leaf bundles and skirts, *doba*, in the crucial *sagali* ceremonies after death (see Lepani and MacCarthy this volume). Weiner pronounced banana leaves 'women's wealth' since they were made, exchanged and controlled by women. For her, they embodied '"womanness": sexuality, reproduction, and nurture' (1976: 119) and intangible, 'eternal female values, women's concern with life, death and regeneration' (Strathern 1981: 673; paraphrasing Weiner 1976: 236). The value of their maternity and of matriliny was materialised in these banana leaf bundles and skirts presented at mortuary ceremonies, through which women reclaimed dead clanspeople from debts to other *dala* (subclans, lineages) accumulated in life. They were a 'cosmic statement of regeneration of pure *dala* substance' (Weiner 1976: 120). In her view, Trobriand women thus exercised power in perpetuity, while men were relegated to a sphere of evanescent power, 'clutching after immortality through objects incapable of regeneration' (236).

Weiner did not ignore Trobriand men, but she de-emphasised the hoary old debates about virgin birth and physiological paternity, about father love versus mother right in matrilineal societies, and rather privileged the brother–sister bond in the intimate synergy between exchanges of yams and of *doba*. Later authors challenged her view of the Trobriand father and gender relations (like Mosko 1992), while some like myself (Jolly 1992a) wondered whether by situating Trobriand women in cyclical or eternal time Weiner had occluded the passage of historical change between Malinowski's season of fieldwork and her own.

Weiner insisted that the Trobriand experience of colonialism was 'rather benign' and that in the 60 years since Malinowski's sojourn, although 'superficially some things had changed (an airstrip, tourists, some western clothing) everything else was as if nothing had changed' (1980: 272). 'Women's wealth' for her assumed a primary place in continuing Trobriand traditions, a strength she characterised as persistence rather than resistance to colonial and Christian influences. She delivered a message to us from Joshua (pseudonym for a young educated health worker who sometimes drove her around): 'We have to get those women to stop throwing their wealth because they take our money' (1980: 274). She interpreted this as a sign of *his* undue western capitalist influence, rather than as suggestive of a broader historical shift in the configuration of the Trobriand exchange system and gender relations. In her first monograph (1976), and in several subsequent publications (1988, 1992), Weiner made broader claims about 'women's wealth' in Oceania—about *bilums* in Papua New Guinea, pandanus textiles in Vanuatu, tapa in Polynesia—critiquing those who, like Malinowski, had failed to see their deep significance. Marilyn Strathern was implicated; she responded in her Malinowski lecture of 1980, 'Culture in a Netbag' (1981).[1]

---

1   *Bilums* have also been called netbags or string bags in the anthropological and material culture literature.

Malinowski and feminist anthropology: Shared universals?

In that lecture, Strathern discerned an uncanny link in Weiner's anthropological genealogy with Malinowski: their shared affinity for universalism. Just as Malinowski (1922) was prone to making grandiloquent generalisations from Trobriand Man to Primitive Economic Man, so Weiner was inclined to leap from Trobriand to Universal Woman (Strathern 1981). Strathern challenged the way in which Weiner, like some other feminist anthropologists of the period, assumed a universal woman's point of view—that because of their gender, women had distinctive, even unique, insights not able to be replicated by men. Presuming naturally grounded continuities between female author and female subject suggested a closure in the manufacture of the subdiscipline of feminist anthropology for Strathern (1981: 669). Not only could we not presume universal 'womanness', connecting Trobriand women and the imagined 'we' of the West, we could not presume what 'womanness' meant within Papua New Guinea.

Strathern offered both a trenchant critique of Weiner's premises and her presentation of Trobriand material and a compelling consideration of differences within Papua New Guinea, comparing Trobriand *doba* with netbags/*bilums* amongst both Hagen and Wiru people. For Hagen, she suggested netbags, although receptacles for women's products, pork and shells, of some value as exchange objects, and loosely signifying 'womanness', were not 'women's wealth', they were focal in public exchanges like *doba*. Indeed, 'Hagen women do not publicly transact with netbags because Hagen women do not publicly transact' (Strathern 1981: 675). In Hagen, Strathern asserted, this was a male prerogative.[2] She argued that netbags were *neither* women's wealth nor men's wealth. It was not the product/object that was sexed but the activity:[3] women produced and men transacted (see also Strathern 1972). For her, netbags and pigs were neither exclusively female nor male objects but conjoint products, in which each sex invested and detached part of itself.

---

2   This distinction is no longer true; Hagen women now publicly transact with *bilums* and other goods sold in the market.
3   In contemporary writing, we might say gendered rather than sexed.

Strathern not only contrasted Trobriand and Hagen contexts, she triangulated them both with Wiru. In this triangulated comparison, the Trobriands were seen as unique in making women's partial contribution to human reproduction a total phenomenon. Strathern concluded:

> We are not dealing with refractions of some universal Womanness whose essential attributes some cultures value and others do not. There are differences both in the qualities attributed to womanhood and in the manner in which symbols are generated out of a male-female dichotomy … the proper focus for analysis becomes not women but the values so assigned. That in the Trobriands women have control over the genesis of life should not be confused with our own biologism (1981: 682).

In this early essay, there is anticipation and prefiguration of the extended comparative argument that Strathern later developed in *The Gender of the Gift* (1988), her influential unravelling of both biological and cultural essentialisms in approaches to gender (see Jolly 1992b); essentialisms that she discerned in Weiner's early writing.[4]

Forty years on: Revaluing 'women's wealth'

In the 40 years since this debate, many things have changed in the scholarly practice of anthropology, our everyday and scholarly perspectives on gender and sexuality and more broadly in our human experience of a shared but deeply unequal and conflicted world. I reflect on these changes and on the innovative contributions of this volume by focusing on three key concepts: woman, wealth and changing values.

Woman

The presumption of a universal, eternal 'woman' has been radically challenged since the 1970s. There has been a widespread acknowledgement of the differences and inequalities between women on the basis of race, class, sexuality (and several other parameters) and an associated embrace of intersectionality in thinking about gender (Henne 2013). Today, even the 'strategic essentialism' advocated in feminist movements of the 1970s is far harder to claim or promote in the context of the complex coalitions in global transnational feminisms (Grewal and Kaplan 1994;

---

4   We might ponder whether that charge of essentialism can be equally applied to Weiner's later comparative work (1988, 1992).

Hilsdon et al. 2000; Mohanty 2003). And, perhaps more fundamentally, universalist, essentialist presumptions grounded in the 'nature' of women, and in particular their reproductive nature have been constantly exposed as western 'biologism', as Strathern intimated. The very distinction between nature and culture fundamental to twentieth-century distinctions between sex and gender has been challenged not just by Marilyn Strathern (1988; Strathern and MacCormack 1980) and Judith Butler (1990, 2004) but by a host of scholars working across many disciplines. Contemporary scholarship stresses gender fluidity, transcending the heteronormative binary of male and female, embracing the inclusion of transgender and intersex people, and the complex relations between gender identity and sexual orientation (for example, see Besnier and Alexeyeff 2014; Jolly 2016).

What are we to make then of the frequent associations that emerge in these chapters and in the broader literature between women's maternity and these distinctive objects they create? The first female ancestor of the Ömie people of Papua New Guinea, famous for their superb barkcloth, is said to have menstruated, cut bark from a tree and soaked it in red river mud, symbolising her blood and her capacity to bear children (Thomas 2012: 484). In many parts of PNG, the capacious, bulging *bilum* is likened to the expansive, protruding womb of a pregnant woman (but see MacKenzie 1991).[5] The red dye used to decorate pandanus textiles in Vanuatu is implicitly but potently linked to the blood of menstruation and parturition (Bolton 1996, 2003; Walter 1996). And, in the Trobriands, banana leaf bundles and skirts symbolise not just maternity but the preeminent value of matriliny and the cosmic regeneration of matter and spirit inherent therein. But how does this compare with western 'biologism'?

As Emily Martin (1991) demonstrated long ago, both popular and more scientific narratives of the conjunction of eggs and sperm in the West encode masculinist conceptions of procreation and pregnancy.

---

5   Unlike *doba*, *bilums* are not preeminently ceremonial valuables but quotidian companions to women, men and children, used for carrying food, firewood, utensils, personal belongings, babies, piglets, puppies and sacred objects (see Gnecchi-Ruscone this volume). A *bilum* is bag, garment, ornament and ritual adornment. As Maureen MacKenzie states, '[T]he bilum is much more than a mundane and useful container … its imagery is used by both women and men to model, and thus confront, dissonance in the paradoxical nature of their relationship' (1991: 1). So, although women are the primary but not the exclusive creators of *bilums*, they are not 'women's wealth' for MacKenzie but rather 'androgynous objects'. She thus supports Strathern in her debate with Weiner, but does so

More recent narratives based on revolutionary developments in reproductive biology, research on genetics, hormones and stem cells and the radical transformations consequent on assisted reproductive technologies are equally entangled with contemporary questions and contests around gender relations (Strathern 1992; Waldby and Cooper 2008, 2014). Indigenous Pacific notions of conception, pregnancy and birth traverse a vast range—from the Sambia diminution of women's wombs as mere receptacles of potent fertile semen, which generate babies and are later transformed into breast milk (Herdt 1981), to the Trobriands where the baby's blood and spirit is thought to derive exclusively from the mother's *dala* while the father is thought to feed and mould the baby's form through intercourse and nurture (see Lepani 2012; Mosko 1992; Weiner 1976).

Such Pacific concepts and practices differ from western 'biologism' in several ways. First, although they do impinge on the intercourse of individual sexed bodies and the body of the individual woman through pregnancy, birth and breast feeding, these are implicated in collective notions of social reproduction that are grounded in ideas of clan-based descent or extended familial regeneration. Women who do not become biological mothers can, still rather easily in many Pacific places, become social mothers through the adoption of the children of sisters or other kin (see Ping-Ann Addo's life story of Kalo in Chapter 9). Moreover, in ways rather different to contemporary European notions of ancestry and generation, Pacific ideas of collective human regeneration are connected to broader processes of regeneration of the nonhuman world and even the cosmos. There are frequent links made between growing babies and growing crops or nurturing pigs; human fecundity and health (and sickness) are often linked to processes that we might think of as ecological vitality (or decay). It is thus intriguing to see that many of the objects Pacific women create and exchange, and which evoke the value of their maternity, are botanical and organic products that emanate from the land—groves of pandanus trees growing near the ocean or in the

---

on the basis of a far more intimate appreciation of the materiality of their making, use and circulation. MacKenzie challenges any exclusive and essentialist association between *bilum* and female fecundity, seeing this as part of a broader conception of fertility. She documents how in Telefol rituals of initiation and death, men transformed *bilums* looped by women into elaborated ritual forms, created in secret but worn in public and used as receptacles for cult objects—they thus signified male sexuality and fertility. It is clear from MacKenzie's analysis that *bilums* do not just signify women's wombs and female fecundity but are drawn into wider models of fertility in which men play an equal, if not privileged, part. Sexual difference is imaged and, through the pliability of the *bilum*, stressed and stretched.

mountains, the bark of paper mulberry or breadfruit trees, the abundant glossy leaves of banana trees, mud and ochres from river and forest, clay from the ground itself. This all suggests that Pacific women are 'mothers of the land';[6] regardless of whether descent is matrilineal, patrilineal or cognatic, the link between women's bodies and these products of the land attaches them to place, country and culture. Below, I ponder what happens when these products of the land are supplemented or even supplanted by materials from elsewhere—*bilums* created from store-bought string already dyed, skirts fashioned not from 'grass' but bolts of cloth, vessels made not from local clay but plastic or aluminium, cloth and quilts created not from bark but cotton, silk, polyester.

We might also ask why the notion of 'womanness' is equated with maternity. Significantly, in her early conception of Trobriand 'womanness', Weiner embraced sexuality alongside maternity (see above). This is understandable given the continuation of sexual practices in the Trobriands, which Lepani (2008, 2012) celebrates as both sex-positive and life-affirming (albeit in a predominantly heterosexual way). This sexual culture persists despite early conversions (from 1894) to a Methodist mode of Christianity and even the spectre of death through transmission of HIV from the 1980s. Katherine Lepani persuasively sees the reciprocal exchange of sex, before and during marriage as integral to broader social reproduction and cultural regeneration (2010, 2012). Other places discussed in this volume—within Papua New Guinea, Tonga and Pacific diasporas in New Zealand—are less celebratory and far more circumspect about, and constraining of, women's sexuality.

Moreover, some of the questions Serge Tcherkézoff raised about being a 'woman' in Samoa are relevant here. Tcherkézoff (1993) argued that the concept and value of 'woman' in Samoa was not unitary but split between the celebration of the sacred (and ideally virgin) sister and the devaluation of the sexualised wife. There has been much debate as to how far Christian conversion entailed a shift from a focus on the brother–sister relation to the husband–wife relation as the privileged dyad in male–female relations, particularly apropos Samoa and Tonga (and more generally in the Pacific, see Gailey 1987; James 1988). In his path-breaking research on Samoan missionary women (in the vanguard of the early evangelisation of the London Missionary Society), Latu Latai argues that the sacred covenant

---

6   This phrase was coined in relation to Bougainville and especially the predominantly matrilineal regions of that island (Tankunani Siviri and Taleo Havini 2004).

attributed to the brother–sister relation in ancient Samoa, although persisting in diluted form, was transposed onto the relation between the pastor and his wife and the congregation (Latai 2014, 2016).

The chapters dealing with Tongans in the islands and the diaspora raise the equally important question of how far women are distinguished and divided, not just in their dual aspects of sisters and wives/mothers, but on the basis of rank. In her chapter, Wonu Veys makes the important point that the precious Tongan valuables called *koloa* (canonically barkcloth, pandanus mats and coconut oil), which were in the past created and controlled by high-ranking or noble women, are now associated with women in general. The ethnographies of Adrienne Kaeppler amongst the aristocrats and royals of Tongatapu (1995, 2005, 2007), of Heather Young Leslie with commoner women from Kauvai (1999) and of Ping-Ann Addo in the Tongan diaspora (2013) all attest to a democratisation of these Tongan valuables, and their contemporary association with women, regardless of rank. But Wonu Veys, like a number of other authors in this volume, eschews the notion that these objects embody a 'female essence', or that they constitute 'women's wealth'. For her, these are 'prestigious objects' not 'women's wealth'. Through a forensic historical examination of the changing meanings of the categories of *koloa* and *ngāue* in Tongan exchange, she argues against a strict demarcation of women's and men's valuables and for contextual fluidity. She queries both the gendering of objects per se and the very notion of wealth.[7]

Wealth

I now turn to this second key concept. In popular English parlance, wealth is usually conceived in monetary terms and implies abundance, or accumulated surplus over what is needed. In contemporary global conversations it is hard to detach 'wealth' from capitalist property relations and notions of value. Weiner's (1976) use of this word to embrace *doba* in the Trobriands was, in my reading, a provocative subversion of the exclusivity or hegemony of a capitalist logic of value. However, its use poses crucial questions as to how the indigenous systems in which

---

7   Her argument echoes a much earlier debate occasioned by Kerry James's (1988) vigorous critique of Christine Ward Gailey's book (1987). James disputed Gailey's translation of *koloa* as 'all goods made by women' and her counterpart translation of *ngāue* as 'men's goods'. James claims *ngāue* means simply work or employment done by either men or women. Women do not make all Tongan *koloa* and, conversely, not all goods made by women are considered to be *koloa* (1988: 33–34). *Koloa* she

these objects were exchanged have variously encountered, incorporated, accommodated and resisted the goods and the values of the capitalist commodity economy.[8]

As the editors suggest in their Introduction, the voluminous anthropological literature on gifts and commodities constitutes an important background to the chapters of this volume. Without rehearsing the terms of that debate engaging authors such as Gregory (1982, 2015), Strathern (1988), Gell (1998) and Appadurai (1986) (but see Hermkens and Lepani this volume; and Jolly 2015), I stress the *copresence* of both gift and commodity values inherent in these objects and the self-conscious and articulate way in which Pacific women deal with the sinuous paths they and these objects travel. Let me take examples of this from the three successive sections of this volume: the first from the Trobriands, the second from Oro Province and the third from Tonga and Pacific diasporas in New Zealand.

---

translates as 'durable goods of value, riches and wealth' (1988: 33), which includes not only decorated *ngatu* (barkcloth), baskets of coiled vine and coconut oil but goods made by men in the past such as ocean-going canoes, store-bought consumer durables and even, metaphorically, children. Conversely, women make many things not considered *koloa*: plain pandanus textiles, coconut-carrying baskets, garlands etc. *Koloa fakatonga*, *koloa* of the highest value, were seen as material manifestations of the gods and their 'earthly descendants and priestly representatives, the *'eiki* (usually translated as chiefs), particularly chiefly women' (1988: 34). So, although decorated barkcloth is made by women and as a privileged form of *koloa* might be linked with the sacred power of chiefly women, it cannot simply be construed as 'women's wealth' in Weiner's terms. Similarly, Adrienne Kaeppler has highlighted the prominence of *ngatu* as a 'high art' in Tongan aesthetic and political values. She suggests decorated barkcloth is a visual art form linked with the verbal arts of *lakalaka* or oratory, which enhances hierarchy (2005). Yet Kaeppler also stresses gendered complementarity:

> Barkcloth and mats were categorized as *koloa* (valuables) and were made by women … *Koloa* is the complementary domain to *ngāue*, products derived from agricultural work and animal husbandry … The *ngāue* of men regenerates people physically, while *koloa* of women regenerates people culturally. Both are necessary, and together regenerate and reproduce society (Kaeppler 2005: 252; see also Kaeppler 2007).

8   In a much earlier paper (Jolly 1992a), I suggested that the difference between Weiner's and Malinowski's analyses of the Trobriands may not just be the difference between a man's and a woman's point of view, but may also reflect differences between their epochs of observation. Weiner (1980) alludes to the holy trinity of foreign influences—colonialism, Christianity and commoditisation— primarily to deny their impact in the Trobriands. The continuing salience of 'women's wealth' is interpreted as persistence rather than self-conscious resistance: 'stability in banana leaves', Weiner proclaimed. Although Weiner constantly laments the alienation and impersonality of western consumer culture, she did not adequately address the question of how the Trobriand gift economy might have been transformed by the experience of a colonising capitalism. I rather suggested (1992a) a sort of celebratory cultural resistance towards commodity values, which I think is evidenced in much recent ethnography that attests to an efflorescence and expansion in Trobriand exchanges (see especially Lepani 2012, and this volume). But, without Trobriand experience, I failed to adequately acknowledge the commensurability of banana leaves and introduced cloth, and the stress on copresence and layering that Lepani discerns (but see Jolly 2008). Ira Bashkow (2011) offers interesting historical insights into a *sagali* in the colonial period witnessed by Alex Rentoul.

Lepani quotes the articulate irony of several Trobriand women who, when presented with the idea that their bundles of banana leaves and skirts were 'women's wealth', chortled and joked—'Oh yes we are very wealthy'—musing on how, despite an abundance of *doba*, Trobriand women are cash-poor, with few kina. The notion of 'women's wealth' is odd both linguistically and culturally in Kiriwina; *na'esaesa* (female wealth) would entail not a woman with accumulated bounty but with the relational capacity to generate and distribute exchange valuables. On the basis of her long-term affinal relationship with the Trobriands and ethnographic fieldwork from 2003, Lepani highlights the continuity of *doba* in the mourning ceremonies of *sagali*, despite the changes in material form. Continuity has been maintained through the commensurability of banana leaves and introduced cloth (*karekwa* in Kiriwina, from the English calico). She traces the historical origin to a *sagali* held within the white coral fence of the Methodist mission station at Oiabia in the early twentieth century. Foreign missionaries discouraged *sagali* as wasteful of time and effort, and opposed *doba* made from banana leaves as dirty. Local converts innovated by substituting clean calico and introduced clothes, those icons of Christian conversion (see Jolly 2014; Keane 2005).

When *sagali* is performed today, introduced cloth has not so much supplanted as *supplemented* banana leaves. The historical sedimentation of the practice is evoked by the layering of baskets of *doba*—immense bundles of patterned banana leaves manufactured by women, but topped with layers of cloth, skirts, blouses and pillowslips created on their Singer sewing machines. The immense variety of women's fibre skirts recorded by Ethel Prisk (a missionary woman at the time of Malinowski's fieldwork c. 1911–1916) has contracted, and flowing, brightly patterned cloth skirts are now becoming more common than the intricate layered and dyed banana fibre *sepwana* skirts worn by close kin of the deceased (clanswomen of the deceased's father and their spouse if married). Today, *doba* bundles can be topped off with money and kina notes, often earned by men in urban centres like Alotau and Port Moresby, which are now seen as an integral part of *doba*. Still, although *doba* made of banana leaves may be given a cash value, *doba* cannot be directly exchanged for cash (except when women acquire banana leaf bundles by donating to the Women's Fellowship). Money is now crucial in searching for *doba*, and in particular the huge bolts of store-bought cloth necessary for contemporary *sagali*. But as cash and commodities are transformed into *doba*, they become valuable gifts in complex systems of exchange, evoking the necessary copresence and complementarity of the indigenous and the introduced, the traditional and the Christian modern.

Lepani stresses that there is no long-term hoarding of *doba* valuables before a funeral, since both indigenous and introduced cloth must be seen as 'fresh'. It is indeed the hard, exhausting *work* of searching for *doba*, of feverishly making banana leaf bundles and sewing cloth that is valued—the process of materialisation rather than the objects themselves, the hard labour of women in giving back to those of other clans/lineages what they have given to the deceased, in neverending spirals of exchange. Thus, Lepani argues for the resilient cultural vitality of *doba* and *sagali*, of changing material forms but the enduring values of maternity and matrilineal regeneration, and of the place of the Trobriands in relation to and *within* a Christian modernity.

Although Michelle MacCarthy starts her chapter with a graphic description of the frenzied vitality, the dazzling display and the decidedly unmournful mourning ceremony of *sagali*, her analysis rather focuses on those villages that for the last two decades have been 'doing away with *doba*'. Echoing those foreign Methodist missionaries who came to the Trobriands in 1894, local evangelical Christians in these villages are critical of the search for *doba* as wasteful. They are either abandoning *sagali* completely or using cash and store-bought goods in lieu of locally manufactured *doba*. For them, Christianity entails a rupture from the 'darkness' of custom and the pursuit of the 'light' through education, individual improvement rather than collective regeneration, and the celebration of cash and the commodity economy as eclipsing the valuables of the past. The present is seen as the time of the 'true church'. Deploying Louis Dumont's model of a hierarchy of values, MacCarthy argues that evangelical Christian values are here hegemonic, and that there has been a radical revaluation of past objects and practices, not just 'satanic' practices like sorcery but even *sagali*, core to Trobriand identity. They criticise the iconic *sepwana* fibre skirts as sexually provocative and sinful. Women like Thelma, a young, devout Pentecostal church member, see such customs as distracting not only from the work needed for daily survival and school fees but also from 'God's work'. They stress the need to look after the living not the dead and to favour the individual and close kin rather than the collectivity of the matriclan. It is clear from the counterpoint between Lepani's and MacCarthy's chapters that there is much flux and contestation not just between tradition and modernity but between those

Trobrianders (usually staunch Catholics and United Church adherents) who think such practices and Christian modernity are compatible and even perforce complementary, and those who assert that these ways of life and values are antithetical. I will return to these questions below in a reflection on changing values.

I now focus on the concept of 'wealth' and the relation of gift and commodity economies in Oro Province, Papua New Guinea, as described in the chapters by Anna-Karina Hermkens, Elizabeth Bonshek and Elisabetta Gnecchi-Ruscone. None of these authors are comfortable with seeing the several objects here created, exchanged and controlled by women—barkcloth, clay pots, *bilums* and pandanus mats—as 'women's wealth'. All offer graphic descriptions of the sensuous, embodied making, wearing, using and exchanging of such things, and attest to their sinuosity as they move between different regimes of value. Indeed, Hermkens argues that preoccupations with imported distinctions between gifts and commodities, subjects and objects have obscured the sensuous materiality linking women's bodies and their creations across diverse contexts.

Hermkens suggests that there is a merging between the substance of women's bodies and the fabric of Maisin barkcloth. This is first embodied in the very process of making the cloth from the bark of paper mulberry trees, the endless beating and pounding as women sit with legs firmly held together for protracted periods. It is again embodied in the merging of the skin of women (with cognate tattoos in the past) and the skin of tapa with its distinctive blood-red and black designs—the inner red signifying women's blood and gender identity, the outer black designs signifying men and patriclan identity (distinctive for each of the 36 Maisin patriclans, these also act as land claims). And there is a merging of barkcloth and women's identity in the use of barkcloth as a garment in life-cycle ceremonies or church festivals and dances, as a basket for carrying sago, as a protective blanket and as a wrapping to bury the dead.

However, Hermkens insists Maisin barkcloth is not best conceived as 'women's wealth' but as a valuable that is daily used by both men and women, and that traverses both gift and commodity circuits in order to signify various layers of being and identity (age, gender, patriclan and Maisin identity), and to create relationships and connections. In Maisin contexts barkcloth is inalienable; in external and international contexts it is alienable. Barkcloth was in the past bartered for a variety of things from other ethnic groups—shells, feathers, obsidian flakes and most proximately for clay pots from Wanigela (see below and Bonshek this volume). Today, only the latter trade persists, if in diminished form. But Maisin barkcloth has become a global commodity in the international art market. Prompted first by Anglican missionaries in the 1930s and then vigorously promoted by Greenpeace and the Peace Corps from the 1990s, Maisin barkcloth has been transformed into an ethnic art that celebrates indigeneity, sustainable green development rather than rapacious logging and the creativity of women's labour. But, Hermkens argues, Maisin women's labour has thereby become alienated and objectified, and the main profits have accrued to the men who control this international trade, such as the male executives of a local cooperative. Thus, she suggests, as barkcloth became a global commodity in the art market, emblematic of generic Maisin cultural property, women were disempowered and the particularistic, intimate identification between women and their barkcloth was devalued.

This celebration of Maisin barkcloth also had dramatic consequences for Wanigela women who have long traded their clay pots for barkcloth. As Bonshek observes, there are now only a few older women who make clay pots and the practice if not dying out is in a 'fragile state'; partly as a result of plastic and aluminium vessels supplanting clay for water storage and cooking, but partly because of changing values in the overlapping regional exchange systems of Maisin and Wanigela. Recounting her experience of a trading expedition with several older women from the Anglican Mothers' Union, Bonshek reveals how the exchange values between clay pots and backcloth have radically shifted in recent times. Wanigela women had to accept not just fewer barkcloths in exchange for their pots but also accepted barkcloth that was not finished, where the red designs were not yet filled in. Maisin barkcloth has recently attained a far higher international value than their clay pots (this has caused some resentment amongst Wanigela women). This differential value dates back to the 1930s when Anglican missionaries collecting for overseas museums preferred the lightweight and less fragile barkcloth to heavy, fragile clay pots. Wanigela clay pots have been sold as flower pots in markets in Popendetta and Port Moresby; they are still regarded as 'craft' or heritage objects rather than art in markets and museums.

Elisabetta Gnecchi-Ruscone's chapter focuses on distinct realms of value *within* the Korafe world as she considers the trajectory of string bags and pandanus mats made by women. Like most of the authors in this volume, she eschews the moniker 'women's wealth' since in her view these are rather clan assets for the patrilineal Korafe. She ponders how such ordinary, everyday objects of use become extraordinary valuables in ritual and interclan exchange. She offers graphic depictions of the making of both *bilums* and pandanus mats, evincing a woman's intimate knowledge and full-bodied interaction with the materials as she cuts, splices, bleaches, softens, spins, sews, plaits or loops. So, 'the intimate, physical actions of the woman's body upon bush pandanus leaves produce an artefact that may be described as creating domesticity'. There is nothing inherent in the materials themselves, but rather matter is transformed through women's intentional creative labour to create things whose differences express different social values. Writing of the nearby Nalik, Graeme Were (2013) observed how two different kinds of pandanus leaf are used for different textiles. The first leaves, the indigenous variant, are sewn together and are seen as protective of persons in life-cycle rituals, and thus have more 'traditional' if evanescent uses. The second, from pandanus plants imported by missionaries from Milne Bay, are plaited and more durable, and are used daily as mundane mats for sitting and sleeping, or in broader individualised exchange networks. Gnecchi-Ruscone observes a similar distinction for the Korafe. Yet both can be seen as creative of safe spaces, as mats are unfolded, rolled out and laid on the ground for family or honoured guests.

In making both string bags (*bilums*) and pandanus textiles, women were/are transforming materials from the bush into objects associated with domesticity, protection and safety. The intentionalities of the women making these objects are embedded in the very transformation of the natural materials. So, for instance, there are string bags of different sizes and textures suitable for carrying tubers from the garden, cloth and pillows and personal things (like money, betel, a knife); for babies and infants, the string bag is both a cradle and a pacifying swing. Women now primarily use imported, dyed string to make string bags, and the colours and designs can reference both clan identity and the individual woman who made it. If women want to stress the values of indigenous practice, or if they have a specific request from kin or tourists for a more 'traditional' *bilum*, they use the far more arduous process of preparing and spinning bark fibres and colouring with resinous black dye or red from mangrove bark. String bags also act as personal adornments, signifying gender and ethnic identities, and are frequently exchanged between kin and friends to express reciprocity, love and attachment. In-marrying wives are often welcomed with string bags by mothers-in-law. But these everyday objects can also be ostentatiously unfurled and transformed into ritual valuables used in interclan exchanges effected by men, and ceremonial occasions such as marriage and initiation. Women contribute to the gifts presented by their husband's clan (especially in concluding a bride price) and, less prescriptively, their brothers' clan. Thus, in tracing the biographies of both *bilums* and pandanus textiles, Gnecchi-Ruscone argues that they are very ordinary things, which can become extraordinary in ritual and exchange, but are always 'inextricably linked' to the world of women: 'They embody the values of women's work and express their intentionality and agency'. But that does not make them 'women's wealth' since women do not compete for power or prestige in gift exchange using these objects, but rather offer them to men as wives or sisters.[9] They thus project more complex gender identities and relations.

The final trio of chapters by Fanny Wonu Veys, Ping-Ann Addo and Jane Horan move us to Tonga and to both Tongan and Cook Islander diasporic communities in New Zealand. Wonu Veys's critical historical interrogation of the changing meaning of *koloa* in Tonga, discussed above, is pivotal to understanding what is happening in Tonga and in the Tongan diaspora. The original link between chiefly women and *koloa* has now been democratised and the creation and exchange of *koloa* is now potentially the provenance of all Tongan women. As Ping-Ann Addo shows in her book (2013), materials, motifs and meanings have been transformed. Barkcloth has been supplemented by synthetic materials (even if these are seen as less authentic and less valuable); the crowns and rows of pine trees associated with tapa linked to royal genealogies have been joined by motifs linked to new homes as well as the ancestral homeland (in Australia images of kangaroos and emus and the Sydney Harbour Bridge, see Reardon Finney 1999). But cloth of all kinds is crucial in the expression of a Tongan identity today, of this modern transnation (Addo 2013).

This is poignantly clear in the life story of Kalo as told by Addo. The precious *koloa* (both fine pandanus mats and barkcloth), which she brought from Tonga to New Zealand and carefully stored under mattresses and packed up in bedrooms, have been complemented by those she has made herself, often in church-based women's groups or received in exchanges at life-

---

9   But, as Katherine Lepani notes, Papua New Guinean women are now selling *bilums* in markets and other commodity circuits, which, as the Introduction evinces so beautifully, is not just an important source of income generation, but contexts in which women display considerable agency and 'entrepreneurial acumen' (personal communication, 22 September 2016).

cycle ceremonies, church or Tongan cultural events. Kalo, like Lepani's interlocutors in the Trobriands, sees herself as cash-poor (her wages from paid work and her pension were mainly donated to the church), but rich in *koloa* valuables. Throughout her life she distributed *koloa* in many contexts, thus raising her commoner status and that of her kin in the Tongan community, and inculcating in her adopted daughters and nieces the value of passing on Tongan values. But, as Addo insists, 'objects, like relationships, are not static' and, as she ages, Kalo divests herself of most of her *koloa*; giving them to her sisters, daughters, nieces and textile-making friends to celebrate births, marriages and even impending maternity outside marriage. She retains only some of her mother's precious *koloa* heirlooms and a couple of pandanus waist mats to wear to church. By redistributing all these valuables, Kalo is expressing not just her love for kin and friends but also her desire that they treasure what she treasures. Although Addo, like all the authors in this volume, interrogates notions of 'wealth', she is more comfortable than most in describing Kalo's *koloa* as women's wealth, insofar as wealth refers to a preeminent value, passed between generations of women. Treasured textiles are for Kalo a way of ensuring that her own traces endure in future sinuous relationships. She has trusted textiles to oblige the Tongan women she knows and loves to live as she did, the Tongan way, the 'straight and narrow way' of the church, to fulfil the destiny she desires for them. Thus, the ultimate value of this 'women's wealth' is, as David Graeber (2001: 142) argues, about the creation of valued persons rather than things (see Introduction this volume).

Jane Horan's chapter on a haircutting ceremony performed by Cook Islanders in Auckland equally exemplifies Graeber's argument. She offers a graphic description of how the seven-year-old who is the focus of this ceremony is transformed from mere boy to a potential Cook Islander man through the dramaturgy of this event. The precious *tivaivai* quilts in which he is enveloped and which adorn his chair, the less precious quilts which drape the stage where he sits, the matching homemade costumes of island fabric in which he and his family reappear after the ceremony, all effect this transformation. The participating audience cut off ribboned locks of his hair and in exchange pass on money (sequestered in envelopes), quilts and store-bought duvets. In the course of this ceremony, cash and commodities are, in Horan's view, moved from the realm of the market to the realm of mutuality. The cash may contribute to the boy's future education, the duvets may be used to warm and cuddle up in during

Auckland winters to come. But, in this context, they, like the precious *tivaivai* cloths, are cultural valuables that materialise the greatest value—the creation and transformation of persons—in a diasporic Cook Islander culture that celebrates kinship and mutual *aro'a*—not just love but the values of kindness, hospitality, compassion and forgiveness.

But, we might ask, why here, as in the Tongan diaspora, are these ultimate values so strongly linked to women, women's creations and abstract notions of womanness (muliebrity, to use Horan's rare term). Clearly other material things or practices can signify being Tongan or Cook Islander—wooden artefacts made by men, tattoos, dance styles. Moreover, the objects that are the precious and efficacious valuables include both textiles that have indigenous origins (barkcloth and pandanus mats) and those that were introduced by Christian missionaries (like *tivaivai* quilts) but which have been thoroughly indigenised (see Jolly 2014). *Tivaivai* quilts, like Papua New Guinean *bilums* made from string imported from Hong Kong, like Trobriand *sepwana* skirts made from bolts of vibrant printed cotton, have through the creative labour of women come to signify place, cultural and national identity alongside barkcloth, bushstring, pandanus and clay. Will they continue to do so in the future alongside store-bought duvets and cash, or will they be replaced by such commodities?

Changing values: Revaluing things, revaluing persons

> Forms of value emerge to regulate a process which is ultimately about the creation of people.
>
> (Graeber 2001: 142)

My rhetorical question frames my final focus on changing values. Here, I ponder on how we might think about transformations of value over the longue durée in the Pacific, transformations of value that pertain to persons and things and their relation. It is vital to see the changing relations of gender and sexuality in the region, and the changing character of these sinuous objects not just on the scale of local, intimate relations but in relation to the macroprocesses of colonialism, Christianity, commodity economics and globalisation (Besnier and Alexeyeff 2014). But it is equally important to see Pacific peoples, and Pacific women in particular, not as passive victims of agents and processes emanating from 'beyond the horizon' but as active subjects encountering, resisting and incorporating, rejecting and indigenising. In these historical transformations, have the notions and values of personhood been transformed from more relational to individual modes (see Wardlow 2006)? Has this process been similar or different for men and women? And how has this impinged on the value of those objects created by women?

In their Introduction, the editors point to how the combined effects of various colonial agents—Christian missionaries, traders, collectors, development practitioners, even anthropologists—entailed a devaluation of objects created by women in relation to those of men, and ultimately a difference in whether these were categorised as 'artefacts' or 'art'. By contrast, they suggest the perspective of this volume:

> allows us to move beyond classificatory distinctions between art and artefacts—objects of symbolic, creative value, and objects of daily utility—that have been valued differently in time, not only by local and international agents but also by the gendered perspectives of observers (Hermkens and Lepani this volume).

Nicholas Thomas (1995: 132) suggested that most early collectors neglected artefacts produced by women, and that this was perpetuated in the tribal art market. But he has also observed that from the first European exploratory voyages in the Pacific, there was an interest in barkcloth, and especially in the fine white tapa of Tahiti (Thomas 1995, 2012). Analogies were early drawn between Pacific women's manufacture and decoration of barkcloth and women's domestic arts in Europe and the Americas—sewing, embroidery and quilting. Still, for most collectors, there was a greater propensity or potential to collect stone and wooden objects made by men (and especially representations of the human form and weapons of war) than objects created by women such as textiles and baskets, which were seen as more mundane, less ritually potent and thus less valuable.

But I suggest there were also important differences *between* colonial agents in relation to objects created by women, and particularly apropos Pacific textiles. Christian missionaries were zealous in condemning the objects men created to manifest divine beings, gods and ancestors, and regularly called for the destruction of such 'idols' or conspired to remove them from converts by collecting them and sending them back to metropolitan museums (see Hermkens 2014). By contrast, missionaries often failed to register the divine dimensions of Pacific cloths and how textiles like barkcloth and pandanus not only covered bodies as clothes and blankets but were used to wrap and protect divine powers inherent in persons and things. Although they promoted new clothes made from introduced cloth as iconic of the acceptance of the new god, they did not attempt to destroy such indigenous textiles but rather eclipse them, perceiving a confluence between them as clothes created by women (see Jolly 1996, 2014).

As the editors argue, the differential valuations and collecting strategies of outsiders laid the historical basis for how objects created by Pacific men were far earlier considered 'art' while women's creations remained 'artefacts' or 'craft'. I will not revisit the protracted and sometimes tedious debates about the problematic universality of the category 'art' and whether it is best seen in terms of beauty or efficacy (see Gell 1998; Layton 2003; Morphy 1994; Myers 2002). But we can witness that those Oceanic objects labelled 'primitive art' in the western canon, and that influenced prominent western artists from the early twentieth century (like Klee, Picasso, Gauguin, Matisse), were usually wooden and stone objects made by men—sculptures of the human form, of ancestors, animals and birds, masks and headdresses (see Price 1989). By contrast, Pacific textiles and pots made by women continued to be curated as 'artefacts' (marking them as nonwestern, of archaeological or anthropological rather than aesthetic interest) or as 'craft' (a category that carries both a quotidian, domestic and feminine association in the world of global art). In their Introduction, the editors stress how, in scholarly writing, the first tend to be interpreted in terms of iconic meanings and symbols, while the latter tend to be analysed in terms of form and function.

It has taken far longer for Pacific women's textiles to be acknowledged as 'art' in the context of museums and galleries. In the Australian context, this has only happened in the last decade or so as they were embraced in larger exhibitions or major dedicated displays were mounted. Pacific women's textiles—tapa, pandanus mats and quilts—were included and celebrated in the Fifth Asia Pacific Triennial in Brisbane in 2006 at the Gallery of Modern Art/Queensland Art Gallery with catalogue essays by Janet Jeffries, Maud Page, Teresia Teaiwa and Nicholas Thomas (Seear and Raffel 2006). Ömie barkcloths were displayed in Sydney, at the Annandale Galleries and the New Guinea Gallery, promoted by the late David Baker and author Drusilla Modjeska (Modjeska 2009) and in Melbourne as the exhibition *Wisdom of the Mountains*, curated by Sana Balai at the National Gallery of Victoria (NGV) from late 2009 to early 2010. A tapa exhibition was mounted at the Monash University Museum of Art, and another, *Talking Tapa, Pasifika Bark Cloth*, at the

Brisbane Multicultural Arts Centre around the same time. *Paperskin*, a comprehensive exhibition of historical and contemporary barkcloth, was displayed at the Queensland Art Gallery in Brisbane in 2010 (travelling from Te Papa Tongarewa in Wellington in 2009). Significantly, in several of these exhibitions individual women were named as the creators of the cloth, although their collective ethnic or ancestral associations were also highlighted. A more recent exhibition of Tongan *ngatu* (painted tapa), *Sui i Moana* (Reaching across the Ocean), mounted at NGV in mid-2016, celebrates both the creativity of contemporary artists Robin White and Ruha Fifita *and* their collaboration with the women of Havelulotu in Tonga. That display of three monumentally large tapa celebrates the connections across Oceania—between Aotearoa/New Zealand, Tonga and the broader Pacific—tracing the paths of people and culture and the movements of fish and other creatures in this vast ocean (see Hermkens and Treagus 2016).

The distinction between 'art' and 'artefact' has also often relied on a perception that art is canonically the inspired creation of an individual author, while an artefact is a more mundane, generic and collective creation. This dubious distinction has been imbricated with gender differences, such that much of western art history from the fifteenth century to the present is a genealogy of pre-eminently male individual artists in relation to particular periods, countries, genres and styles. 'Primitive' or tribal art rather relies on a suppression of the signature of an individual artist, with a tendency to privilege the collective character of the work and associate its authenticity with greater age and a pristine state (see Jolly 2011; Thomas 1995).

This series of complicit binaries—between art and artefact, western and 'primitive' art, individual versus collective authorship—poses the question of how far the values ascribed to objects are in fact materialisations of values pertaining to persons. There has been a prevailing tendency in the anthropology of the Pacific (as in much western social theory) to counterpose the value of western individualism with the value of relationality or collectivism in the Pacific. Even though such binaries have been propounded as 'heuristic fictions' (Strathern 1988) rather than a description of lived realities, there has been a vigorous debate in the anthropology of the contemporary Pacific as to whether we are witnessing an increase in the value of individualism, if so what might be catalysing such changing values and whether such tendencies towards individualisation might be gendered, or different for men and women (see Hermkens, Taylor and Morgain 2015;[10] Jolly 2015; Wardlow 2006).

Several processes have been implicated in arguments about increasing individualism in the Pacific—commodity economics, Christianity (especially evangelical forms), biomedical health systems, state politics, human rights discourses and practice, etc. By far the greatest attention has been paid to the combined influences of the first two—commodity economics and Christianity. Significantly, these emerge as dominant forces in *local* discussions of changing values throughout this volume, both in past and present periods. In the colonial period in the Pacific, Christianity and capitalism were strange bedfellows—both utterly conjugated in terms of the global expansion of European colonialism but also prone to huge fights (for example, about slavery and systems of indenture on plantations) and lesser struggles (for example, in the western Pacific, over the use of indigenous languages in conversion as against lingua franca like pidgins, which emerged from early extractive trade and stabilised through plantation labour systems). But in places where capitalism and Christianity cohabited most harmoniously (as in Hawai'i), their combined forces entailed land dispossession, conversion to new gods and new goods and, ultimately, the promotion of new laws and western values in a settler colonial state (e.g. Merry 2000).

Throughout this volume, Christianity and commodity economics are coupled in local perceptions of 'changing values'. In the Trobriands, the coming of the new god in the successive waves of Methodism, Catholicism and now evangelical Christianity is seen as perforce accompanied with new goods (iconically new clothes and cloth). In analysing the latest phase of the 'coming of the light' in the last two decades, MacCarthy links conversion to evangelical Christianity, the pursuit of cash and commodities and a heightened individualism (echoing Robbins 2004). Lepani is less persuaded of fundamental changes in the values pertaining to persons—insisting on the persistence of relational personhood and collective regeneration in the face of the challenges of modernity, including that of HIV and the individualist biomedical model promoted to redress it

---

10 This volume arose out of research funded by the Australian Research Council, which was dedicated to exploring that question, namely 'Engendering Persons, Transforming Things: Christianities, Commodities and Individualism in Oceania' (FL100100196), an ARC Laureate project on which the editors were valued colleagues.

(see Lepani 2008, 2010, 2012, 2015). Like many other authors, she observes how the introduced things and values associated with Christianity have become indigenised so that rather than individualisation we witness new clothes, imported fabrics and quilts signalling a persisting relational moral economy and a reconfigured collective ethnic or national identity (as Trobrianders, Papua New Guineans, Tongans and Cook Islanders). Just as the Hawaiian quilt has been indigenised and has served nationalist, anticolonial purposes (Jolly 2014), so we might see Kalo's *koloa*, or the *tivaivai* quilts made and used by Cook Islanders in Auckland, not just as stressing the persistence of the Tongan or Cook Islander values in the diaspora but as a resistance to the hegemony or even the encompassment of the values of the market and of isolated individuals.

An elegy for the future?

We might ask then whether the supplanting of 'sinuous objects' made by women (albeit indigenous or introduced) by store-bought commodities like duvets or cash in envelopes (as in Horan's chapter) portends dramatically changing values in the future. The editors suggest not.

> Horan's example is an indication of the way that recently introduced commodities *replace* the objects of women's wealth. But does this also mean that the value of gift exchange is rendered gender neutral? Commensurate measures of value continue to frame gift giving in gender-specific ways. Transactions retain the gendered nature of the gift along relational lines and through the work of women in organising and staging ceremonial events. Whether gifts are purchased commodities and envelopes of money, or objects that have come into being through women's creative labour, the coherent value in meaning making is still legitimated by gender [emphasis in original] (Hermkens and Lepani this volume).

and

> Throughout this volume is the observation that the relationality at the core of women's gift giving confers commensurate value and meaning in exchanges, whether the objects are created through women's embodied labour or purchased and transacted as commodities (Hermkens and Lepani this volume).

Only time will tell if this supreme value of relationality is perpetuated. Pacific women living both in their home islands and in the diaspora are dealing not just with the powerful forces of globalisation but with a world facing the perils of dramatic climate change. In Papua New Guinea in particular, extractive industries have already felled huge forests, mined precious ores and tapped the country's expansive reserves of gas and oil. While these industries may have contributed to national wealth measured as gross domestic product, the possibilities of employment in the commodity economy and the consumption of desired things (like trucks and mobile phones), the benefits of such industries have been unevenly distributed, and class and gender inequities are steadily increasing (see Jolly et al. 2015). Moreover, although the islands of the Pacific contribute little to the raised levels of carbon emissions in the atmosphere, compared to countries on the rim like Australia, the effects of climate change are already apparent. As sea levels rise with climate change, groves of pandanus and mangroves growing near the ocean have already sustained damage while the changing patterns of rainfall in the region, the likely increased severity of storms and cyclones, floods and droughts will perhaps imperil ecologies in which paper mulberry, breadfruit and banana trees thrive (as well as the indigenous cultivation of taro, yams, sweet potato and sago). In 2007, gardens across Collingwood Bay were submerged and buried under silt in a devastating flood that affected much of Oro Province. The flood not only forced Maisin people and their neighbours to live on government rations of rice and the contributions of working relatives until the gardens could recover, but it also affected tapa. The paper mulberry saplings would not grow in the boggy soil, and hence tapa was not made and exchanged for some time (Barker and Hermkens 2016: 202). The consequences of climate change if not redressed will perforce affect the whole world, including those overdeveloped countries like the United States, China, India, Europe and Australia, which are the primary source of the problem (see Jolly forthcoming) This, together with more critical attitudes towards free trade and policies favouring protectionism within several major global powers, may stall or even reverse some of the hurtling pace of globalisation. Again, only time will tell.

References

Addo, Ping-Ann. 2013. *Creating a Nation with Cloth: Women, Wealth, and Tradition in the Tongan Diaspora*. Oxford: Berghahn.

Appadurai Arjun (ed). 1986. *The Social life of Things: Commodities in Cultural Perspective*. Cambridge: Cambridge University Press.

Barker, John and Anna-Karina Hermkens. 2016. 'The Mothers Union Goes on Strike: Maisin Women, Tapa Cloth and Christianity'. In *Gender and Christianity in Melanesia: Towards a Unifi ed Analysis*, ed. Michelle MacCarthy and Annelin Eriksen. Special issue of *The Australian Journal of Anthropology* 27(2): 185–205. DOI: 10.1111/taja.12193.

Bashkow, Ira. 2011. 'Old Light on a New Controversy: Alex Rentoul's Account of the Trobriand Women's Sagali'. *History of Anthropology Newsletter* 38(2): 9–18.

Besnier, Niko and Kalissa Alexeyeff (eds). 2014. *Gender on the Edge: Transgender, Gay and Other Pacific Islanders*. Honolulu: University of Hawai'i Press.

Bolton, Lissant. 1996. 'Tahigogona's Sisters: Women, Mats and Landscape on Ambae'. In *Arts of Vanuatu*, ed. Joël Bonnemaison, Kirk Huffman, Christian Kaufmann and Darrell Tryon, pp. 112–119. Bathurst: Crawford House Publishing.

——. 2003. *Unfolding the Moon: Enacting Women's Kastom in Vanuatu*. Honolulu: University of Hawai'i Press.

Brunt, Peter and Nicholas Thomas (eds). 2012. *Art in Oceania: A New History*. London: Thames & Hudson.

Butler, Judith. 1990. *Gender Trouble: Feminism and The Subversion of Identity*. New York and London: Routledge.

——. 2004. *Undoing Gender*. New York and London: Routledge.

Gailey, Christine Ward. 1987. *Kinship to Kingship: Gender, Hierarchy and State Formation in the Tongan Islands*. Austin: University of Texas Press.

Gell, Alfred. 1998. *Art and Agency: Towards a New Anthropological Theory*. Oxford: Clarendon Press.

Graeber, David. 2001. *Toward an Anthropological Theory of Value: The False Coin of our own Dreams*. New York: Palgrave.

Gregory, Chris. 1982. *Gifts and Commodities*. London: Academic Press.

——. 1997. *Savage Money: The Anthropology and Politics of Commodity Exchange*. Amsterdam: Harwood Academic Publishers.

——. 2015. 'Preface to the Second Edition'. In *Gifts and Commodities* (2nd edition), pp. xi–xli. Chicago: HAU Books.

Grewal, Inderpal and Caren Kaplan (eds). 1994. *Scattered Hegemonies: Postmodernity and Transnational Feminist Practices*. Minneapolis: University of Minnesota Press.

Henne, Kate. 2013. 'From the Academy to the UN and Back Again: The Travelling Politics of Intersectionality'. In *Grounding Travelling Concepts: Dialogues with Sally Engle Merry about Gender and Justice*, ed. Hilary Charlesworth and Margaret Jolly. Special issue of *Intersections: Gender and Sexuality in Asia and the Pacific*, 33. Online: intersections. anu.edu.au/issue33/henne.htm (accessed 23 February 2017).

Herdt, Gilbert. 1981. *Guardians of the Flutes: Idioms of Masculinity*. New York: McGraw Hill.

Hermkens, Anna-Karina. 2013. *Engendering Objects: Dynamics of Barkcloth and Gender among the Maisin in Papua New Guinea*. Leiden: Sidestone Press.

——. 2014. 'The Materiality of Missionisation in Collingwood Bay, Papua New Guinea'. In *Divine Domesticities: Christian Paradoxes in Asia and the Pacific*, ed. Hyaeweol Choi and Margaret Jolly, pp. 349–380. Canberra: ANU Press. Online: press-files.anu.edu.au/downloads/ press/p298891/pdf/ch152.pdf (accessed 19 January 2017).

Hermkens, Anna-Karina, John Taylor and Rachel Morgain (eds). 2015. *Gender and Person in Oceania*. Special issue of *Oceania* 85(1).

Hermkens, Anna-Karina and Mandy Treagus. 2016. 'Review of Robin White and Ruha Fifita *Siu i Moana: Reaching across the Ocean*'. In *Artlink*. Online: www.artlink.com.au/articles/4514/robin-white-and-ruha-fifita-siu-i-moana-reaching-a/ (accessed 19 February 2017).

Hilsdon, Anne-Marie, Martha Macintyre, Vera Mackie and Maila Stivens (eds). 2000. *Human Rights and Gender Politics: Asia–Pacific Perspectives*. London and New York: Routledge.

James, Kerry. 1988. 'O, Lead us Not into "Commoditisation": Christine Ward Gailey's Changing Gender Values in the Tongan Islands'. *Journal of the Polynesian Society* 97(1): 31–48.

Jeffries, Janis. 2006. 'Texts and Textiles: Pacific Encounters'. In *The 5th Asia-Pacific Triennial of Contemporary Art*, ed. Lynne Seear and Suhayana Raffel, pp. 180–183. Brisbane: Queensland Art Gallery Publishing.

Jolly, Margaret. 1992a. 'Banana Leaf Bundles and Skirts: A Pacific Penelope's Web?' In *History and Tradition in Melanesian Anthropology*, ed. James G. Carrier, pp. 38–63. Berkeley: University of California Press.

———. 1992b. 'Partible Persons and Multiple Authors' (contribution to Book Review Forum on Marilyn Strathern's *The Gender of the Gift*). *Pacific Studies* 15(1): 137–149.

———. 1994. *Women of the Place:* Kastom*, Colonialism and Gender in Vanuatu*. Chur and Reading: Harwood Publishers.

———. 1996. 'European Perceptions of the Arts of Vanuatu: Engendering Colonial Interests'. In *Arts of Vanuatu*, ed. Joël Bonnemaison, Kirk Huffman, Christian Kaufmann and Darrell Tryon, pp. 264, 267–77. Bathurst: Crawford House Publishing.

———. 2008. 'Of the Same Cloth: Oceanic Anthropologies of Gender, Textiles and Christianities', Invited Distinguished Keynote Lecture for the Association of Social Anthropology in Oceania, The Australian National University, Canberra, 14 February 2008.

———. 2011. 'Becoming a "New" Museum: Contesting Oceanic Visions at Musée du Quai Branly'. *The Contemporary Pacific* 23(1): 108–139.

———. 2014. 'A Saturated History of Christianity and Cloth in Oceania'. In *Divine Domesticities: Christian Paradoxes in Asia and the Pacific*, ed. Hyaeweol Choi and Margaret Jolly, pp. 429–454. Canberra: ANU Press. Online: press.anu.edu.au/?p=298891 (accessed 22 September 2016).

———. 2015. '*Braed Praes* in Vanuatu: Both Gifts and Commodities'. In *Gender and Person in Oceania*, ed. Anna-Karina Hermkens, John Taylor and Rachel Morgain. Special issue of *Oceania* 85(1): 63–78. DOI: 10.1002/ocea.5074.

———. 2016. 'Engendering Vertigo in Time-space Travel'. Contribution to Review Symposium on Marilyn Strathern, *Before and After: Sexual Mythologies of Everyday Life*, ed. Sarah Franklin. Special issue of *Hau: Journal of Ethnographic Theory* 6(3): 393–399. DOI: dx.doi. org/10.14318/hau6.3.025.

———. forthcoming. 'Horizons and Rifts in Conversations about Climate Change in Oceania'. In *Pacific Futures*, ed. Warwick Anderson, Tony Ballantyne, Barbara Brookes and Miranda Johnson. Honolulu: University of Hawai'i Press.

Jolly, Margaret, Katherine Lepani, Anna Naupa, Michelle Rooney and Helen Lee. 2015. *Falling through the Net: Gender and Social Protection in the Pacific*. Discussion Paper for UN Women New York, *Progress of the World's Women, 2015–16*. Online: www.unwomen.org/ en/digital–library/publications/2015/9/dps–gender–and–social– protection–in–the–pacific (accessed 23 February 2017).

Kaeppler, Adrianne. 1995. 'Poetics and Politics of Tongan Barkcloth'. In *Pacific Material Culture*, ed. Dirk A.M. Smidt, Pieter ter Keurs and Albert Trouwborst, pp. 101–121. Leiden: Mededelingen van het Rijksmuseum voor Volkenkunde, Leiden 28.

———. 2005. 'The Tongan Lakalaka as Sociopolitical Discourse'. In *Polynesian Paradox: Essays in Honour of Professor 'I Futa Helu*, pp. 154–167. Suva: Institute of Pacific Studies, University of the South Pacific.

———. 2007. 'Me'a Lalanga and the Category Koloa: Intertwining Value and History in Tonga'. In *Vastly Ingenious: The Archaeology of Pacific Material Culture, in honor of Janet Davidson*, ed. Atholl Anderson, Kaye Green and Foss Leach, pp. 145–154. Dunedin: University of Otago Press.

Keane, Webb 2005. 'The Hazards of New Clothes: What Signs Make Possible'. In *The Art of Clothing: A Pacific Experience*, ed. Susanne Küchler and Graeme Were, pp. 1–16. London: UCL Press.

Latai, Latu. 2014. 'From Open *Fale* to Mission Houses: Negotiating the Boundaries of "Domesticity" in Samoa'. In *Divine Domesticities: Christian Paradoxes in Asia and the Pacific*, ed. Margaret Jolly and Hyaeweol Choi, pp. 299–324. Canberra: ANU Press. Online: press. anu.edu.au/?p=298891 (accessed 22 September 2016).

——. 2016. 'Covenant Keepers: A History of Samoan (LMS) Missionary Wives in the Western Pacific, 1839–1979'. PhD thesis. The Australian National University.

Layton, Robert. 2003. 'Art and Agency: A Reassessment'. *Journal of the Royal Anthropological Institute* (n.s.) 9: 447–464. DOI: 10.1111/1467-9655.00158.

Lepani, Katherine. 2008. 'Mobility, Violence and the Gendering of HIV in Papua New Guinea'. *The Australian Journal of Anthropology* 19(2): 150–164. DOI: 10.1111/j.1835-9310.2008.tb00119.x.

——. 2010. 'Steady with Custom: Mediating HIV Prevention in the Trobriand Islands, Papua New Guinea'. In *Plagues and Epidemics: Infected Spaces Past and Present*, ed. Ann Herring and Alan C. Swedlund, pp. 305–322. Oxford: Berg Publishers.

——. 2012. *Islands of Risk, Islands of Love: Culture and HIV in the Trobriands*. Nashville, TN: Vanderbilt University Press.

——. 2015. '"I Am Still a Young Girl if I Want": Relational Personhood and Individual Autonomy in the Trobriand Islands'. *Gender and Person in Oceania*, ed. Anna-Karina Hermkens, John Taylor and Rachel Morgain. Special issue of *Oceania* 85(1): 51–62. DOI: 10.1002/ocea.5073.

MacKenzie, Maureen A. 1991. *Androgynous Objects: String Bags and Gender in Central New Guinea*. Chur: Harwood Academic Publishers.

Malinowski, Bronisław. 1922. *Argonauts of the Western Pacific: An Account of Native Enterprise and Adventure in the Archipelagoes of Melanesian New Guinea*. Studies in Economics and Political Science, no. 65. London: Routledge.

Martin, Emily. 1991. 'The Egg and the Sperm: How Science has Constructed a Romance Based on Stereotypical Male-Female Roles'. *Signs: Journal of Women in Culture and Society* 16(3): 485–501. DOI: 10.1086/494680.

Merry, Sally Engle. 2000. *Colonizing Hawai'i: The Cultural Power of Law.* Princeton, NJ: Princeton University Press.

Modjeska, Drusilla. 2009. 'Fabric of Wisdom: The Context of Ōmie Nioge'. In *Wisdom of the Mountain: Art of the Ōmie.* Melbourne: National Gallery of Victoria Press.

Mohanty, Chandra Tolpade. 2003. *Feminism without Borders.* Durham, NC: Duke University Press.

Morphy, Howard. 1994. 'The Anthropology of Art'. In *Companion Encyclopaedia of Anthropology, Humanity, Culture and Social Life,* ed. Tim Ingold, pp. 648–685. London: Routledge.

Mosko, Mark. 1992. 'Motherless Sons: "Divine Kings" and "Partible People" in Melanesia and Polynesia'. *Man* (n.s.) 27(4): 697–717. DOI: 10.2307/2804170.

Myers, Fred 2002. *Painting Culture: The Making of an Aboriginal High Art.* Durham, NC: Duke University Press.

Price, Sally. 1989. *Primitive Art in Civilized Places.* Chicago: University of Chicago Press.

Prisk, Ethel M. 1919. *About People in Papua.* Adelaide: G. Hassell.

Reardon Finney, Frances. 1999. 'I Thought it Would be Heaven': Migration, Gender, and Community Amongst Overseas Tongans'. Masters in Anthropology thesis. The Australian National University.

Robbins, Joel, 2004. *Becoming Sinners: Christianity and Moral Torment in a Papua New Guinea Society.* Berkeley: University of California Press.

Seear, Lynne and Suhayana Raffel (eds). 2006. *The 5th Asia-Pacific Triennial of Contemporary Art.* Brisbane: Queensland Art Gallery Publishing.

Spriggs, Matthew. 2009. 'Oceanic Connections in Deep Time'. *PacifiCurrents: eJournal of the Australian Association for the Advancement of Pacific Studies* 1(1): 7–27.

Strathern, Marilyn. 1972. *Women in Between: Female Roles in a Male World: Mount Hagen, New Guinea*. London: Seminar Press.

——. 1981. 'Culture in a Netbag: The Manufacture of a Subdiscipline in Anthropology'. *Man* 16(4): 665–688. DOI: 10.2307/2801494.

——. 1988. *The Gender of the Gift: Problems with Women and Problems with Society in Melanesia*. Berkeley: University of California Press.

——. 1992. *Reproducing the Future: Essays on Anthropology, Kinship and the New Reproductive Technologies*. Routledge: New York.

Strathern, Marilyn and Carol P. MacCormack (eds). 1980. *Nature, Culture and Gender*. Cambridge: Cambridge University Press.

Tankunani Siviri, Josephine and Marilyn Taleo Havini. 2004. *As Mothers of the Land: The Birth of the Bougainville Women for Peace and Freedom*. Canberra: Pandanus Books.

Tcherkézoff, Serge. 1993. 'The Illusion of Dualism in Samoa: "Brothers-and-Sisters" are not "Men-and-Women"'. In *Gendered Anthropology. Proceedings of First Conference of European Association of Social Anthropologists, August 1990*, ed. Theresa del Valle, pp. 54–87. London: Routledge and Kegan Paul.

Thomas, Nicholas. 1995. *Oceanic Art*. London: Thames and Hudson.

——. 2012. 'Spiderweb and Vine: The Art of Ōmie'. In *Art in Oceania: A New History*, ed. Peter Brunt and Nicholas Thomas, pp. 484–485. London: Thames & Hudson.

Waldby, Catherine and Melinda Cooper. 2008. 'The Biopolitics of Reproduction: Post-Fordist Biotechnology and Women's Clinical Labour.' In *Australian Feminist Studies* 23(55): 57–73. DOI: 10.1080/08164640701816223.

——. 2014. *Clinical Labour: Tissue Donors and Research Subjects in the Global Bioeconomy*. Durham, NC: Duke University Press.

Walter, Annie. 1996. 'The Feminine Art of Mat-weaving on Pentecost'. In *Arts of Vanuatu*, ed. Joël Bonnemaison, Kirk Huffman, Christian Kaufmann and Darrell Tryon, pp. 100–109. Bathurst: Crawford House.

Wardlow, Holly. 2006. *Wayward Women: Sexuality and Agency in a New Guinea Society*. Berkeley: University of California Press.

Weiner, Annette B. 1976. *Women of Value, Men of Renown: New Perspectives in Trobriand Exchange*. Austin, TX: University of Texas Press.

——. 1980. 'Stability in Banana Leaves: Colonialism, Economics and Trobriand Women'. In *Women and Colonization: Anthropological Perspectives*, ed. Mona Etienne and Eleanor Burke Leacock, pp. 270–293. New York: J.F. Bergin.

——. 1988. *The Trobrianders of Papua New Guinea*. New York: Holt, Rinehart and Winston.

——. 1989. 'Why Cloth? Wealth, Gender and Power in Oceania'. In *Cloth and Human Experience*, ed. Jane Schneider and Annette Weiner, pp. 33–72. Washington, DC: Smithsonian Institution Press.

——. 1992. *Inalienable Possessions: The Paradox of Keeping-While-Giving*. Berkeley and Los Angeles: University of California Press.

Were, Graeme. 2013. 'On the Material of Mats: Thinking Through Design in a Melanesian Society'. *Journal of the Royal Anthropological Institute*, 19(3): 581–599. DOI:10.1111/1467-9655.12051.

Young Leslie, Heather. 1999. 'Traditions, Textiles and Maternal Obligation in the Kingdom of Tonga'. PhD thesis, York University, Toronto.

Young Leslie, Heather E., Ping-Ann Addo and Phyllis Herda (eds). 2007. *Hybrid Textiles: Pragmatic Creativity and Authentic Innovations in Pacific Cloth*. Special issue of *Journal of Pacific Arts* 3(5).